BRITISH LOW CULTURE

From safari suits to sexploitation

Leon Hunt

London and New York

First published 1998
by Routledge
2 Park Square, Milton Park, Abingdon, Oxon, OX14 4RN

Transferred to Digital Printing 2004

Simultaneously published in the USA and Canada
by Routledge
29 West 35th Street, New York, NY 10001

Typeset in Joanna and Bembo by
Ponting–Green Publishing Services
Chesham, Buckinghamshire

British Library Cataloguing in Publication Data
A catalogue record for this book is available
from the British Library

Library of Congress Cataloguing in Publication Data

Hunt, Leon
British Low Culture : from safari suits to sexploitation /
Leon Hunt.
p.   cm.
Includes bibliographical references and index.
1. Great Britain—Social life and customs—20th century.
2. Popular culture—Great Britain—History—20th century.
I. Title.
DA589.4.H86   1998
306'.0941'09045—dc21   97–37619

ISBN 0–415–15182–1 (hbk)
ISBN 0–415–15183–X (pbk)

BRITISH LOW CULTURE

Hunt's analysis of the soft-core porn and horror film genres of the 1970s, of mass market literature exploiting emergent youth subcultures, and of television shows such as The Persuaders!, offers up the sort of meticulous archaeology which cultural studies needs at the present time.

Will Straw, McGill University, Montreal

To read Leon Hunt's book is to visit a half-forgotten world of glam rock, sitcoms, pulp fiction and soft porn. The reader is both captivated and appalled by Hunt's clear-eyed portrait of a past cultural era that still echoes in the present.

John Street, University of East Anglia

Flares, lava lamps and safari suits and a national cinema dominated by smutty comedy and cheap softcore have all made 1970s popular culture appear too gruesome to recycle as nostalgia and too offensive for academic study. But the generic artefacts of the 1970s, such as sexploitation films, skinhead novels, glam rock and the mythology of wife-swapping suburbia have become important reference points and are now embraced by contemporary popular culture.

British Low Culture revisits the 1970s through some of its least respectable texts: television programmes such as Jason King, The Persuaders! and On the Buses; films such as Surburban Wives, House of Whipcord and Confessions of a Window Cleaner, and the prime-time titillation and smut of comedians such as Benny Hill. Identifying 'permissive populism', the trickle down of permissiveness into mass consumption, as a key feature of the 1970s, Leon Hunt considers the values of an ostensibly 'bad' decade and analyses the implications of the 1970s for issues of taste and cultural capital. Hunt explores how the British cultural landscape of the 1970s coincided with moral panics, the troubled Heath government, the three-day week and the fragmentation of British society by nationalism, class conflict, race, gender and sexuality.

Leon Hunt is a lecturer in film and television studies at Brunel University. He has contributed to Velvet Light Trap, Necronomicon and You Tarzan: Masculinity, Movies and Men.

CONTENTS

ILLUSTRATIONS

ACKNOWLEDGEMENTS

The author and publisher would like to thank the following for permission to use stills: The Kobal Collection for *Confessions of a Window Cleaner* and *Confessions of a Pop Performer*, Polygram/Pictorial Press for *Jason King* and *The Persuaders!*, Thames Television for *Man About the House* and London Weekend Television for *On the Buses*; stills from *On the Buses* reproduced by BFI Stills, Posters and Designs. Every effort has been made to obtain permission to reproduce the photographs and posters. If any proper acknowledgement has not been made, we invite copyright holders to inform us of the oversight.

Several people read draft chapters from this book and I would like to thank Carol Jenks, Tanya Krzywinska, Andy Medhurst and Mike Wayne for their comments and suggestions. They may not agree with everything in the book (translation: *don't blame them*), but their input was invaluable. Ian Abraham, Steve Chibnall, Ian Conrich and Ian Hunter helped locate or provided important primary materials. Thanks also to Richard Tomes for his 'Writer's Block' cartoon – yes, I *did* 'Get Well Soon'. Finally, I am grateful to Rebecca Barden for supporting and encouraging what must have sounded like a pretty wayward book.

This book is dedicated with love to Margaret and Beth Hunt, my mother and my sister.

1

'THE DECADE THAT TASTE FORGOT'?

Revisiting the 1970s

There is a kind of self-hatred in the eager embrace of mediocrity which characterises so much contemporary nostalgia. The spiritual impoverishment on show in *Are You Being Served?* makes you worry for a decade that could have found pleasure in it, but even more for one that would want to watch it again.

Ben Thompson (1993: 59)

Like a 'return of the repressed', the 1970s have in recent years come to exert a grip on the popular imagination. The signs of it have been everywhere; nostalgic archival television such as *Sounds of the 70s* (BBC 1993), Channel 4's 'Glamrock Weekend' (1995) and *Match of the Seventies* (BBC 1995), a series of football snapshots where sideburns shared equal billing with golden goals; the glorification of period muzak in the so-called 'easy listening' scene; reprints of 'youthsploitation' fiction published by New English Library; the recirculation of 1970s television on video and cable, with sitcoms and safari-suit crime-busting (*Jason King*, *The Persuaders!*) particular favourites; the annual spectacle of Gary Glitter prising himself back into his silver suit for his Christmas Gang Show; the rediscovery of British cinema's last popular cycle, the sexploitation film; the rehabilitation of lava lamps and flares.

In popular accounts of the period, it's the 'decade that style/taste forgot', an object of pleasurable, kitsch embarrassment. In 'serious' cultural histories, the two most frequently used words are 'crisis' – political/cultural crisis, *Policing the Crisis* – and 'closure'. The latter is embedded, albeit quizzically, in the title of Bart Moore-Gilbert's anthology *The Arts in the 1970s: Cultural Closure?* which considers the 1970s as a crisis in the grand narrative of progressive, politically and aesthetically enlightened culture. In his introduction, Moore-Gilbert offers the concept of 'post-avantgardism' as a negotiation of this 'closure', a more fragmented cultural production associated both with the impact of black, feminist, gay and lesbian politics and with new outlets and material bases for such work (workshops and specialist bookshops, for example) – 'the context of reception and modes of address offered by a given work of art thus becomes at least as important as subversion of stylistic norms in determining political effectivity' (Moore-Gilbert 1994: 21). Inherent in this progressive narrative is the legacy of the 1960s, characterised by an earlier volume (again with a qualifying question mark) as a 'cultural revolution' (Moore-Gilbert and Seed 1992). This is an important narrative, but not the one with which the present book is directly concerned.

1

If, 'post-avantgardism' notwithstanding, 'high' modernist narratives flounder or pause to re-gather their forces in the 1970s, the 'low' flourishes, particularly through an unholy alliance with the ostensibly progressive notions of sexual liberation and permissiveness. A central organising theme in this book is what I shall call 'permissive populism', the popular appropriation of elitist 'liberationist' sexual discourses, the trickle-down of permissiveness into commodity culture, the 1970s as a particularly cruel parody of the 1960s.

This book revisits an important and comparatively neglected part of British cultural history, examining shifts in understandings of class, sexuality and 'Britishness' through a variety of critically disdained texts. But my own positioning has some relevance here. I'm in my mid-thirties – a teenager when this material first appeared – and very much part of the target audience for the nostalgic recycling of the 1970s. Consequently, this isn't simply a cultural history – it isn't just about 'then' – but considers, also, that important component of any nostalgia, the way that memory 'directs our attention not to the past but to *the past–present relation*' (Popular Memory Group 1982: 211). In other words, how do the 1970s speak to the 1990s and how do they figure in its popular imaginary?

Such a project inevitably overlaps with the critical remapping of British culture, and particularly, in the final three chapters, of British cinema history, which tends to skip hastily from the 1960s 'boom' to the alleged renaissance initiated by *Chariots of Fire* in 1981. The metaphor of unexplored territory is a recurring one in accounts of British cinema – large areas remain 'unknown', or constitute, in Julian Petley's words, a 'lost continent' (1986). Some of these continents are generic, some belong to 'lost' historical moments (silent cinema, for example) or marginalised audiences (women's pictures). This critical remapping has, however, tended to congeal into a new orthodoxy – out with documentary and kitchen-sink realism, in with Powell and Pressburger, Gainsborough melodrama, Hammer horror. If something like *Carry On* is still comparatively marginal, it's because this process of recuperation has often been dominated by a rather simplistic opposition between an implicitly 'realist', critically respectable British cinema and 'non-realist' genres such as horror and melodrama which were critically despised but often very popular. Barr (1986) and Cook (1996) have taken issue with this opposition; Barr observes the way the two strands intersect and coexist within a range of films, while Cook identifies 'a kind of reverse elitism ... the reclaiming of critically despised films for an alternative pantheon of the Romantic/Gothic smack of a distaste for commercialism and entertainment' (23). But even she can't avoid it entirely, and simply replaces the word 'realist' with 'consensus'. It's a stubbornly persistent conceptualisation of British popular fictions. Petley, for example, characterises the critical underdog as a 'repressed side of British cinema, a dark, disdained thread weaving the length and breadth of that cinema, crossing authorial and generic boundaries, sometimes almost entirely invisible, sometimes erupting explosively. always received critically with fear and disapproval' (1986: 98).

This is a very specific 'lost continent' – fantastic, poetic, flamboyant, unrestrained and pretty damn sexy. The problem is not with Petley's metaphor; rather, that so many 'lost continents' begin to look more like the Bermuda Triangle. Reclaiming melodrama and the Gothic is one thing, but sexploitation and low-budget sitcom movies are clearly something else.

A useful point of reference would be *Peeping Tom* (Michael Powell, 1960), the recuperated text in British film history. Its qualifications are impeccable – the right kind of 'bad taste' (the bourgeois press were suitably appalled), a misunderstood auteur and a theory-friendly subject (even the characters talk about scopophilia); a victim of repressed, dreary, pathologically literal-minded Britain. But *Peeping Tom* belongs to another trajectory within British popular culture, one its detractors recognised more successfully than its rescuers. The film's historical moment is also that of the emerging British sex film, a generic link it acknowledges in the casting of Pamela Green, one of the most famous 'glamour' models of the 1950s/ 60s. The film's publicity made great capital out of her presence – a forty-foot-high cut-out of her was placed above The Plaza, Piccadilly, at the film's premiere. Green was best known for her work with George Harrison Marks, an 'art' photographer/pornographer whose career encompasses 8mm striptease loops like *Xcitement* (1960), the nudist film *Naked as Nature Intended* (1960) – both featuring Green – Mary Millington's most successful film, *Come Play With Me* (1977) and, more recently, artefacts even further downmarket than this book travels, 'CP' (corporal punishment) videos. *Peeping Tom* meticulously reproduces Marks's sleazy *mise-en-scène* in the nude photography sequences – Powell was an admirer, and employed him as stills photographer on the film. In so far as *Peeping Tom*'s relationship with pornography is acknowledged, it is assumed to be a critical one – one of the aggressive 'regimes of looking' it pathologises – but it is doubtful whether audiences in 1960 would have seen it like that. Powell's film is a rich and fascinating one, as its numerous rereadings attest, but it's also a sleazy, exploitative one and its canonisation has in some ways closed off some alternative routes through British cinema which would include the more titillating 'social problem' films (*Beat Girl*, 1960, *The Yellow Teddybears*, 1963), the censor-friendly 'instructive' nudist films, Hammer's downmarket rivals Tigon, who also made skin flicks, and Pete Walker's grim horror-thrillers.

Popular memory and the 1970s

In *The Seventies: Portrait of a Decade*, Christopher Booker asks, 'what in years to come will evoke the sober, gloomy Seventies ... What was the Seventies sound, the Seventies look? What was the Seventies "image"?' (1980: 4). His answer may come as a surprise to retro-stylists, for he argues that it is 'hardly a time which in years to come is likely to inspire us with an overpowering sense of nostalgia ... we may in short remember the Seventies primarily as a kind of long, dispiriting interlude' (ibid.: 5). While the latter would have found few dissenters in the immediate aftermath of the period, it now seems extraordinary to say that the 1970s are not stylistically recognisable. Music, film and fashion of the 1970s are ineffably time-bound, and most retrospective pieces at some point include a list of artefacts and garments (some consist of little else) – flares, hot pants, platform shoes, tank tops, Ronco Buttoneers, feather cuts and lots of crushed velvet.

Nostalgia about the 1970s tends to focus on specific parts of the decade – largely pre-punk, pre-Jubilee, pre-Winter of Discontent, and above all, pre-politically correct – and thus offers a distinctive set of pleasures. In May 1995, Channel 4 scheduled a 'glamrock' celebration, 'one night of everything we love to hate about the 70s', against BBC's more sober VE Day celebrations. This was a striking opposition: Vera Lynn versus Gary Glitter – a sense of competing nostalgias, one 'authentic', the other self-consciously ironic. Only the more visibly contested 1960s come close to competing with the Second World War in terms of the nostalgia industries, whereas the 1970s are not only linked to overtly 'bad' memories (power cuts, three-day weeks, terrorism at home and abroad, 'mugging' panics) but the epitome of 'bad taste', the lack of that thing that the 1980s placed so much emphasis on – 'style'.

'Our reaction to Seventies fashion,' wrote Jon Savage towards the end of the 1980s, 'is as much a result of conditioning as it is a considered reaction to their cut, style and texture, for they are now directly associated with attributes that have no place in Success Culture' (1988b: 67). Glam remains an important reference point for 1970s fashion, its excesses and recession-defying bohemianism. When Hebdige (1979) argues that white subcultural style was often a complex negotiation of the impact of black culture, he leaves glam out of the equation, calling it 'Albino camp'. Yet Polhemus at least notes the sartorial similarities between glam and Afro-American funk styles in the early 1970s, the 'pimp' suits and 'hustler' style not only worn by musicians like George Clinton and Bootsy Collins but committed to celluloid cultdom by North American 'blaxploitation' classics like Shaft (1971) and Superfly (1972). 'Funky chic' fits a familiar 'aspirational' reading of in-your-face black subcultural style:

> enormous flares in the trouser legs served to focus the eye on the contrast-
> ing ultra-tight fit around the crotch and bottom (while the use of expen-
> sive materials like suede and snakeskin underlined the Dressing Up,
> aspirational aspect of the message.)
>
> (Polhemus 1994: 72)

It might be stretching a point to see glam style as white 'funky chic'. Polhemus links it to the 'prosperity' of Swinging London, and yet glam's historical moment is far from economically prosperous – it coincides with the troubled Heath government and a major recession. Moreover, the more populist appeal of Gary Glitter and The Sweet – Charles Shaar Murray calls them 'purest meatball' (1991: 225) – can be seen as part of an aspirational, white dressing-up culture in the face of both an unpromising economic climate and the sense that the original bohemian party had not included them on the guest list.

Nostalgia, according to Stuart Tannock:

> invokes a positively evaluated past world in response to a deficient present
> world. The nostalgic subject turns to the past to find/construct sources of

identity, agency or community, that are felt to be lacking, blocked, sub-
verted or threatened in the present.

(1995: 454)

How did the 1970s get to be a 'positively evaluated past-world'? The Popular Memory
Group's 'past–present relation' is useful here. Tannock sees nostalgia as a 'periodizing
emotion' (ibid.: 456), implying that the past–present relation is one of plenitude
and lack. He identifies three motifs in imagining this configuration: 'a prelapsarian
world (the Golden Age, the childhood Home, the Country); second, that of a "lapse"
(a cut, a Catastrophe, a separation or sundering, the Fall); and third, that of the
present, postlapsarian world (a world felt in some way to be lacking, deficient, or
oppressive)' (1995: 456–7).

I want to suggest that 1970s nostalgias construct the period as both 'golden age'
and 'Fall', sometimes simultaneously. In the first version, the period is a pleasurable
'Fall' within a 'structure of progress' (the 1960s were more 'hip', the present more
'enlightened'), recuperable only from a position of irony. In the second, 1970s
gaucheness is a signifier of innocence before a Thatcherite, style-obsessed Fall. In
the third, we find a pre-politically correct 'golden age', and embedded within this
is a kind of male heterosexual fin de siècle.

'If you can remember the seventies, you were there,' pronounced host Jack Dee
with characteristic dourness on Channel 4's Glam Quiz. Indeed, what such programmes
seem to offer is some collective experience of looking at embarrassing pictures of
oneself from an earlier time. The subtext of these packaged reminiscences is How
Far We Have Come to the sophisticated present day.

Lynn Spigel argues that television's use of popular memory 'aims to discover a
past that makes the present more tolerable':

popular memory is history for the present; it is a mode of historical consciousness that speaks to the concerns and needs of contemporary life.
Popular memory is a form of storytelling through which people make
sense of their own lives and culture.

(1995: 21)

For example, old television is repackaged or 'quoted' as camp, so that 'the past
becomes a cartoonish masquerade' (ibid.: 18) in contrast with contemporary enlightenment. Here's the Radio Times on Jason King:

Jason King – author, private investigator and offshoot of Department 'S' – was
the personification of seventies man. Sporting a ludicrous moustache, flamboyant shirts, velvet catsuits and the largest of medallions, he leapt from
bed to bed, purring catchphrases like 'Whenever I feel the need for exercise I lie down until it passes.' It's now the most popular show on Bravo, so
turn on, tune in and dust off those flares.

(21–7 October 1995: 96)

Spigel is thinking of the way North American cable channels juxtapose sitcoms from different decades, thereby constructing 'a vision of the past that implicitly suggests the "progress" of contemporary culture' (1995: 19). This implies a kind of inoculation – laughing at the past to celebrate the present – and there is something of this dynamic about 1970s nostalgia; no need to interrogate 1970s masculinity because it's too kitsch to take seriously.

Already inherent in the first nostalgia – a superior, knowing relationship with the past – is the sense of a time when things were simpler, even if this involved men talking about 'crumpet' and 'knockers'. In this version, 'the decade that style forgot' is less a souring of the bohemian 1960s than a carnivalesque orgy of vulgarity before the designer decade, before Thatcher, before style bibles and Armani-pundits like Peter York. In *Peter York's Eighties* (BBC 1996), the eponymous besuited sage celebrated the 'designer decade' as 'an end to everything seventies; the 3-day week, dull clothes, corporatism'. This refrain was also taken up by Robert Elms – 'Britain in the seventies was somehow a celebration of grottiness. We didn't know *anything* in the seventies.' The idea of 'not knowing' becomes potentially attractive within a nostalgic structure of feeling, which requires a certain amount of disavowal. Nostalgia, in Simon Frith's words, remembers 'a time when we didn't know what would happen to us, a time before disappointment ... A nostalgic judgement is a historical judgement, whether personally, in terms of our own regrets, or socially (so that nostalgia for the 1970s is shaped by the Thatcherite 1980s)' (Frith and Gillett 1996: 3). This pre-Thatcher nostalgia is evident in Ashley Heath's largely celebratory account of 'that tank top feeling' in *The Face*:

> Post-Thatcher and post-yuppie, our struggling nation is looking back to all that came before the matt-black shoulder-pad talk, back to a time when the miners went on the march – and managed to bring down a government. We were a bit goosed on the economic front then, and we're a bit goosed economically now, so you can kind of relate to Citizen Smith and his Tooting tank top, back on the BBC shouting 'Power to the People!' If the Seventies was all about having a good time and trying to get your 'look' together with no money and no decent hairdressers, then the Nineties is looking pretty similar.
>
> (1993: 50)

We can't pretend that this is any less of a false historical consciousness than the first one. It ignores the possibility that the 1970s – with the emergence of the New Right and (as yet unsuccessful) attempts to crush the trade unions – might have shaped the Thatcherite 1980s. Looking back on his influential 'Skins Rule' essay, Pete Fowler detects a development from the working-class populism he cautiously celebrated – Labour-voting but racist and pro-death-penalty – to Thatcher's ability to incorporate such a populism into successful political discourse. In 1976, he claims, he wondered what would happen if:

instead of feeling embarrassed by the excesses of the working class, the Conservatives simply embraced the crassness of the proletariat right. If they stuck a dagger into the heart of what I was rapidly coming to see as the real false consciousness, as opposed to the wished-for Marxist false consciousness that I had talked about with such conviction in the late 1960s. It happened, of course, in 1979.

(Fowler 1972/1996: 170)

A *Loaded* heritage

There is a 'sexual political exactness' (Medhurst 1995: 16) about a lot of recirculated 1970s popular culture, so that the period has become a reference point for a kind of unfettered straight masculinity – the 'Fall', clearly, was via the 'castrated' New Man of the 1980s. In the first episode of *Match of the Seventies*, Dennis Waterman wistfully recalls a time when 'men were men, and George Best proved it ten times a night!'. *Loaded* magazine often looks back to its 1970s prototypes – Stan Bowles, George Best, Robin Askwith. In the 'Video Marathon' devoted to Askwith, the sexual nostalgia comes into focus at one particular moment: '"Proper '70s tits!" cries one of our scoundrels as a lady in a comfortable fitting T-shirt flits past on screen' ('The Loafer' 1995: 102).

Somewhere between 1993 and 1994, British masculinity was perceived as having spawned a new type, the 'New Lad'. His media 'sighting' could arguably be traced back to a less congenial late-1980s figure, the 'lager lout', a 'young male with too much money to spend and too much lager inside him' (Redhead 1990: 4). This 'well-heeled hooligan' (ibid.: 5) shed his more violent qualities and was transformed from a folk devil into a consumer category. For one thing, he had a 'lifestyle' and, in 1994, a magazine to prove it – *Loaded*, the most successful British men's magazine of the 1990s. The New Lad was middle class (or trad-rock *nouveau riche* like Oasis), but in love with working-class masculinity and irresponsible hedonism. New Lads included pop stars (Blur), comedians (Baddiel and Skinner's *Fantasy Football League*) and most importantly journalists. They even had their own sitcom to confirm that they were *Men Behaving Badly*.

There is already a strong link between nostalgia and certain versions of masculinity. In the US men's movement, there's a longing for a mythic past, a time before the 'soft' men who capitulated to the emasculatory onslaught of feminism, and who had already been 'feminised' themselves by industrialisation. Mark Simpson calls it 'heritage masculinity, an Olde Worlde natural virility with added bran' (1994: 254). The New Lads are like a kind of 'secularised' men's movement, a hedonistic inversion of all that bonding and primal screaming. The men's movement has its roots in 'the anthropological and/or historical; the mythopoetic or Jungian-archetypical; and the psychotherapeutic' (Pfeil 1995: 168). New Lads look to alcohol, football and 'birds', a refusal of any serious agenda. Mass culture is one of the castrating forces for men's libbers like Robert Bly – 'real' masculinity is positively archaic, outside culture and history. New Lads don't need to go back quite so far to find

7

their 'wild' archetype – only as far as George Best or a repeat of *The Professionals*. In one episode of the latter, a female psychologist mocks Bodie and Doyle for their 'hairy masculine fun'. Being 'hairy' and 'masculine', for the men's libbers, isn't supposed to be fun – it's positively sacred, a Hairy Grail. Meanwhile, for *Loaded*-man – actually more lairy than hairy – instead of ritual wounding, there's the hangover, both the painful evidence of having *lived* the night before and a commitment to never learning from one's mistakes. The New Lad doesn't want to separate from the mother – on the contrary, he needs her to tell him that yes, he is a very naughty boy. He is, after all, the man 'who should know better' (*Loaded*'s motto), implying a need for maternal authority, the only kind which allows his rebellion to make sense.

Popular culture of the 1970s has largely been excavated as an orgy of unsoundness, both an uneasy 'coming to terms' with feminism and 'permissiveness', and what looks like a sort of last major assault in the face of impending ideological policing. In a great deal of 1970s nostalgia, this male heterosexual utopia is the central defining point. The current 'easy listening scene' has on the one hand been characterised in terms of 'mellowing out to authentic late '60s/early '70s lounge music and making your carefully selected wardrobe of bygone style horrors feel 25 years younger again' (Laura Lee Davies, 'Say Cheese', *Time Out* 1285, 1995: 92). But for others these late 1960s/early 1970s slices of kitsch summon up a more specifically gendered scenario. This is 'Suburban wife-swapping music' in which 'visions of a cravat-sporting Leslie Phillips leering from a Jensen Interceptor at a hot-panted "lovely" do spring readily to mind' (Andrew Collins, Q 104, 1995: 130).

'Rubbish amongst the gold': the popular and the 'low'

The title of this book refers not to 'popular' but to 'low' culture, a distinction I have made to point to patterns of distinction and critical judgements made within the larger and by no means uncontested field of the 'popular'. The 'low' can be distinguished both as a doubly marginalised district within the popular and as an ostensibly irrecuperable textual community.

If studying popular culture was once a way of challenging traditional cultural hierarchies and distributions of cultural capital, cultural studies has more recently wrestled with a new orthodoxy, namely 'the intellectual assumption, made by some students of popular culture, that the symbolic experiences and practices of ordinary people are more important analytically and politically than Culture with a capital C' (McGuigan 1992: 4). In other words, 'popularity' has taken on a kind of cultural capital in itself. However, 'cultural populism' hinges on an assumption shared, paradoxically, with cultural traditionalists; that there are homogeneous and stable fields which can be called 'high' and 'low' or 'canonical' and 'popular' culture existing in an eminently reversible hierarchy. John Frow, on the other hand, suggests that no such 'stable hierarchy of value' exists any more (1995: 1). Rather, consumer capitalism has re-located the 'high' as a kind of niche market, one amongst many. Value and cultural capital are negotiated, instead, within distinct textual fields:

for consumers of 'low' culture the sense of illegitimacy or of cultural infe-
riority that characterized previous regimes of value has now largely dissi-
pated. Indeed, it might make more sense now to argue that, rather than
designating definite domains of texts, the terms 'high' and 'low' represent
a division that is operative within all cultural domains.

(ibid.: 25)

With this in mind, cultural relativism – cultural studies' very own 'folk devil', endlessly inverting Shakespeare and soap (we've all seen them!) – is nothing of the sort.
Distinct cultural fields – soap, pop, sitcom, pulp fiction, even pornography – can be
taken as relative, but their texts clearly never are. Texts are always sites of evaluative
struggle between the 'high' and the 'low', whatever the presumed hierarchical positioning of their overall domain.

An article in *The Guardian* by Nick Hornby brings these issues closer to home.
Hornby shadowed a first-year student at a British university, and, as the day wore
on, made a clearly eye-opening visit to the library, and, in particular, its video collection:

I went to an old, snooty university which probably still despises and dis-
trusts popular culture, and while I'm browsing, I become envious; I wish
I had been given the opportunity to spend a couple of terms ploughing
my way through Fellini and Altman and Woody Allen.

('Busy Doing Nothing', *The Guardian*, 4 December 1995: 5)

Warning bells are ringing here – Hornby thinks Fellini, Altman and Woody Allen
are 'popular culture'.[1] Either way, he has a surprise coming:

But then I come over all William Rees-Mogg; there is some real rubbish
amongst the gold. Have we, the taxpayers, really shelled out for 'two classic episodes' of *George and Mildred*? And *Abba – The Movie*? And *The Very Best of On
the Buses*? Apparently so, but why? Structuralism is to blame, I reckon.

(ibid.: 5)

An autobiographical 'confession' is necessary here – it wasn't structuralism, Nick, it
was me (I ordered the videos in question and frequently use them in classes). But
there are some interesting perceptions in Hornby's article of the relationship between academia and popular culture.

First, we have the relativising 'levelling-down' of high theory. As it happens, I do
have some reservations about the juxtaposition of Lévi-Strauss and Reg Varney or
Lacan and 'Dancing Queen' too, but not because they open the cultural floodgates
to a sea of effluent. Bourdieu suggests that one of the reasons why the 'popular' is
despised by those richest in cultural capital is precisely because of its 'easiness':

The refusal of what is easy in the sense of simple, and therefore shallow,
and 'cheap', because it is easily decoded and culturally 'undemanding',

9

1   'Raucous' pleasures: (*Top L to R*) Michael Robbins, Bob Grant; (*Bottom L to R*) Anna Karen, Reg Varney, Doris Hare, Stephen Lewis in *On the Buses*. (Courtesy of LWT.)

> naturally leads to the refusal of what is facile in the ethical or aesthetic sense, of everything which offers pleasures that are too immediately accessible and so discredited as 'childish' or 'primitive'.
>
> (1979/1984: 486)

'Facile' tastes appeal to the senses, act on the body, while 'legitimate' taste offers the promise of intellectual distance from the object being consumed.[2] Bourdieu uses a provocative phrase to describe the aesthetic violence threatened by the despised 'popular' object with its insistence on the corporeal site of pleasure, and one I shall return to: it 'annihilates the distanciating power of representation' (*ibid.*: 489). While high theory may offer many useful insights – Bakhtin, Theweleit and Bourdieu have allowed me to say things I could not have done otherwise – there is a danger of its use simply re-inscribing that 'distanciating power'.

But Hornby's take on culture isn't monolithically anti-popular. For one thing, he is best known for his eulogisation of football, and 'the beautiful game' has all the right 'authentic', folk-tinged qualifications for inclusion in a popular canon. And the 'real rubbish amongst the gold' isn't sitcom – it's *certain* sitcoms. I have the advantage of knowing that the video collection in question also includes *Hancock, Steptoe and Son, Blackadder, Fawlty Towers* and *The Young Ones.* Sitcom is a good example of a popular hierarchy. In the first division, we might find discernible auteurs (Ray Galton and Alan Simpson, Dick Clement and Ian Le Frenais, Johnny Speight), a link either with 'realist' drama (*Steptoe, Till Death Us Do Part, Porridge*) or fringe/'alternative' comedy (*Fawlty Towers, Blackadder, Absolutely Fabulous*). Following that, there's a zone for a kind of 'civilised', often nostalgic light entertainment – the work of Croft and Perry (*Dad's Army, Hi-De-Hi*) comes to mind, as does the interminable *Last of the Summer Wine.* And 'the rest' might include what Tise Vahimagi calls the 'bland, by-the-numbers programming of *On the Buses, Bless This House, Are You Being Served?* and *Man About the House* … cosy, studio-bound situation comedy' (Vahimagi 1994: 185). Two other factors are worth mentioning. ITV sitcoms don't usually make it into the first two categories – 'There is, one cannot but feel, something incontrovertibly … well … ITV, about ITV comedy', said *The Guardian* of *Man About the House* (August 1973). And, of course, quality is implicitly bound up with audience, as the following *On the Buses* review suggests: 'you can always get a laugh out of a mass audience if you aim low enough, and maintain a cynically witless level of high spirits and raucous silliness' (*Daily Mail*, 18 March 1970). Another pointed to the 'raucous evidence' of the show's success: 'A high-pitched feminine shriek' (*Daily Mail*, August 1973.)

As for Abba, to whose charms Hornby is clearly impervious, pop's hierarchies are particularly complex and fluid (Thornton 1995 provides a useful account of how youth taste formations accumulate what she calls 'subcultural capital' and distinguish themselves from an imaginary 'mainstream'). In the early 1970s, 'serious' pop music was rock – this cultural prestige was still very new – album-centred, anti-commercial, 'progressive' or folk-related. A genre like glam focused on singles, producers over 'artists' (Nicky Chinn and Mike Chapman, Mike Leander), labels like RAK (home of Mud, Suzi Quatro, Kenny), Larry-Parnes-style pop creation (a Dickensian name – Glitter, Stardust – a larger-than-life image, a genius-of-the-producer sound). Glam lacked that signifier of cultural capital within pop discourses – 'authenticity', a notion forever problematised, but never eradicated, by punk's cut-up aesthetics and Year Zero hostility to prog-rock's portentous posturing.

Glam was doubly inauthentic, as evinced by a comparatively rare subculturalist account by Taylor and Wall (1976). Its convergence with most rock histories' marginalisation of glam should not come as too much of a surprise. Thornton notes the similarity between subcultural theory's and youth culture's own hostility to an abstract 'mainstream' – 'While youth celebrated the "underground", the academics venerated "subcultures"; where one group denounced the "commercial", the other criticized "hegemony"; where one lamented "selling out", the other theorized "incorporation" ' (1995: 119). Taylor and Wall see glam as the first and, it seems, most insidious 'universal style' generated by consumer capitalism (1976: 110), with Bowie, in particular, 'strategically marketted as a new kind of media product – a bisexual short-haired mod who preaches a spiritual nihilism (in countercultural form) to an audience across the class and age groups, but to the backing of a working class rock beat' (ibid.: 111). Leaving aside the question of what exactly constitutes a 'working class rock beat' and the fact that they don't find mass-marketed bisexuality at least provocative (they generously 'concede that this requires further empirical investigation elsewhere', 123), they find two serious absences in glam rock's 'subcultural capital'. It is neither an 'authentic' subculture nor a product of middle-class counter-culture – rather, it mimics and incorporates elements of both. First, it rides on the coat-tails of the skinheads – Taylor and Wall quote Slade's manager Chas Chandler who claimed that the band belonged to 'the same wage-packet type of background as the football fans' (ibid.: 110). But second, the mass media are seen as anathema to 'authentic' subcultures, negating as they do the key defining element of 'homology', 'the symbolic fit between the values and life-styles of a group, its subjective experience and the musical forms it uses to express or reinforce its focal concerns' (Hebdige 1979: 113). Teds, Mods and Skins 'made themselves, and made their styles', according to Mungham and Pearson (1976: 7) – and their clothes, presumably. But in the case of glam, the:

> creators of the new 'classless' product for consumption by a class appear to have successfully neutralized any liberating potential there might have been in the condition of youth in the 1960s, and have achieved this in no small measure by marketting a product that is economically obtainable by the masses (cheap clothes, clubs and records).
>
> (Taylor and Wall 1976: 112)

Taylor and Wall offer an intriguing opposition to represent the triumph of consumer capitalism over spontaneous cultural formations – the declining sales of football magazines like Goal and Shoot in contrast with the ascendancy of pop and teen magazines. It's easy to smirk at the assumptions here, in an age of colossal football merchandising franchises – what's more symptomatic is the gendering of popular culture. It's difficult to think of a more appropriate genre to 'emasculate' male subcultures. Subsequently, pop history could be perpetually rewritten, often reclaiming the artificial, the contrived and the disposable. In the British music press, glam is virtually canonical, a recurring reference point for 1990s pop.

However, even within glam, there was a sense of 'high' and 'low', something ignored by Taylor and Wall. Bowie, Roxy Music and, to a lesser extent, T. Rex with Marc Bolan (a 'folkie' who 'sold out' to chart success) had the right art-school credentials to qualify as authors of their synthetic images,[3] but Gary Glitter and The Sweet clearly didn't. Slade, the glam success story in terms of Top Ten singles (thirteen between 1971 and 1975, the year glam fizzled out) were something else again.[4] The logo on Dave Hill's guitar – 'SuperYob' – gave us a clue to their contingency, as did their skinhead/suedehead past. Their glam trappings – Noddy Holder's mirror top hat, Hill's extraordinary silvery little numbers – clashed with the unrepentant illiteracy of their titles and their Midlands laddishness. More than any other band, they suggested the 'trickle-down' of men 'glamming up' until it was, in fact, nothing of the sort. Holder's voice was cock rock incarnate, not the fop rock of 'high' glam, as lascivious an expression of rampaging, slightly grotesque male desire as Sid James's laugh.

If certain popular forms are admitted into the canon, another way of valuing the 'low' is precisely through its resistance to rehabilitation, often embodied in the search for 'a final textual frontier that exists beyond the colonizing powers of the academy' (Sconce 1995: 379). 'If I had to think of one reason why the Carry Ons matter so much,' writes Andy Medhurst, 'it's because they aren't really recuperable for proper culture' (1992: 19). The same desire for a good–bad object seems evident in Peter Hutchings's fear that rendering Hammer horror films 'worthy and respectable would be doing them a disservice. More, it would be like forcing them into the light and watching helplessly as they crumble into dust' (1993: 187).

This desire for the 'irrecuperable' can be as elitist as anything emanating from within the academy. Jeffrey Sconce, for example, has examined the fanzine culture surrounding 'trash' cinema, or, as he calls it, 'paracinema', a 'most elastic textual category' which includes 'all manner of cultural detritus' from Godzilla to government hygiene films to Edward D. Wood (Sconce 1995: 372). The 'paracinematic' is identified less by generic-formal qualities (although 'badness' seems fairly important) than as a 'particular reading protocol, a counter-aesthetic turned subcultural sensibilty' (ibid.: 372). In other words, we're talking subcultural capital again. The 'paracinema' brigade are usually middle-class and university educated, and these trash connoisseurs are not populists, by any stretch of the imagination – they are as contemptuous of mainstream entertainment as they are of 'art' cinema. And while they set out to 'trash the canon', they nevertheless invest a great deal in cultural distinction – only a select few will 'get' the counter-aesthetic virtues of Curse of the Swamp Creature.

Sconce's is the most useful exploration of 'trash' in relation to taste and value. But paracinema is redeemed through two notions which are not easily transplanted on to British 'low' culture – 'style' (especially in relation to authorship) and 'excess'. 'Excess' implies something in the process of representation, and British (s)exploitation, for example, is not an excessive cinema; if anything, it's a recessive one, in more ways than one. True, there are exceptions. Horror Hospital (1973) betrays some of director Antony Balch's mixed background in avant-garde film-making and exploitation distribution – 'Search no longer for the missing link between William Burroughs and "Confessions of a Taxi Driver" [sic],' suggested Time Out (June 1996: 165). And Zeta One (Michael Cort, 1969) – Carry On Barbarella, in a nutshell, even down to Charles Hawtrey – contains a strip poker sequence so long and inconclusive that it does take on a fascination verging on the 'paracinematic'. Largely, however, these texts do, indeed, 'annihilate the distanciating power of representation', as Bourdieu puts it. If there is an 'excess', it is in the represented; the 'carnivalesque debaucheries' (Medhurst 1992: 16) which would encompass the raucous laughter of On the Buses, Robin Askwith's thrusting buttocks, Slade's wall-of-sound terrace anthems, The Sun's lascivious headlines.

But the academic investment in the popular/'low' raises other issues about affiliations, cultural positioning and aesthetic priorities. Andy Medhurst captures some of these dilemmas particularly well in his declaration of allegiance to the 'irrecuperable' Carry Ons:

one of the strongest attractions of the *Carry Ons* for me is that through them I can pretend I'm not a university lecturer any more and bolt back to another time and life. More than that, I suspect I use films like this precisely to summon up and sustain fantasies about origins and affiliations that are no longer uncomplicatedly mine.

(1992: 17)

Jostein Gripsrud describes such an investment as a 'symbolic "homecoming" ' (1989: 197), and it does suggest a longing for a time before cultural capital. Gripsrud attempts to historicise a generation of academics 'from working-class or non-academic petit-bourgeois backgrounds, also from geographically "peripheral" areas' (ibid.: 196) whose cultural mobility left them ambivalent about their newfound enculturation. He puts this down to 'the prevailing complacency of the academic proponents of high culture', but I can think of other reasons – Gripsrud is as alarmingly unreflexive about the superiority of high culture as he claims the populists are about the 'low'. The return to a low cultural 'home', he argues, is an attempt both to negotiate a 'socio-cultural limbo' and to disavow the cultural capital they have obtained, a class privilege he characterises as 'double access' to low and high culture – 'Some people have access to both high and low culture, but the majority has only access to the low one' (ibid.: 199). So far, so good – I couldn't claim that this is anything other than a 'double access' book. What Gripsrud seems less comfortable with, however, is the possibility that the return to the 'low' is potentially empowering in itself, an informed aesthetic investment rather than a loss of nerve in the face of Culture with a capital C. He does, in any case, distinguish between two forms of 'high' cultural capital – a set of media texts and 'a discourse on these and other social phenomena' (ibid.: 197). While there are undoubtedly pitfalls, this 'mixed economy' of low (textual) and high (critical/theoretical) capital seems to me to allow for new cultural affiliations and fresh aesthetic agendas. Sconce, for example, likens the 'paracinema' fans to Bourdieu's 'new style autodidact':

> The autodidact is a person who invests in unsanctioned culture either because he or she can 'afford' to, having already made a successful conversion of legitimate cultural and educational capital into economic capital, or who feel, because of their tentative and at times alienated relationship with 'legitimate culture', that such disreputable investments are more durable and potentially more 'rewarding'.

(1995: 379)

Interestingly, some of the trash connoisseurs' more resistible characteristics – their subcultural elitism and contempt for the 'herd' – are the ones drafted in from 'high' discourses. But they do point to a potentially fruitful 'impurity' in contemporary reading strategies and an appropriately fragmented sense of cultural belonging. Gripsrud, like Hornby, seems uneasy about such cultural mongrelisation, as well as being annoyingly and unsupportably confident that he knows what would really prove to be 'rewarding'.

Conclusion

'Comedy', says Richard Dyer – although he could also be talking about related popular phenomena – 'is unruly – it can no more be secured for the right-on than it can for the right-wing' (1993: 117). Clearly, a book on 'British low culture' will make some investment in this 'unruliness', but not an uncritical one. There are certain traps to beware of – handling 'unsound' objects with theoretical tweezers or indulging in populist bullying – but I think it will be apparent that I value some of these texts, for all their 'unacceptable' baggage. Other material falls into the all-too-convenient residual category of 'the interesting', by saying disagreeable things in illuminating ways. At the end of the day, value cannot be separated from use, and all of these objects have a capacity to produce knowledge of one sort or another.[5] And if their popularity doesn't automatically translate into 'quality' (of whatever kind), I have no reservations about asserting their importance.

In Hiding in the Light, Dick Hebdige acknowledges a tension between the abstractions of theoretical discourse and a semi-empirical 'reverence for the irreducibility of the thing-in-itself' (1988: 12), but ultimately nails his colours to the mast. 'If I have a preference at all,' he writes, 'it is that obdurate English preference for the particular, for the thing itself' (ibid.: 12). I have chosen to structure my book, too, around 'the thing itself', in this case sitcoms, skinhead novels, sexploitation films – most of the chapters can be read as relatively self-contained case studies. The generic landscapes are Soho, wife-swapping suburbia, football terraces, garishly decorated 'pads' and creepy country houses. The cast of characters includes Robin Askwith, Roger Moore, Benny Hill, Slade, Mary Millington and pulp anti-hero Joe Hawkins. Certain priorities in primary material require some comment. You will notice that the book's 'foreground' is comprised of narrative texts – films, television shows, pulp novels – while crucial components of 1970s popular culture like pop, fashion and sport tend to fill in 'background' detail. The material nature of music, in particular – and any medium formed substantially by non-representational codes (rhythm, melody, colour, movement) – brings a lot of theoretical baggage with it, as the continuing subculture/musicology debates testify, more than I can really do justice to here. This is also a very British version of the 1970s, I'm afraid, but I hope to compensate for this both by exploring largely uncharted territory and by using it to raise some more broadly applicable issues around gender, class, popularity and nostalgia. I hope you find it an illuminating excursion – read it, if you wish, by the light of a lava lamp.

2

PERMISSIVE POPULISM

Low cultural production in the 1970s

What exactly were the 1970s, given that calendar decades rarely offer neat accommodation to political developments, cultural trends and shifts in fashion or taste formation? 'If anything,' suggests David Toop, 'fashions last about five years, or maybe five months ... To complicate the issue, fashions overlap' (1988: 64). Toop has pop music in mind here, where the disparate strands of glam, folk-rock, prog-rock, heavy metal, teeny- and weeny-bopper pop, soul, punk, ska and disco certainly don't cohere into a unified aesthetic moment. Glam and punk, in particular, offer contrasting responses to Britain's worsening state: the former's optimism and fashion overload flying in the face of the recession, the latter an end-of-its-tether soundtrack to the 1977 Jubilee and the 'Winter of Discontent' (1978–9). It's pop, above all, which creates the impression of a broken-backed decade, one which takes four or five years to notice that the 1960s are over and, from 1976, starts to face up to some harsh realities. But there is a danger of overestimating punk's commercial importance rather than its impact in bohemian circles or as tabloid 'shock'. Dave Harker notes that even the big punk sellers like The Sex Pistols' *Never Mind the Bollocks* (1977) took ten years to get a gold disc and paled beside hippies like Fleetwood Mac, whose *Rumours* (also 1977) sold 13 million copies (1994: 243). Harker singles out Elton John at the most consistent 'sound of the seventies' with fourteen Top Twenty albums in the UK (four at number one) – even on the pop scene, there were as many continuities as ruptures.

The slide from optimism to 'surliness and introversion' (Gibbs 1993: 38) turns up in a number of accounts, but the dates vary. Dave Harker observes rock history's fondness for the Woodstock music festival and The Rolling Stones' Altamont concert (both 1969), respectively, as signifiers that the-times-they-were-a-changing, the latter conspicuously devoid of love-and-peace and lethally policed by Hell's Angels – 'In between a lot of people rolling around in a muddy field and the murder of a black man, Meredith Hunter, *something* happened' (1994: 245). Hewison and Booker see the early 1970s as a continuation of the 1960s – for the former the failure to con-solidate the upheavals and protests of 1968 (Hewison 1986), for the latter through Edward Heath's 'fantasy solutions' to Britain's economic ills: decimalisation, health service reforms and 'big projects' (Concorde, the Channel Tunnel, Milton Keynes) (Booker 1980: 108).[1] For Booker, 1975 was an 'explosion into reality' (*ibid*.: 110) and, with the new Tory leadership under Margaret Thatcher, the end of 'the

Wilson–Heath–Wilson era ... a distinct historical, political and social "sub-period" '
(ibid.: 136). Hewison's book concludes in the same year.

Politically, however, the 1970s do lend themselves to a seemingly self-contained
narrative. The Tories, under Heath, returned to power in 1970; a marginal Labour
government floundered in a sea of compromises from 1974 to 1979, under first
Harold Wilson and then, from 1976, James Callaghan; and Thatcher ushered in the
1980s in 1979 after a 'Labour isn't Working' campaign and a period of paralysing
industrial action conceptualised in political and media discourses as the 'Winter of
Discontent'. Cultural studies' account of the 'crisis' (most notably Hall et al. 1978)
fleshes out this faltering rightwards trajectory, although Policing the Crisis could hardly
have known, in 1978, what was just around the corner. Heath's government already
represented a marked swing to the right, identifiable by the 'tendency to "criminalise"
every threat to a disciplined social order and to "legalise" ... every means of containment' (ibid.: 288). Arguably, the Thatcher government extended this legalised
containment even further to a 'moral' domain in such initiatives as Clause 28 (pro-
hibiting the 'promotion' of homosexuality), perhaps the most symbolic reversal of
post-war permissiveness.

There were important liberalising victories in the 1970s – the Equal Pay Act (1970)
and Race Relations Act (1976), for example. But if the 'permissive' 1960s were made
possible by a proliferation of liberalising legal reforms, the early 1970s witnessed a
counter-strike of punitive legislation – the Industrial Relations Act and the Criminal
Damage Act to rein in the unions and pickets, the Emergency Powers Act and Pre-
vention of Terrorism Act to deal with the IRA's mainland bombing campaign,[2] the
Misuse of Drugs Act and the subtly racist Immigration Act.[3] This law-and-order package
grew out of Heath's pre-election Selsdon Park conference, giving rise to Harold Wilson's
'Selsdon Man' epithet for the new get-tough Tory, 'a hairy, primeval beast threatening to gobble alive the benefits which socialism spread around postwar British society' (Hugo Young, quoted by Savage 1991: 43). 'Selsdon Man' saw lawlessness and
impending chaos everywhere – in trade-union power, terrorism at home and abroad,
in the transformed ethnic make-up of Britain. The latter fuelled a 'mugging panic'
in the media, the subtext of which was black crime against white middle-class victims, a mythology which already had a voice within the government in the person
of Enoch Powell and which the National Front exploited in a poster campaign in
the late 1970s. 'Perhaps violence, race tension and terrorism are the most important
social phenomena of the seventies,' suggests Arthur Marwick (1982: 249), and Savage (1991) attests to a sense of impending apocalypse. Events as diverse as the IRA's
1974 bombing campaign (Tower of London, Guildford, Woolwich and Birmingham), the violent Grunswick film-processing factory dispute of 1976-7 and the NF's
deliberately provocative march through the predominantly black area of Lewisham
in 1977 might support such a feeling. Yet equally significant was the response to
what was perceived as an 'ungovernable Britain': 'the law-and-order campaign of
1970 had the overwhelming single consequence of legitimating the recourse to the
law, to constraint and statutory power, as the main, indeed the only, effective means
left of defending hegemony in conditions of severe crisis' (Hall et al. 1978: 278).

The empowering of the police through the notorious 'sus' law and the activities of the Metropolitan Special Patrol Group at demonstrations also contributed to the 'breakdown' they were supposedly meant to be containing.[4]

The 'crisis' is not without its refracted textual reverberations in contemporaneous popular narratives. It's not uncommon to read television crime shows like The Sweeney and The Professionals in this way (Hurd 1981; Donald 1985; Clarke 1992). But law-and-order tremors can also be detected in New English Library's youth cult pulp novels, in exploitation films like House of Whipcord (Pete Walker, 1974) and two crime films released during the same year, Get Carter (Mike Hodges, 1971) and Villain (Michael Tuchner, 1971). Together, they reveal what Alexander Walker memorably calls 'a vividly conceptualised view of life as a state of constantly impending doom only tempered by periods of grievous bodily harm' (Walker 1985: 25). Walker is thinking of a television play, Rumour, written by Mike Hodges prior to Get Carter, but he could just as easily be describing the mean Metropolitan streets walked by The Sweeney's Jack Regan or the dog-eat-dog world of Richard Allen's Skinhead (NEL, 1970).

The radical right took different forms, not always unaffiliated to parliamentary politics. Moral campaigners like the Festival of Light scored censorship victories of varying degrees, most tellingly over Gay News (1977), against whom they were able to mobilise the seemingly slumbering blasphemy law. Radical right-wing groups like the National Association for Freedom took a hands-on approach to curbing picket power (at Grunswick, for example), and, along with the ever-visible National Front, were granted a degree of respectability by the post-1975 Tory leadership. Thatcher spoke at the former's inaugural dinner, and in a 1978 television interview claimed that many people were 'rather afraid that this country might be rather swamped by people with a different culture' – as for the NF, 'at least it's talking about some of the problems' (Whitehead 1985: 235). She wasn't slow in joining in.

If there is a 'cultural closure' in the 1970s, perhaps it manifests itself particularly in a partly enforced insularity in British, and particularly English, culture; at war with Irish Republicans and witnessing a rise in Scottish and Welsh nationalism. A great deal had been invested in the chic cultural pre-eminence of (mainly southern) England during the 1960s, but that particular bubble had burst. The 'Swinging' myth required a capitalist 'boom', not a recession. The three-day week, power cuts and, in early 1974, a 10.30 television curfew imposed by the energy crisis all contributed to the image of an ever-dwindling 'sad little island'.[5] Both Booker and Moore-Gilbert, amongst others, perceive a cult of nostalgia in the 1970s – the obsession with restoring old buildings, Laura Ashley, Upstairs Downstairs on television.[6] Pop and fashion succumbed to a 1950s revival – Malcolm MacLaren's Let it Rock sold Ted fashions, David Essex starred in That'll Be the Day (Claude Whatham, 1973), arguably the British American Graffiti, and glam had a retro wing in groups like Mud, the Rubettes and New Faces winners Showaddywaddy. Above all, in 1977 there was the Jubilee, the epitome of English insularity, 'Jack Warner in a new haircut and a flared suit ... an edited, English version of what it was to be British' (Savage 1991: 352). Britain had, indeed, never been more (sometimes violently) fragmented – by nationalism, regionalism, class conflict, race, gender and sexuality.

Apart from the 'crisis' texts I've cited, (early) 1970s popular culture often seems to display an optimism at odds with this impending chaos, a sense of not noticing that the 1960s were over. One reason, of course, is that this is partly what entertainment is supposed to do – offer an escape from and palliative for grim realities. But, as Laing suggests, another reason might lie with the long-term experience of those born in the postwar baby boom – the welfare state and the much-trumpeted but precarious affluence of the 1950s and 1960s helped fuel 'an almost unconscious certainty that, by its very nature, the post-war world was one of infinitely expanding prosperity and full employment' (1994: 29). While power cuts and television shutdowns made the recession a tangible reality for even the more prosperous, one of the enduring impressions of the period is the belief that the 'permissive' legacy of the 1960s would manifest itself in a more democratically distributed form. This vulgar hedonism could be found in tabloid populism, not least in its appropriation of pornography and 'sex education' guides, television light entertainment, widely distributed sexploitation films, all testifying to a mythology of lowbrow (male) sexual 'liberation'. It is this post-permissive culture that I want to contextualise in the rest of this chapter.

Our smutty revolution

> The sexual revolution didn't affect my business much. It was the average bloke in the street who's always bought my stuff … Anyway, what was the sexual revolution? Fucking everybody without worrying. That's about it.
>
> George Harrison Marks[7]

Bob and Terry haven't seen each other for five years. They had vowed to join the army together, but Bob's flat feet rescued him at the last moment, freeing him to leave his working-class origins behind – he's about to marry Thelma and move to a new, barely finished housing estate. They have already unknowingly bumped into each other, appropriately enough, in a Soho strip club, the Knave of Hearts, but now they are face to face on a train. Terry, to say the least, is not pleased. Not only did his best friend abandon him, but an important cultural-historical moment has happened without him:

Terry: I missed it all! Swinging Britain was just hearsay to me, something I read about in the overseas edition of The Daily Mail. The death of censorship! The new morality! Oh! Calcutta! Topless waitresses in see-through knickers!

Bob: They never caught on … Er, topless waitresses.

Terry: Well, that's a crumb of comfort. At least I'd like to have been here to see them not catching on. Permissive society? I missed it all. I get back and it's Malcolm Muggeridge, Lord Longford and the Jesus Revolution.

Bob succeeds in placating and consoling him – this is, after all, one of sitcom's great love stories. Terry is thinking of moving to London to 'catch the tail end' of 'permissive' Britain – he 'caught a glimpse of it today in Soho'. 'Aye,' says Bob sagely, 'well the permissive society's still going on down there, much more than up our way.'

The scene is from 'Strangers on a Train', the first episode of *Whatever Happened to the Likely Lads?* (BBC 1973-4). The series was a sequel to *The Likely Lads* (1964-6), which, as Andrew Pulver puts it, used Bob (Rodney Bewes) and Terry (James Bolam) 'to epitomise the nose-against-the-window frustration of north-of-Carnaby Street Sixties Britain' (1996: 165). Strictly speaking, it's a bit classy for this book – although it is the most time-bound of 1970s 'classic' sitcoms, the one most concerned with its historical moment – but it represents an important way of thinking about 1970s popular culture as a negotiation of the 1960s (particularly sexual) revolution. Permissiveness left a lot of people behind, but 'trickled down' in the 1970s, albeit in a rather different form. For people like Terry and Bob – northern and, respectively, working-class and *nouveau*-suburban – the real legacy of permissiveness was to be found in Soho, not the Royal Court Theatre, in Maltese girls with boa constrictors rather than in Kenneth Tynan's 'erotic' review *Oh! Calcutta!* (1970). Terry's litany of missed opportunities is clearly constructed on an ascending scale – the death of censorship and 'new morality' are purely instrumental in paving the way for topless waitresses and see-through knickers.

There is an agreement across the political spectrum that the 1960s, for better or worse, had something to do with 'permissiveness', but what was it? Part of the problem with arriving at some kind of definitive summation is that, as Jeffrey Weeks observes, the word was used more by its detractors than by those considered to be its adherents; it 'became an almost scatological word of abuse, a phrase which welded together a number of complex, and not necessarily connected, changes, into a potent symbolic unity' (Weeks 1989: 249). The Festival of Light's 1971 'Rally Against Permissiveness' could be seen as such an imaginary unification, while Mary Whitehouse's *Whatever Happened to Sex?* constructs an unlikely alliance between 'the pornocrats who present the unacceptable face of capitalism and the dogma-riddled lefties who see the undermining of morality as the prerequisite of take-over' (Whitehouse 1977: 243). In the same book, she resorts to a genetic metaphor – 'in-breeding' – to characterise the conspiratorial links she perceives between the National Council for Civil Liberties, the Abortion Law Reform Association, gay liberation and the paedophile 'movement' who could always be drafted in to discredit other sexual political agendas (ibid.: 71).

Weeks offers two senses of the term *permissiveness*. First, there is a political/juridicial definition, a 'legislative moment' stretching from the late 1950s to the early 1970s (Weeks 1985: 21). This would include such liberal reforms as the Obscene Publications Act (1959), Betting and Gaming Act (1960), Abortion Act (1967), Sexual Offences Act (1967) and Equal Pay Act (1970). But 'permissiveness' also describes a sociological shift, a consequence of the postwar economic boom which encouraged a kind of controlled hedonism, a democratic liberalisation in the name of capitalism.

In this light, the 1970s start to look like both an economic and a moral recession; except, of course, that some post-permissive 'culture industries' suffered less of a recession than others.

We can make a further distinction here, between a 'permissiveness' which had repercussions for diverse sections of the population and the rather more exclusive 'permissive society', 'a middle-class, arts-related, metropolitan phenomenon' (Healy 1995: 246). The 'permissive moment' arguably splits in the early 1970s. On the one hand, there is the growing visibility of more specific sexual political discourses. The feminist and gay movements, in particular, perhaps sensed that they had not been intended as the main beneficiaries of 'liberation' – '"Sexual liberation" was confined to the heterosexual libido, and the belief in the release of the "real" man and "real" woman could have its bizarrely oppressive effects' (Weeks 1989: 293). At the same time, there was a commodification of permissiveness, which allowed a less elite crowd to 'catch up', albeit sometimes via forms equally oppressive to those not driven by the male heterosexual libido. The ambivalent popular cultural reception accorded feminism – or 'women's lib' – is a case in point. 'Second wavers' were often represented in the form of two contrasting images – promiscuous availability and humourless aggression. Both turn up in Carry on Girls (1973), in the usual parade of 'crumpet' for Sid James and Bernard Bresslaw to leer at longingly but unproductively and in the topically sabotaged beauty contest staged at the film's climax. Germaine Greer's The Female Eunuch was, of course, a bestseller in 1970, and more cautious negotiations of feminism's impact (if not politics) could be found in the magazines Nova (1965–75) and Cosmopolitan, whose first British issue appeared in 1972. Nova was nominally closer to the 'permissive society' than its rival, but its middle-class, heterosexist assumptions are evident in the 'How to undress in front of your man' flickbook published in the May 1971 issue. The early 1970s is a 'coming to terms' phase, in which the second wave coexists with Miss World, domesticated softcore and casual misogyny in the media.

For the arts and the media, the most important piece of permissive legislation was arguably the 1959 Obscene Publications Act, which formed the semantic battlefield for many a struggle. Here was the beginning of a distinction between a 'high' and 'low' permissiveness; its preamble set out its aim: 'to provide for the protection of literature; and to strengthen the law concerning pornography'. It introduced the defence of 'public good' – artistic, scientific or some other kind of merit which distinguished the meritorious from the exploitative. If that wasn't contentious enough, it retained the ambiguous 'tend to deprave and corrupt' definition of obscenity. In any case, pornography, too, could be interpreted as being for the 'public good' by an astute counsel, as a series of therapeutic masturbation defences proved. In 1972, The Longford Report proposed ominous reforms for both of these loopholes: 'the plea of public good should cease to be available as a defence on a charge of publishing an obscene article' (Longford Committee Investigating Pornography 1972: 370) and 'an article or a performance of a play is obscene if its effect, taken as a whole, is to outrage contemporary standards of decency or humanity accepted by the public at large' (my emphasis) (ibid.: 371).

21

The liberalisation of British film censorship certainly grew out of the Act's implied cultural distinction. Guy Phelps notes that John Trevelyan, the British Board of Film Censors' secretary througout the 1960s, 'succeeded in ... persuading the industry to accept that films of "artistic quality and integrity" should be treated "with respect" ' (Phelps 1975: 45), and Anthony Aldgate (1995) has shown how Trevelyan used the 'kitchen sink' and social problem films of the 1950s and 1960s to create a 'responsible' 'X' certificate film in opposition to the exploitation of the 'Adults only' category by Hammer and others. History has cast Trevelyan's beleaguered successor Stephen Murphy (1971–5) in the role of anti-censorship liberal, but he worked on the same principles. The controversial passing of *A Clockwork Orange* (Stanley Kubrick, 1971), *Straw Dogs* (Sam Peckinpah, 1971), *The Exorcist* (William Friedkin, 1973) and *Last Tango in Paris* (Bernardo Bertolucci, 1972) replayed the same priorities in less congenial times – at least two of them (Kubrick, Bertolucci) were respected auteurs and Peckinpah had his critical followers, too. Phelps (1975) and Dewe Matthews (1994) suggest that the Murphy-era Board overcompensated for their controversial choices by cutting heavily into less respectable films. Even then, 'quality' was erratically conceived. Few eyebrows would be raised by Michael Winner's failure to convince the board of *The Nightcomers'* (1971) credentials; but while Andy Warhol had been a favourite of Trevelyan's, Murphy was not enamoured of *Trash* and both cut it and delayed its certification.

Interestingly, the most sustained attacks by Festival of Light acolytes and similar interest groups were on 'high' permissiveness in the early part of the decade – *Oh! Calcutta!* (1970), the underground magazine *Oz* (prosecuted in 1971), *The Little Red Schoolkids Book* (1971), Martin Cole's sex education film *Growing Up* (1970). But Whitehouse's *Whatever Happened to Sex?* is haunted by a geographically specific Other that seemed to represent a blueprint for Britain's future – a transgressive Scandinavian jungle of unrestricted pornography and compulsory (and polymorphously perverse) sex education. *The Longford Report*, too, looks aghast at 'the Danish experiment', crudely interpreted as the belief that sex crime decreased in inverse proportion to pornography's uncensored expansion. In 1976, Whitehouse's ultimate nightmare came to Britain. Jens Jorgen Thorsen proposed to film the sex life of Christ in Britain, a project which threatened the ultimate secularisation of sex. He was roundly seen off by a coalition of parliamentary, religious and royal moral gatekeepers. In any case, by 1976, Britain had its own love–hate relationship with pornography firmly in place.

The pornification of Britain

> 'Capitalism', by its anarchic nature, has no controlling will. Its central
> imperatives – expansion, realisation of surplus value, profit – ensures
> a certain indifference to the terrain it is working on and through.
>   Jeffery Weeks (1985: 21)

In the early 1980s, another 1970s narrative was closed, at least for the time being – the once unstoppable growth of the sex industries, both in but increasingly also beyond the porn ghetto within Soho. In 1981, the Indecent Displays Control Act served notice on pornography's visual transformation of the West End and the provincial high street. Its predecessor was the aborted 1973 Cinematograph and Indecent Displays Bill – lost during the transition to a Labour government. Porn was 'spilling over' from its ostensibly private consumption – the cinema club or sex shop – through its increasingly explicit front-of-house advertising. 'It's become increasingly difficult to take a child to the London cinema,' fumed Michael Heseltine in 1975, 'The place is sex mad' (Screen International 3, 1975: 9). In 1982, the Local Government (Miscellaneous Provisions) Act toughened up the licensing of sex shops, while the new Cinematograph Act of the same year put paid to what were, in effect, hardcore film clubs.

By the 1970s, the sex industries were flourishing while the moral campaigners were making short work of what was left of the 'underground'. There were two reasons for this. First, the pornocrats worked with capitalism – they were, as Whitehouse observed, 'the unacceptable face of capitalism'. No one tested out free-market libertarianism more than the porn barons, and this was a significant growth industry in an otherwise ravaged economy. Its most lasting tycoon was David Sullivan, a 'Thatcherite before Margaret Thatcher' (Killick 1994: 50). The second reason was that the law was, by and large, on their side.

The Obscene Publications Act was floundering in a sea of inconsistencies over its 'tend to deprave and corrupt' definition. What could it mean in such a rapidly changing sexual climate? In 1974, top-shelf magazines like Penthouse, Mayfair and 'advice' mag Forum were ruled indecent in Bath. But hardcore film-maker John Lindsay was unsuccessfully prosecuted in 1974, 1977 and 1981 for 'publishing' films like Jolly Hockey Sticks, Juvenile Sex and Girl Guides Rape. Each prosecution was for the same films, and in each case he was acquitted.[8] Lindsay incorporated his symbolic victories into the marketing of the films, so that they began with the following authenticating boast:

> I, John Lindsay, was prosecuted at Birmingham Crown Court in 1974, and at the Old Bailey, London, in 1977, under the Obscene Publications Act 1959 and 64. I was acquitted in both cases and the jury found my films not to be obscene under the aforementioned Act.

The Act did not cover private cinema clubs, which could be prosecuted only under common law – consequently, Lindsay was able to exhibit the films once they had been cleared. Cinema clubs had also been let off by a loophole in the 1952 Cinematograph Act which rendered them virtually exempt from all but its safety regulations – in other words, they were answerable neither to the British Board of Film Censors nor to the local councils, who actually wielded more power than the BBFC. During the 1960s, clubs such as the Gala, Compton and Tatler groups opened with a mixed menu of 'continental' cinema and American softcore, and, in 1975, Lindsay opened the first hardcore cinema in Britain, the Taboo.

It's possible to trace two broad developments in the 'pornification' of Britain during the 1970s. The early part of the decade saw a 'mainstreaming' of pornography, indeed, a shift in what might be categorised as pornography, through *The Sun's* absorption of top-shelf material on Page 3, the *Confessions* films and the widespread acceptance (Bath notwithstanding) of magazines like *Penthouse*, *Men Only* and *Mayfair*. The latter were constructed, like *Playboy*, as 'lifestyle' magazines, where the consumption of nude pin-ups was part of the membership of an exclusive and very modern men's club; a *Penthouse* feature on 'How to Pull Birds in London' offered telling advice on how to make the most of 'liberation':

> Last but not least do not miss out on that other British sport – *demos*. Watch the press for announcements. *Left wing* demos are ideal. There is always a considerable body of amenable young ladies of highly progressive and permissive inclination.
>
> (Guirdham and Allen 1971: 18)

Both Whitehouse (1977) and Thompson (1994), from contrasting viewpoints, see 1976 as a turning point. The failure to convict the film *Inside Linda Lovelace* seemed to spell the end for prosecuting the written word as obscene, thus the shift in tactics (from obscenity to blasphemy) against *Gay News*. But it seemed to galvanise anti-porn campaigners. The final chapter of *Whatever Happened to Sex?* is called 'Days of Hope' – the Court of Appeal removed the 'public good' defence for porn (no more therapeutic wanking!), a decision upheld by the House of Lords; Thorsen was sent packing and *The Times* published an editorial on 'The Pornography of Hatred'. Whitehouse also played the paedophile card again, just to stack the censorship deck a little. But in any case, the feminist anti-porn campaign was achieving a greater visibility. Thompson (1994) traces (not very sympathetically, it has to be said) the sometimes uneasy alliance betwen feminist and Christian fundamentalist campaigners – but victory was by no means a foregone conclusion until the new legislation of the early 1980s. If anything, the sex industries seemed to thrive on such opposition, an impression reinforced by the characteristically insolent title of one of David Sullivan's magazines, *Whitehouse*.

The second half of the 1970s, then, is marked by an aggressive expansion of the porn industries, through Soho property-grabbing unchecked by Westminster Council, but, more significantly, through a marked expansion into the provinces. From 1976 to 1982, Soho had '54 sex shops; 39 sex cinemas and cinema clubs; 16 strip and peep shows; 11 sex-orientated clubs; and 12 licensed massage parlours' (Thompson 1994: 44). The fear of 'provincial Sohos' (*ibid.*: 58) had already been anticipated by the scandal surrounding sex supermarkets in 1970. Like any thriving capitalist industry, the pornocrats wanted to expand, above all into suburbia. In 1978, Sullivan opened his chain of Private Shops across Britain, usually in the face of massive resistance from locals powerless to prevent the transformation of their high streets. Mrs Kathleen Davey of Tunbridge Wells was one of many to express disquiet at this environmental upheaval:

> I have to pass the sex shop in Vale Road to go and get my pension and I think it looks sinister. I don't know what's behind the dark windows but

I'm quite sure it encourages undesirable people to come into this part of the town.

(quoted in Killick 1994: 36)

An interesting distance had been travelled between *No Sex Please, We're British* (Cliff Owen, 1973) – originally a box-office hit on the stage in 1971 – and *The Playbirds* (Willy Roe, 1978). *No Sex ...* 's central premise is the impact of a sex shop on a suburban high street. The Aphrodisia Bookshop is tellingly flanked by the Christian Reading Room and Barclays Bank – 'Honestly, I don't know what these British are coming to!' exclaims an American tourist whose husband's gaze is visibly wandering. The farcical mechanics of the plot – a bank clerk (Ronnie Corbett) receives the porn shop's delivery by mistake – evolve out of a 'return of the repressed' logic not dissimilar to the dynamics of innuendo. The more he tries to get rid of it, the more he ends up with; the most unyielding of the anti-porn campaigners (Arthur Lowe) inadvertently screens a blue movie to an audience of bird-watchers, including a rapt vicar, and the same character is 'recognised' by two prostitutes as a regular customer. This 'repressive hypothesis', to borrow Foucault's phrase, can be found also in the representations of anti-porn campaigners in films like *Eskimo Nell* (Martin Campbell, 1974) – puritans are secretly gasping for porn and kinky sex, just like their Victorian predecessors. But the film testifies also to porn's uncontainability, the way it 'spills over', even from behind the darkened windows of sex shops or the intricacies of blue movie distribution.

The Playbirds, on the other hand, speaks from within the sex industries – it's one of a series of films produced by David Sullivan, and its story takes place within a porn empire managed by an apparent Sullivan surrogate (Alan Lake). The title sequence is an extraordinary document of Soho at the height of its domination by commodified sex; history has bestowed a semi-documentary status upon it. As Mary Millington walks through the district, we see an unchanging, never-ending background of sex shops, cinema clubs, strip clubs and massage parlours – the effect is of *seeing* the statistics cited by Thompson. In a different kind of film, one could read this as a dire warning – Soho as a model for every high street. But The Playbirds is the most un-apologetic of films – a quality I shall explore in more detail in Chapter 7. This is how things are now, it seems to suggest, and this is how things will continue. Anti-porn campaigners of varying political persuasions and the incoming Conservatives with their 'family values' had different ideas.

The *Sun*-sational 1970s

For Jonathan Green, the 1960s were a 'bourgeois front-runner' to the 'true, pro-letarian uprising' of the 1970s (Green 1993: 9). There is a sense of trickling down – to working- and lower-middle-class consumers – and out, to suburbia, a virtually mythic locale during the period. In the 1970s, permissiveness collides with Orwell's 'voice of the belly protesting against the soul' (1941: 152). No-where is this shift more apparent than in the most lasting legacy of the decade, the newspaper read by Robin, Chrissie and Jo in *Man About the House*: the sexy, soaraway *Sun*.

The Sun poses huge problems for cultural populists – 'It is populist in the worst sense' (McGuigan 1992: 184), and 'destroys the assumption that if something is popular it must be ideologically sound' (Medhurst 1989b: 41) – but its cultural and historical importance should not be underestimated. Its low-permissive credentials are evident in its demonisation in *The Longford Report* for its 'sex and punchy radicalism' (Longford Committee Investigating Pornography 1972: 323). Rupert Murdoch relaunched it as a tabloid in 1969, but its swing to the right did not become apparent until the later rise of Thatcher – in 1971, it coined the famous phrase 'Maggie Thatcher – Milk Snatcher' when the then Education Secretary withdrew free school milk, her first claim to media fame. It backed Labour in 1970, supported the miners' strike in 1972 and opted out of the 'Ted and Harold show' in 1974, but, from 1975, recognised a tougher, more pragmatic populism in the form of the one-time Milk Snatcher, who seduced the editorial board once and for all. But this shift was tailored in editorials to fit a brash, young, modern image: 'The Sun is not a Tory newspaper ... *The Sun* is above all a RADICAL newspaper. And we believe that this time the only radical proposals being put to you are being put by Maggie Thatcher and her Tory team' (quoted by Chippindale and Horrie 1990: 61). On the other hand, *The Sun's* sexual politics were in place from the start. The first Page 3 girl, Stephanie Rahn, appeared in November 1970, but it set out to popularise the 'sexual revolution' in other ways, too – articles on orgasms and losing one's virginity often extracted from 'better sex' books like Jane Garrity's *The Sensuous Woman*. Above all, there were the 'saucy' stories which drew on a familiar popular mythology and transformed it into a 'never had it so good' sexual utopia. Chippindale and Horrie (1990: 38) cite the story, published in 1972, of the 'OMO Wives', Swindon housewives who signalled their sexual availability in supermarkets with packets of OMO washing powder – 'OMO' was allegedly an acronym for 'Old Man Out'.

Sex was part of a discursive notion of 'fun', one with rigidly drawn boundaries which positioned readers in specific ways. Men were in on the joke; women could play too, so long as they weren't 'frigid', lesbians, humourless feminists or ugly, like Olive in *On the Buses*. As Patricia Holland put it, sex was 'one of the rights of the consumer' (Holland 1983: 102), snatched from the jaws of do-gooders and moralistic spoilsports who wanted to deny the consuming working classes their momentary pleasures. Sex comedies – in which Robin Askwith's Timmy Lea was constantly meeting 'OMO Wives' – were all about such momentary pleasures, the compensatory 'fun' for performing undervalued labour – thus the importance of window cleaners, plumber's mates and milkmen in popular sexual mythologies. 'Crumpet' was now available to the poorer, the older and the unglamorous. Robert Murphy discerns a 'magnetic but unsavoury myth' in the later *Carry Ons*, 'where middle aged men could at last share the favours of sexually liberated young women' (Murphy 1992: 252).

Central to *The Sun's* readership were the C2s – conceived as young, skilled, ITV-watching, Labour-by-default but politically unmotivated. It has been argued that it was the mobilisation of these 'weak' voters that won success for Thatcher during the

'Winter of Discontent' (another *Sun* epithet). But first they were mobilised as new kinds of consumers:

> a working class whose rise to prosperity is still a living memory ... *The Sun* addresses a working class defined by its modes of consumption rather than its place in production. It unifies and organises its readers in terms of their forms of entertainment, by cultural attitudes rather than by class solidarity.
>
> (Holland 1983: 101)

Television

Murdoch and editor Larry Lamb also benefited from a new relationship with television: 'not to compete with television but to feed off it (with programming details, gossip and scandal)' (Laing 1994: 36). *The Sun* was the first popular daily to exploit advertising on television fully – a strategy rejected by its rival, *The Daily Mirror*. Its rapid-fire ads, fronted by Christopher Timothy, further consolidated the generic world they had marked out for themselves – 'cheeky' delivery, scandal, suburban slap-and-tickle and titillating 'glamour'. Meanwhile, ITV was sustained by flourishing advertising revenues at a time when the recession and the transition to colour cut cruelly into the BBC's budget. By the mid-1970s, the major networks (ATV, Granada, Thames, LWT and Yorkshire) enjoyed net advertising revenues of between £15 million and £27 million.

Whannel describes the 1968–82 period as 'the longest period of industrial stability in British television history' (1994: 176), but this is also the story of ITV's ascendance over the BBC. In 1982 the re-organisation of British broadcasting began – Channel 4, cable and satellite and the 'consumer sovereignty' debates which followed the Peacock Report (1986). The 1960s carry the critical burden of being a 'golden age of broadcasting', characterised particularly by the post-Reithian liberal benevolence of Hugh Carleton Greene, Director-General from 1960 to 1969. Ridgman (1992) qualifies this representation a little, but his account of the period is still predominantly the story of the BBC. The single play was its contribution to 'high' permissiveness, sufficiently so for Mary Whitehouse to single out Greene as the person 'who, above all, was responsible for the moral collapse which characterised the sixties and seventies' (1977: 15). Meanwhile, programmes like *Z Cars* and *Steptoe and Son* combined critical and commercial kudos. Of the ITV companies, only Granada has been allowed to crash this public service party via *World in Action*'s crusading zeal or *Coronation Street*'s virtual invention of the modern soap opera.

Not too surprisingly, events in the 1960s paved the way for 1970s broadcasting. BBC2's arrival in 1964, specifically as a 'high culture' channel, effectively cast BBC1 as even more of a competitor with ITV. Colour arrived on BBC2 in 1967 and spread to the other two channels in 1969. The consolidation of colour television was a progressive development – the percentage of colour sets increased from 1.7 to 70 per cent during the decade. Ridgman (1992) notes colour's impact on competitive scheduling and international sales, most visibly through a kind of 'heritage television' (Upstairs, Downstairs, Edward the Seventh), and one could also point to Lew Grade's glossy adventure shows like The Persuaders!

The ITV contracts were re-allocated in 1967, and four new companies (Thames, LWT, Yorkshire and Harlech) began broadcasting in 1968. LWT and Thames are of particular interest, in this context. Ridgman pinpoints LWT's shaky start as the 'official closing date' for the idealistic 1960s (1992: 142). An attempt to consolidate the legacy of commercial and intellectual respectability, LWT was dogged by bad ratings – Potter (1990) attributes this to a personnel whose strengths lay primarily in current affairs, but there were some notable exceptions. LWT was consistently beaten by BBC1 in the ratings at weekends, so that other regions lost confidence and picked up fewer of their programmes (including some of their bigger hits, such as Please Sir!, which had to be subsequently relaunched). In 1970, LWT was criticised by the ITA for one 'thoroughly bad weekend' (Potter 1990: 70) which included On the Buses, Frost on Sunday and a nude scene from Godard's film British Sounds on the arts programme Aquarius. The company was re-organised and relaunched in 1971, yet, paradoxically, the one area in which they had scored high ratings was light entertainment, especially sitcom, in the expert hands of Frank Muir. On the Buses hit the top spot in 1970 and was voted Top ITV Show in The Sun – it was rarely out of the Top Ten until its decline in 1973, and generated three successful films. Please Sir! and Doctor in the House, the latter a huge improvement on its insipid cinematic predecessors, were also big hits.

Thames was arguably the British television success story of the 1970s, both ITV's biggest programme-maker and the company which dominated the ratings by the start of the decade. While Thames encroached on the BBC's 'serious' programming, two types of programme gave it its highest viewing figures and turn up most frequently as reruns. On the one hand, it evolved a new, tough approach to crime drama, increasingly shot on 16mm, and later forming the basis of its film subsidiary, Euston films – Callan, Special Branch, Van Der Valk, The Sweeney (see Alvarado and Stewart 1985). But Thames, too, excelled in light entertainment programming: This Is Your Life, Opportunity Knocks, an unbeatable succession of sitcoms including Bless This House, Man About the House (which begat the even more successful George and Mildred and the not-quite-so-successful Robin's Nest) and Love Thy Neighbour. Above all, it had Benny Hill, who joined Thames in 1969. His one-off specials were ITV's top-rating show in 1970, 1971 and 1973, and he received a BAFTA award as Best Light Entertainer in 1971. His shows were an institution and consistent crowd-pleaser throughout the 1970s and a politically incorrect albatross for Thames by the end of the 1980s. But he, too, could be constructed as a kind of unprecedented 'heritage' television – half-hour versions of his hour-long shows became one of Thames's most successful exports, not least in North America.

Meanwhile, the BBC achieved its highest viewing figures for one-offs – the royal wedding (1974) and the Jubilee (1977), for example – and Christmas shows like Morecambe and Wise and Mike Yarwood. From 1966 to 1971, Miss World was their top-rating programme; the legendary 1970 contest, which included an unbilled flour-throwing feminist protest, achieved the highest ratings of the year (with Thames's *Benny Hill Show* in second place). For two years, the Eurovision Song Contest displaced Miss World, as the New Seekers and Cliff Richard, respectively, came second, but it remained in the Top Twenty up to and including 1977. Of the BBC's regular programmes, *The Generation Game* held a particularly formidable position in viewers' affections.

The BBC's most successful sitcoms were a continuation of traditions established during the 'golden age' – Croft and Perry's nostalgic character comedy (*Dad's Army, It Ain't Half Hot Mum*), the continuing and still popular *Steptoe* and *Till Death Us Do Part* and an update of the sitcom-as-character-drama tradition with *Porridge* and *Whatever Happened to the Likely Lads?* On the other hand, the critically praised *Fawlty Towers* was only a moderate success with viewers, until successive reruns built up its following. With its Oxbridge credentials and generic self-consciousness, *Fawlty Towers* anticipates the post-'alternative' sitcoms of the 1980s and 1990s.

Up Pompeii and *Are You Being Served?* looked to smuttier traditions – both had links of one sort or another with the *Carry On* films. Talbot Rothwell wrote *Up Pompeii* and most of the *Carry Ons*, but drew more on the latters' historical and generic parodies, which had mixed their innuendo with something verging on satire. In any case, Frankie Howerd was already being courted by the Oxbridge comedy establishment. *Are You Being Served?*, on the other hand, was a writing-on-the-wall sitcom; the Thames/LWT formula appropriated and refined. The 'pussy' jokes of Mrs Slocombe (Mollie Sugden) went further than its ITV rivals, and the show reclaimed *Carry On*'s potential queer heritage through John Inman's Mr Humphreys.[9] The *Carry On* films were in big trouble by the mid-1970s – they were starting to get the unpopular 'AA' certificate (for over-fourteens and therefore neither neatly 'family' nor 'adult') and ... *Behind* (1975), ... *England* (1976) and particularly ... *Emmanuelle* (1978) saw them struggling to keep up with the *Confessions* and *Adventures* films while holding on to an identity of their own.[10] But on television it was a different story – the BBC's screening of *Carry On Doctor*, for example, was viewed by 20.6 million people in 1979, and their screenings were invariably in the Top Twenty. At the same time, Thames TV specials like 1971's *Carry On Christmas* achieved similar success, suggesting an institutional shift for sex-free 'low' comedy rather than its death – *Are You Being Served?* survived well into the 1980s.

British cinema

British cinema had its very own 'crisis' in the 1970s. Clearly, battles over censorship distinguish the period from the 'Murphy Must Go'[11] era to James Ferman's pragmatic diplomacy in ensuring the Board's survival – it's a measure of Ferman's astuteness that he survived the even more volatile video explosion of the early 1980s. More damaging were the industry's irreversible financial difficulties, a combination of falling admissions and the withdrawal of American finance. Two consequences were particularly visible. First, the gulf widened between a limited number of large-budgeted, usually internationally financed productions – like the Bond movies or films by Ken Russell and Stanley Kubrick – and small-budgeted films aimed squarely at a domestic audience – primarily comedy, but also horror and the work of the Children's Film Foundation. Second, British cinema was visibly losing what limited commercial ground it had gained both to Hollywood blockbusters and to a thriving popular international cinema. In 1971 and 1972, British cinema was healthily represented in end-of-year box office lists; more than half of the Top Twenty were British. But by 1974 and 1975, the Top Twenty was dominated by American films like *The Sting*, *The Exorcist* (numbers 1 and 2 in the list, respectively, in 1974), *Towering Inferno* (number 1 in 1975) and notable international hits like *Enter the Dragon* (number 3 in 1974) and, of particular interest here, *Emmanuelle* (number 4 in 1975 and number 5 in 1976), the most successful softcore film at the British box office. As the decade developed, the Bond films, not too surprisingly, held their own most consistently – *Diamonds Are Forever* (number 1 in 1972), *Live and Let Die* (number 1 in 1973 – so much for Roger Moore being an 'inferior' Bond), *The Man With the Golden Gun* (number 3 in 1975), *The Spy Who Loved Me* (number 1 in 1977) and *Moonraker* (joint number 1 with *Superman* in 1979). Alexander Walker calls the mid-1970s 'the lowest point in British film-making' (1985: 135), and the 'lowest, the most shameful nadir of film industry fortunes' (*ibid.*: 136), and crosses his fingers for that nice David Puttnam to turn everything around. For Andrew Higson, 'the 1970s can be regarded as a transitional period for cinema, caught between two more significant moments' (1994: 217). Certainly, most British film histories support this prioritising of 'significant moments'.[12] Higson sees *Chariots of Fire* (1981) as a 'revival of British film production' (*ibid.*: 217), and it *is* a revival of the international marketability of 'Britishness'. But in terms of a popular indigenous genre cinema in Britain, the 1970s offer a final phase and a dovetailing of a number of significant traditions. This is the last period to date in which British audiences saw a comparatively large number of British films.

Three genres are particularly important, often in varying hybrid forms – horror, comedy (particularly drawing on television) and sexploitation, all relatively cheap and all reliable fare for British audiences.[13] The history of British horror tends to be written as the history of Hammer films (see Pirie 1973 and Hutchings 1993), and, while this is only part of the story, they did initiate the most productive phase for the genre, from the late 1950s to the mid-1970s. Hammer was still fairly prolific in the early part of the decade, but on reduced budgets – it had enjoyed backing from American studios during the 1960s and was now dependent on the more modest funds that EMI and Rank could offer. However, another company associated with horror was considerably more buoyant in the early 1970s, sufficiently so to have come close to buying Hammer from Sir James Carrerras for £300,000 in 1972. Tigon developed out of the Compton organisation under producer Tony Tenser and property developer Laurie Marsh. Hammer seemed to gaze longingly at sexploitation in films such as the 'Karnstein' cycle of sex-vampire films (*The Vampire Lovers*, 1970, *Lust for a Vampire*, 1971, *Twins of Evil*, 1971), but they had achieved a degree of respectability at odds with their early reviews, extending to the Queen's Award for Industry in 1968. In terms of 'quality', Hammer might as well have been MGM compared to Tigon, who combined cult horror films like Michael Reeves's *The Sorcerers* (1967)

30

and the subsequently acclaimed *Witchfinder General* (1968) with *Monique* (John Bown, 1970), *Zeta One* (Michael Cort, 1969) and *Au Pair Girls* (Val Guest, 1972). The endearing tattiness of Tigon's output barely hinted at the extent of its growing empire. By 1971, it was vertically integrated and bought the Classic chain, the third largest distributor in the country, which included ninety-one cinemas, twenty-one bingo clubs, one sauna, one casino, two coffee bars and three chocolate shops. The Tigon group's interests included film production and distribution, film music publishing, property development, educational/training films and cinema development. It was a precarious empire, as it turned out, but Tigon continued as a distributor of sexploitation, including the Sullivan films starring Mary Millington. Elsewhere, horror films drew on sexploitation personnel and directors – in particular the films of people like Pete Walker, Norman J. Warren, Antony Balch, José Larraz and James Kenelm Clarke.

One of the most productive comedy cycles was the television spin-off. Television spin-offs also included two *Sweeney* films, Euston Films' first theatrical features, the first of which – the emphatically titled *Sweeney!* (David Wickes, 1977) – was particularly successful (number 14 in the end-of-year Top Twenty list). Higson describes the television spin-off as an 'important if under-valued' strand in British cinema:

> Made on a low budget specifically for the domestic market rather than for export, and recruiting their performers and their audience from pre-existing entertainment forms such as music-hall, revue, variety and theatrical farce, 'low' comedy was a means of maintaining a stake for British film-makers in production and for British films in exhibition.
>
> (1994: 233)

Unfortunately, he then seems to join in with the under-valuing when he describes the spin-off as 'a rather desperate strategy'. To be fair, for all sorts of reasons, the television spin-off proved to be a dead-end – it depended, like exploitation movies, on the quota system (abolished in 1983), the Eady levy (withdrawn in 1984) and low production costs.[14] Yet two points need to be made. For one thing, television spin-offs had been a part of British film production since the 1950s – Hammer discovered its most bankable genre via *The Quatermass Experiment* (or *Xperiment* as the film version renamed it to emphasise its adults-only credentials), and sitcoms like *The Larkins* and *Whacko!* became *Inn for Trouble* and *Bottoms Up*, respectively (see Medhurst 1986). In terms of longevity, it isn't immediately clear that this cycle was more 'desperate' than, say, social problem or 'Swinging London' films – they were, admittedly, less exportable. Second, it would be misleading to understate just how successful they were, especially in the early part of the decade; and, even as late as 1979, *Porridge* could still make it into the Top Twenty films of the year. In 1971, *On the Buses* was the second most popular film at the British box office (to LWT's chagrin, I would imagine, given that the company refused to back it – EMI funded it as 'A Hammer Comedy Special'). It grossed £600,000 in its first month, and only *The Aristocats* had made more by the end of the year; *Up Pompeii* and *Dad's Army* were joint eighth and tenth, respectively. In fact, British comedy was a strong presence at the

31

1971 box office, with *There's a Girl in My Soup* at number 4 and the prophetically popular *Percy* at number 5. *Steptoe and Son* (1972), *Mutiny on the Buses* (1972), *Please Sir!* (1972) and *Up the Chastity Belt* (1972) all achieved Top Twenty positions.[15] Furthermore, one might usefully see the *Confessions* films as a fusion of sexploitation and the sitcom movies, which is why I shall sometimes refer to them as 'sexcoms'. They featured similar stars and personnel – the team of Greg Smith (producer) and Norman Cohen (director) also made the *Dad's Army* film. *Confessions of a Window Cleaner* (1974) made the Top Twenty two years running, in 1974 and 1975, and I would suggest that it absorbed its sitcom rivals rather than displacing them. The central character's family had a sitcom familiarity about them, an impression reinforced by the casting of television regulars like Dandy Nicholls, Doris Hare, Anthony Booth and Bill Maynard.

'The British people do not like dirty films,' John Trevelyan predicted towards the end of the 1960s, 'and they will never prosper' (Dewe Mathews, 1994: 186). As predictions go, this was not one of the more insightful ones. British cinema would barely have survived without 'dirty films'; as David McGillivray puts it, 'the last and most devastating downswing in British film production coincided with the cessation of the sex film business at the end of the Seventies' (1992: 15). While I have already sketched in the development of the porn industries, we need to consider specifically cinematic developments to account for this growth. By the start of the 1970s, all of the major cinema chains had accepted the 'X' certificate, which, from 1970, was now for over-eighteens; the new 'AA' (over-fourteens) certificate had been introduced as an intermediary category. Of the films reviewed in *CinemaTV Today* in 1974, 140 were 'X' films, compared with 46 'AA', 66 'A' and 25 'U'. Of that 140, 49 were sexploitation. Ten West End cinemas made a total of £15,861 in one week showing sex films at the end of 1974. It wasn't just films like *Emmanuelle* which accounted for such takings. In November 1975, a seemingly unprepossessing double-bill like *Love in a Women's Prison* and *Sins Within the Family* could make £6,600 at the Classic, Piccadilly, in one week, making it number 9 in that week's West End Top Ten. In 1977, the first British porn complex, the five-screen Classic Moulin, opened – Mary Millington's most successful film, *Come Play With Me* (1977), played there continuously for four years.

The above were all BBFC-passed films, and therefore the softest of softcore. Commercial softcore – especially prior to video – was an odd commodity. Its ostensible use-value (masturbatory gratification) was rarely granted by an individual text, if at all. Rather, like so much of the porn industries, it was a tease to lead into further consumption – with some notable exceptions, porn was a larger text, irreducible to a feature-length movie. Long-forgotten but successful imports like *French Love* (nearly £72,000 in twenty-two weeks at the Classic Moulin) and *How to Seduce a Virgin* didn't need to deliver – they were part of a larger loop in perpetual unsatisfying motion. The real merchandise in Soho's fleapits was the promise of pleasure for the curious, the visitor or the persistent 'connoisseur' – perhaps a star established in men's magazines (Mary Millington), a poster (hence the Cinematograph and Indecent Displays Bill), titles hinging on pornotopian buzzwords (confessions, virgin, intimate, secrets – words which embodied a tension between repression and release). Euro-smut's exchange value was not unlike primitive cinema, virtually sold by the yard, or rather by interchangeable title and poster. British sex comedies increasingly offered a more stable product, through stars and through comedy itself. No less important was the twinning and tripling of cinemas which eased sexploitation's journey into the provinces – the ABC circuit had an unexpected hit with I Am a Nymphoniac in 1972, paving the way for the wider distribution of the mid-1970s sexcoms.

The production base of Percy (1971) had been unusually close to the respectable heart of the British film industry – it was made for EMI by the Ralph Thomas/Betty Box team responsible for the Doctor films.[16] The Confessions films indicated a larger shift in the industry – they were distributed by Columbia. Promoted on television and through tie-in paperbacks, they made a bigger impact on the box office than their spottily distributed predecessors had been able to. Salon's cheaper Adventures films achieved similar success – Salon merged with Target International to distribute films as Alpha. Adventures of a Taxi Driver narrowly beat Confessions of a Driving Instructor in 1976 – car sex was clearly generically fashionable that year. This mainstream success didn't entirely conceal the genre's exploitative origins – one of the publicity suggestions for Confessions of a Window Cleaner's exhibitors was to display a ladder, a bucket and a pair of knickers in the foyer. But those knickers, significantly, had found their way into Odeons and other major chains and would stay there for the next few years.

The remainder of this book looks in more detail at some of the texts produced by this cultural-historical moment. Chapter 3 looks at the meeting of post-permissiveness and 'low' comedy – Carry On films, Benny Hill, television sitcoms – and also considers the way race and racism moved on to the agenda of prime-time light entertainment. Chapter 4 returns to the question of 1970s masculinity, and considers some of the dominant media types: as glam androgyny met swaggering laddishness in a shower of competing aftershaves, was this the first 'crisis' in masculinity? Chapter 5 considers youth pulp fiction both in the light of the law-and-order discourses of the period and in relation to its 'high' counterpart, subcultural theory. The final three chapters take on the 'lost continent' of 1970s British cinema – sexploitation and related horror films made outside the semi-respectable confines of Hammer. Taken together, they offer intriguing insights into the sexual and political culture of the period and how it was mediated through popular generic forms.

3

FROM CARNIVAL TO CRUMPET

Low comedy in the 1970s

Two things are happening in this chapter. First, I pick up on aspects of the 'high'/'low' distinction in relation to 1970s comedy, drawing on writing by Orwell, Nuttall and Carmichael and Bakhtin and looking at the *Carry Ons, On the Buses*, Benny Hill, *Man About the House, Rising Damp* and *Love Thy Neighbour*. Second, I pay particular attention to two developments in 1970s comedy – the different manifestations of permissive populism, or 'low' permissiveness, and the growing visibility of race as a subject for mainstream humour.

An obvious stopping-off point for any reclaiming of low British culture is George Orwell's 'The Art of Donald McGill' (1941), the most frequently cited text in defences of the tradition of mass-produced low comedy. Orwell was unexpectedly ahead of his time in celebrating some of the most despised aspects of the low-popular. First, there was *familiarity*, as opposed to the new and innovative – seaside postcards were 'as traditional as Greek tragedy' (a concession to 'proper' culture), 'a sort of sub-world of smacked bottoms and scrawny mothers-in-law which is part of Western European consciousness' (1941: 144). Second, there was their *vulgarity*, taken as a sign of their good health. Third, there was a revelling in *irresponsibility*, an irresponsibility which was the by-product of a predominantly repressed, compliant culture – the jokes appealed to an 'unofficial self, the voice of the belly protesting against the soul' (ibid.: 152).

Some of these themes and priorities were updated over thirty years later in a book which went very much against the grain of most critical writing in the 1970s. Jeff Nuttall and Rodick Carmichael's *Common Factors/Vulgar Factions* (1977) – 'bafflingly neglected', according to Medhurst and Tuck (1982: 44) – virtually invents cultural populism, with all of its weaknesses but also some of its refreshing, canon-baiting traits well to the fore. Here was a book about Blackpool, sex, pubs, sport, Harry Ramsden chip shops, 'laffs'. On the minus side, Nuttall and Carmichael's handling of taste and culture now seems simplistic – high culture represents death, an 'elephants' graveyard' reflecting 'the pale levels of good taste', while the repressed 'ruling class' will 'form a bulwark against the vigour and vinegar of the ascendant working class, a wall built of respectability' (1977: 4). Gender is even more of a problem – this is a muscle-flexing, masculine populism, and the writers find signs of resistance in the most ghastly violence and misogyny.

It comes as little surprise that Orwell is silent on matters of gender and ethnicity, and even class has a way of slipping in and out of this British low self, a 'lazy, cowardly, debt-bilking adulterer who is inside all of us' (1941: 53). Class is to the fore in Nuttall and Carmichael, however – the survival of vulgarity romantically parallels that of the 'ascendant working class'. But vulgarity has given way to ugliness and obscenity, and the former, in particular, is valued in two ways. First, it is linked to survival and identity: 'We use ugliness to fight back the smothering blankets of refinement. We use ugliness to revenge ourselves on the inevitability of death' (1977: 5). On the Buses is worth citing here, and we need look no further than the destination of the number 11 bus, which goes to the cemetery gates. That's the ultimate terminus, after all, and Stan and Jack drive there several times a day to remind themselves to have a good 'laff' first. Lest they forget, there's also the waxen-faced, sunken-cheeked inspector, Blakey, to signify death, a body devoid of the flatulent, guffawing lechery which functions like a life-support machine.

Second, ugliness becomes an aesthetic criterion, a kind of low-sublime, in its own right: '"Ugliness" is not so much the absence of the aesthetic but constitutes an alternative aesthetic. A cultural force whereby the vulgar can embrace their intrinsic merits, whereby the living can spit in the face of devastation' (1977: 9). Perhaps their richest intervention is in the specific field of comedy. Their distinction between 'me' and 'us' humour stands in for a number of oppositions – south versus north, wit versus 'necessity', cleverness versus community. Mikhail Bakhtin makes a similar distinction between 'official' laughter, private and individual, 'cut down to cold humour, irony, sarcasm' (1984: 37–8), and the public, collective laughter of carnival: 'Carnival is not a spectacle seen by the people; they live in it, and everyone participates because its very idea embraces all the people' (ibid.: 7). High theory/low culture caveats notwithstanding, it would be difficult to keep Bakhtin apart from the Carry Ons, On the Buses or Benny Hill, with their insistence on the 'lower bodily stratum' – he does give us some purchase on the politics of vulgarity. Nevertheless, Nuttall and Carmichael's 'survival' humour allows more scope for the coexistence of subversive and reactionary practices and ideologies. Bakhtin, roughly contemporary with Orwell (Rabelais and his World was written between the late 1930s and early 1940s), is one of the first romantic populists – he is unequivocal about the noble vulgarity of 'the people' and his longing for peasant folk cultures sometimes suggests Leavis in a Kiss-Me-Quick hat.

'Me' humour is founded on wit, an important sign of cultural capital:

a witty man is always in some way demonstrating his superiority. He has the skill to bend words, he has the special knowledge to make the right obscure reference that only you or I, of course, will recognise, in our deeply exlusive way ...

Wit is ambitious, it courts finesse. It seeks to leave behind human fallibility for which it holds an ultimate contempt ...

(Nuttall and Carmichael 1977: 24–5)

On the other hand, 'us' humour, 'survival laughter', 'the humour of necessity', rests on 'the perpetual celebration of common factors':

> Survival humour clings to the rock, embraces its own imperfections, set- tles for living at any price on the off-chance of pleasure or relief at some future date. Survival humour clings together with other folk, whilst for the best wits there is no safety in numbers or anything else, except escape.
>
> (*ibid*.: 25)

On the face of it, this marks out the celebrated and the critically marginalised in British comedy – the 'raucous' laughter despised by *The Daily Mail*. 'Me' humour encompasses, most obviously, the Oxbridge (and later 'alternative') tradition – by the 1970s, *Monty Python's Flying Circus* was obviously clever humour for clever people; the comic reference points had an almost unprecedented exclusivity (European philosophers, art cinema). But the more populist programmes in the 'great tradition' (*Hancock*, *Steptoe and Son*, *Porridge*) hinge on the wit of a central character, and, by implication, the writing team. 'Us' humour is trickier, already disappearing into the past. Even the *Carry Ons* cannot be viewed as pure 'us' humour, for all their music hall smut. Talbot Rothwell's 1960s scripts, like his work on *Up Pompeii*, combine familiar, recycled puns and innuendo with historical/generic parody, which implies the presence of a degree of 'wit' (the Latin jokes in *Carry on Cleo*, for example). Not for nothing is *Carry On Up the Khyber* (1968) the 'one *Carry On* that almost gets its foot in the door as a classic of respectable British cinema ... a film that crosses the boundaries' (Ross 1996: 73) – its burlesquing of British imperialism is at least knocking on the door of satire, even if it runs away when the door opens. Nuttall and Carmichael, in any case, cast Kenneth Williams in the 'me' camp – 'literacy, articulation, rambling inventiveness ... innuendos that "only you and I" can understand' (1977: 37). This, of course, raises other issues about who 'only you or I' might be. As Medhurst (1992) and Healy (1995) have shown, Williams's use of the gay slang *parlare* on the radio show *Round the Horne* perhaps constructs a more specific, locally defined 'us'. Sid James, on the other hand, was the *Carry Ons*' most consistent invocation of a more traditional 'us', and the most frequent to enjoy top billing. In other words, by the 1970s, 'me' and 'us' humour were already strains within British comedy rather than entirely separate textual domains. Nevertheless, there is a predominance of 'us' over 'me' in the texts considered in this chapter, even if, in the 'race' sitcoms of the period, it becomes harder to determine who 'we', the subjects of comedy (and 'Britain') are – exclusively white? White and sometimes Afro-Caribbean, but never Asian? Middle-class and liberal, not working- class and bigoted?

Carrying on

The *Carry Ons*, 'the last major cinematic flourish of "us" humour' (Medhurst 1986: 183) are often seen at one remove from cultural history, already a little anachronistic when they began in the late 1950s, increasingly so as 'the sixties' happened. The series can be broken down into three overlapping phases. The early, institution-based films such as ... Sergeant, ... Nurse and ... Teacher featured anecdotal plots in which 'the causal logic of classic narrativity is replaced by a more loosely motivated plot, less developmental than episodic ... weak in dramatic accumulation, functioning more as a thinly disguised pretext for the display of comic set-pieces' (Hill 1986: 142). During the second phase, generic/historical parodies offer the series even more of a holiday from social and cultural change – the sequence of ... Jack (1963), ... Spying (1964), ... Cleo (1964), ... Cowboy (1965), ... Screaming (1966), Don't Lose Your Head (1966), Follow That Camel (1967) and ... Up the Khyber (1968) is broken only by a return to bedpans and blanket baths with Carry On Doctor (1967). It's the third phase with which we are especially concerned here, beginning with Carry On Camping, the most successful British film of 1969 and an unexpectedly self-reflexive one.

That ... Camping marks a shift is rarely disputed, and one scene is usually taken as emblematic of this turn: 'After Barbara Windsor's brassiere had at last burst ... where was the humour in teasing about the possibility of such an occurrence?' (Medhurst 1986: 183). But two points need to be made here. First, nudity and innuendo had coexisted in British popular culture for some time outside the cinema. The Windmill Theatre in Soho, from 1932 to 1964, combined nude tableaux (and later strip-tease) with stand-up comedy – Morecambe and Wise, Dick Emery and Harry Worth all passed across its stage, while Benny Hill, inappropriately, failed the audition.

Second, when the Carry Ons first capitulated to (brief) displays of nudity, they did so not by looking forward, or even sideways, but backwards. Babs's breast-propelled bra does indicate a point-of-no-return, but the opening and closing of the film suggest that the film's lowbrow determinants are more historically complex.

We are at the cinema – it ought to be a Jacey or a Compton, but in fact it's the Picture Palace. The poster announces Nudist Paradise, and the dialogue refers to Naked – As Nature Intended. Inside the fleapit are Sid James and Bernard Bresslaw with their 'dates' Joan Sims and Dilys Laye – it goes without saying that they all have ice lollies. Sid can't wipe the grin off his face, nor suppress delighted guffaws; Bresslaw's jaw is touching carpet. Dilys Laye is nauseous – a condition later linked to motion sickness, appropriately enough for a film considering a journey into new territory. And Joan Sims is equal parts outrage and indifference at all that judiciously staged volleyball:

Joan: It's disgusting, that's what it is, it's disgusting!
Sid: What are you talking about, disgusting? It's artistic.
Joan: Artistic?
Sid: Certainly!
Joan: What, with all those big bottoms bobbling about all over the screen?
Sid: Ah, you wouldn't think anything of it if we were walking about like that all the time – free, unfettered, unashamed.
Joan: Oh no? I suppose you'd rather we all sat here stark naked.
Sid: Wouldn't bother me.
Joan: It would if your ice lolly fell in your lap.

The nudist film is perfect for *Carry On* – a British institution in which high (surface) ideals masked base lechery.[1] But by 1969, they were already consigned to history – the 'nudies' had fizzled out six or seven years earlier. The nudist camp, however, had been institutionalised as a comic locale in seaside postcards by the mid- to late-1960s, now displaying naked breasts – a helpful 'Nudist Camp' sign was always visible to explain why the British were taking their clothes off. The comic potential of (invisible) male genitals found new generic outlets – 'Ginger Nuts! I knew I'd Forgotten Something!' exclaims a woman as her red-headed husband bends over to stir the soup. Sid and Bernie take their partners to the camp featured in the film – 'back to nature, all that freedom!' – but find that it's no longer a naturist club. There they are joined by suburban Terry Scott and his wife, with her neighing, honking car-accident of a laugh, hanger-on Charles Hawtrey and a bus full of St Trinian's jailbait from 'Chayste Place' presided over by Kenneth Williams and Matron Hattie Jacques. We're back on familiar ground until the arrival of a Hippy Free Festival in an adjacent field, successfully expelled but not before they make off with Babs and the other girls. The camp is a socio-sexual space in transition – naturism has moved on, free love is on its way; the former takes itself seriously enough to be debunked, the counter culture is an unknown quantity and visibly Not Welcome.

Carry On Loving (1970), ... *At Your Convenience* (1971), ... *Matron* (1971) and ... *Girls* (1973) require some comment as the most of-their-moment of the 1970s entries. ... *Loving*'s parade of miserable couples, linked by Sid and Hattie's dating agency, are contrasted both with commercialised sex ('Everyone's Raving About – SEX!' 'Twice Nightly' declares a bus display)[2] and uninhibited youth – a running gag finds the same teenage couple on a bus, in the back of a car, in a lift and in a telephone box ('Please be quck. Others may be waiting for it'). ... *Matron* is about a plot by a work-ing-class gang to steal the contraceptive pill, a felicitous metaphor for hijacking the permissive bus. The Family Planning Act was passed in 1967, and ITV was screening family planning advice in 1970, the year that the pill was officially available to the unmarried, and available on the National Health from 1973. But its use even by married couples was limited – a 1970 survey revealed that only 19 per cent of couples un-der forty-five used it, 29 per cent used condoms and 37 per cent didn't use any-thing (Marwick 1982: 117). According to Jeffrey Weeks, 'its incidence of use decreased down the social scale and in a movement from the south-east of England towards the north-west' (1989: 260). But the pill was a totem of social change, largely from a male definition: 'The eroticisation of modern culture could focus on the female body without most of the consequences which in earlier days had been feared and expected' (*ibid.*: 260). The motivation in ... *Matron* is ostensibly to sell the contra-ceptive pill abroad, but there's an enduring sense of the lower orders redistributing permissive wealth.

As the 1970s *Carry Ons* returned to the institution, they also seemed to have re-located to a place called Planet Smut, a region (a lower region) populated by towns like Much-Snogging-on-the-Green and Fircombe and landmarks such as the Finisham Maternity Hospital and Rogerham Mansions. The institution, according to Marion Jordan, cannot accommodate 'the animal nature of human beings: their sexuality

... their excretory functions, their preference for idleness as opposed to pointless physical strain' (1983: 316). But the institution is now largely given over to 'animal nature' – the hospital was always a safe bet for this, and the toilet factory in ... *At Your Convenience* certainly doesn't function as the body-denying institution Jordan is talking about. In ... *Matron*, Sid is preoccupied with his pill-snatch, so it's left to Terry Scott's Dr Prodd, 'the taxidermist' (there are trophies celebrating each sexual conquest), to keep the lecher's end up, not least when sexually harassing a dragged-up Kenneth Cope. The film plays fast and loose with gender, even by the standards of the series. Cope, posing as a nurse, changes his name from Cyril to Cyrille ('It's a surreal ... a real name!') – 'Cor, I could really fancy you,' says Bresslaw admiringly, later donning a dress himself. Kenneth Williams's hypochondriac doctor learns that he has an unusually large pelvic cavity and convinces himself that he's changing sex. 'Your mail,' says Matron Hattie, handing him some letters – 'Yes, I am,' shrieks Williams, 'and I can prove it, do you hear me? Prove it!'

One consequence of carnivalising the institution is that the 'spoilsports' have to be found elsewhere – the targets become more specific (feminism, trade unions) and the community less easy to hold together. The earlier films, John Hill observes, ultimately unite authority and the group into a collective, unified effort 'binding together diverse social types through an "imaginary" dissolution of real authority relations' (1986: 143). In ... *At Your Convenience* and ... *Girls*, this becomes harder to do: ... *At Your Convenience*, very much a Heath era movie, was an unexpected flop at the box office, a failure attributed by Rigelsford (1996) and Ross (1996) to its I'm All Right Jack anti-union stance. Kenneth Cope's Vic Spanner (in the works) largely denies human 'nature' in the interests of the union rulebook. Only 'animal nature' can re-unite the group, not only on a riotous Brighton outing but by the dissolution of Vic's one-man strike by a sexy new canteen girl. Even so, and for all its considerable pleasures, ... *At Your Convenience* is a worryingly top-down narrative, playing like a grubby *Metropolis* to unite capital and labour – boss's son Richard O'Callaghan and foreman's daughter Jacki Piper stand in for Gustav Fröhlich and Brigitte Helm respectively. Sid's class affiliation – admittedly self-delusory in real terms – is the casualty. He plays a foreman who can nevertheless 'speak the language' of the workers. Earlier, he gets them laughing and almost back to work, before O'Callaghan utters the fatal line, 'All right, that's enough fun.' Having already saved the company with his racing winnings, his daughter's marriage to O'Callaghan ensures that 'you're management yourself' – 'No, no, I'm a worker!' he protests, but to no avail. One can only speculate on the reasons for the film's commercial failure, but it is worth contrasting with the trade union populism of *On the Buses*, whose first cinematic offshoot enjoyed very different fortunes in the same year.

Carry On Girls, meanwhile, fragments fascinatingly before our eyes. This time, the plot is a confrontation – a beauty contest versus women's libbers, led by June Whitfield's Augusta Prodworthy. Interestingly, it's the latter who win, and, while Sid's trademark laugh is the last sound we hear, there's a slightly desperate ring to it. The feminists are a diverse group, older than popular representations of second wavers tended to be. Augusta combines women's rights with puritanism, and seems ripe for a humiliation that never arrives – 'there can never be anything proper in young women being shown off like cattle for the sexual gratification of drooling men'. 'Proper' is killjoy talk in Carry On land, and the sabotage is appropriately called Operation Spoilsport.[3] Second in command is Angela, coded lesbian with her bobbed hair, shirt-and-tie and cardigan – a policeman calls her 'this gentleman' by mistake. There's even a bra-burning ritual which swiftly deteriorates into a conflagration. But the feminists offer empowerment to a familiar Carry On type – the put-upon wife or partner, here represented by Mayor's wife Patsy Rowlands, who joins the group, and, by implication, the taken-for-granted Joan Sims who has her revenge on Sid by stealing the takings during the beauty contest fracas. Augusta is mocked for opposing a men-only toilet – 'We will squat on this erection to man's so-called superiority' – but Rowlands's weak bladder politicises bodily functions; for her, there is truly something at stake. Unusually, as Frances Gray suggests, 'joining the women's movement has been a way into humour, not a way out' (1994a: 9), and the film allows her considerable pleasure at the humiliation of husband Kenneth Connor.

Regular rises and Bus Driver's Stomach:
On the Buses

> I think fuckin' laffing is the most important thing in fucking everything. Nothing ever stops me laffing.
> 'Joey', Learning to Labour (Willis 1977: 29)

The word 'raucous' recurs in descriptions of On the Buses (LWT 1969-73), the word applied both to its audience and to the show itself, 'filled to the brim with noisily unlikeable stereotypes' (Crowther and Pinfold 1987: 71). Certainly, the show's most enduring image is of driver Stan (Reg Varney) and conductor Jack (Bob Grant) laughing, endlessly, terrifyingly – nothing can stop them. At work, it's the sign of their power over the Hitler-moustached Blakey (Stephen Lewis), while at home it's usually directed at Stan's lank-haired, milk-bottle-spectacled sister Olive (Anna Karen), who is funny simply because she is unattractive. But Stan and Jack have another reason to laugh – no oil paintings themselves, they never go short of 'crumpet', and Jack, in particular, has his pick of the sexy young clippies.[4] As Jordan says of the Carry Ons, 'there is no need ... for men to be attractive' (1983: 332). This is the epitome of permissive populism – anti-authority, based on male camaraderie (like all those 1970s ads showing ugly men drinking beer), delighted at the availability of modern young women. Few short scenes in British film history empower the male gaze quite like the opening of the first On the Buses film (Harry Booth, 1971). Wherever they look, there are cleavages to look down and miniskirts to look up – Stan is so distracted by one such 'view' that he drives through a puddle, sending an ejaculatory spray over Blakey. In 'The New Uniforms', one of the most popular episodes, first transmitted in 1970, they are forced to wear bell-bottomed trousers and flared tunics. They mince about in a mock fashion show, but their disgust turns to delight when their pulling power increases as a result. The uniforms put

40

them up a class – they're mistaken for pilots by two Swedish girls – and down a generation.

Paul Willis's *Learning to Labour* (1977), a classic cultural studies text, follows a group of working-class 'Lads' from school to factory floor. Along the way, Willis provides some incidental but valuable insights into comedy and power. The Lads, boisterous and disruptive, distinguish themselves from another group, the 'Ear 'oles', effete and conformist, who have capitulated to the formal hierarchies of school or work. For the Lads, on the other hand, the informal must be asserted against the hegemony of the formal, and a crucial vehicle for doing so is the 'laff', 'the privileged instrument of the informal, as the command is of the formal' (Willis 1977: 29). Blakey is very much the 'Ear 'ole', utterly subservient to the bus company while forever bleating out ineffectual commands – his famous catchphrase, 'I 'ate you, Butler!', is the very embodiment of powerlessness. He's the weak link in working-class masculinity, the portal through which women drivers, poncey uniforms and bureaucratic interference gain entrance.

Willis could easily be describing *On the Buses* when he characterises the 'laff' as: 'part of an irreverent marauding misbehaviour. Like an army of occupation of the unseen, informal dimension, "the lads" pour over the countryside in a search for incidents to amuse, subvert and incite' (ibid.: 30). Bakhtin's notion of the 'carnivalesque' revels in the reversal of hierarchies of power, debunking and humiliating authority, just as Blakey is tormented so ritualistically – in 'Foggy Night', they amuse themselves by throwing peanuts into his snoring mouth until he wakes up, choking. Jack, in particular – a leering hedonist, cigarette in one hand, head thrown back like a shark on laughing gas – is the maestro of 'marauding misbehaviour'. It's particularly significant, therefore, that he is also Shop Steward. Apart from modulating his voice to 'speak' from this position, there is no indication that the union rulebook interferes with beer, 'birds' and laffs; rather, it bolsters up the (male) working class's right to physical pleasures, to fun and misbehaviour. Writers Ronald Wolfe and Ronald Chesney had incorporated trade unionism into an earlier sitcom, *The Rag Trade* (BBC 1961–3) – 'Everybody out!' was Miriam Karlin's catchphrase. In the very first episode of *On the Buses*, there's already an impending strike over the canteen – 'We're the bosses now, you know,' Stan tells Blakey. When Tom Lappin describes the show as 'a telling witness to the Britain of the Heath era', he doesn't mean it as a compliment – rather patronisingly, he describes it as 'all vulgar fumbling and struggling to come to terms with the wider world' (1994: 18). But its vulgar populism contextualises it as part of that moment – did the miners make Heath look like the proverbial 'Ear 'ole'? *Carry On At Your Convenience* recoils from 1970s militancy, and, while picket line duty isn't much fun in *On the Buses* – Stan has to get up earlier than he would for work – it acknowledges that the working classes might have to fight for their pleasures, good-natured skiving and clippie-pulling included.

Of course, these 'laffs' aren't equally distributed – when are they ever? If the *Carry Ons* contain more diverse representations of women than tends to be acknowledged, *On the Buses* constructs its biggest boundaries around gender. The point of the clippies seems to be that they don't need to be seen as workers; rather, as busmen's perks.

2 'Bus Driver's Stomach' and 'Ear 'oles'; the carnivalesque bodies of *On the Buses*. Stan (Reg Varney), Blakey (Stephen Lewis) and Jack (Bob Grant). (Courtesy of LWT.)

When Stan's girlfriend becomes a driver (in the 1971 film), she's off limits to him until she's demoted again, whereupon Jack gives him the green light – 'She's crumpet, mate – she's available.' In so far as the film has a plot, it deals with Blakey's scheme to bring in women drivers, who pose a threat to Stan's overtime as well as the sexual economy of the depot. Middle-aged and 'masculine', they are humiliated in a particularly vicious way, tormented with spiders and laxatives, subjected to homophobic innuendo:

Blakey: They'll be able to do your job properly, and they won't waste time trying to
         pick up the clippies.
Jack: By the look of 'em, I'm not so sure.

But it's Olive who is the butt of the show's domestic cruelty – she is, quite simply, the most abject female figure in British comedy. The more she attempts to accentuate her sexuality with false eyelashes ('They're too big – every time you blink, you'll knock your glasses off') or an improbable blue frilly mini-nightie, the more we are invited to recoil. When she puts on a bikini in *Holiday on the Buses* (Bryan Izzard, 1973), the camera looks her up and down as though it can't believe its eyes – when she dives into the pool, the bottom half inevitably comes off, to much ribaldry. Married to the lugubrious Arthur (Michael Robbins), she inhabits the most extravagant version of the sexless, discontented comic couple:

Olive: My wedding dress was very beautiful.
Mum: Yes, love, it did something for you – made you look very glamorous.
Arthur: The veil did.
Olive: What do you mean by that?
Arthur: Gawd, that veil was so thick you didn't know which way you were facing.
        Half the time you'd got your back to the vicar.
Olive: It wasn't the veil. It was so hot my glasses got all steamed up. And when the
        vicar started talking, I thought I was gonna sneeze.
Arthur: I must be the only bridegroom who lifted up the veil of his bride to kiss her
        and found an inhaler stuck up her nose.

The treatment of Olive is truly merciless and unremitting. Unlike Yootha Joyce's
Mildred or the 'bad' wives in *Carry On*, she is never the subject of humour, only its
object. But she is also the central site of the show's 'aesthetic of ugliness', its prime
grotesque body. She first enters the series coughing, a constant inscription of corporeal frailty and intestinal determinants – 'Watch it love, you'll burst your boilers.'
The grotesque female body gets pride of place in Bakhtin's carnivalesque aesthetic,
not least in the terracotta figurines of pregnant, cackling hags. Mary Russo is more
cautious – these female grotesques are 'more than ambivalent ... loaded with all of
the connotations of fear and loathing around the biological processes of reproduction and of aging', but at least 'exuberant' (1994: 63), not the word which comes
to mind with Olive. But she accommodates (a suitably ambivalent word) the series's most sublime aesthetic reversal in 'Brew It Yourself', where Stan's home-made
beer initiates a carnivalesque transformation of the largely desire-free zone of the
Butler household. Arthur, in his drunken stupor, finds Olive 'a bit of all right!' and
they kiss passionately, she in her baroque nightie, curlers and Stan's cap. 'Blimey,
mate, she'll kill him!' marvels Stan – Arthur has had an unspecified but much-cited
'operation' – as they go upstairs for a rare and presumably riotous taxing of the
bedsprings.

The carnivalesque body operates as a kind of anti-abject, celebrating its precarious borders as empowering rather than identity-threatening.[5] The mouth, the genitals, the bowels and the womb are privileged sites in this anatomical agenda:

> the grotesque image ignores the closed, smooth, and impenetrable surface
> of the body and retains only its excrescences (sprouts, buds) and orifices,
> only that which leads beyond the body's limited space or into the body's
> depths.
>
> (Bakhtin 1984: 318)

These 'sprouts' and orifices belong to a polymorphous body, so that sex, eating and
defecation are not fully distinguishable from one another. In one of Benny Hill's sketches,
he hides a goose down his trousers and it keeps popping out, front and back, to steal
food, pinch bottoms and generally misbehave; an unruly penis one minute then an
animated turd or a hungry mouth. In *On the Buses*, everything comes back to the digestive

system, recalling Nuttall and Carmichael's description of comedian Frank Randle as 'a visibly overflowing sewerage system', a reminder to the audience that they were 'mere alimentary systems, mere overgrown infants, mere flesh and blood' (1977: 38). Male sexuality is not phallic, but situated, instead, in the stomach – ''Scuse fingers,' apologises Stan as he gropes a clippie on her way into his cab. The very first image in the first episode is sausages being cooked for breakfast, and by episode six we've been through the full high-cholesterol diet just in the opening scenes. No episode is complete without a meal-time discussion, words and half-chewed food flying every which way. But while a stomach full of fried food keeps the cemetery gates symbolically at bay, it also brings them literally closer, as evinced by 'Bus Driver's Stomach', the combined consequence of excessive fry-ups and bad posture. Stan complains that the bus 'puts a froth on my gastric juices', while Arthur warns him that 'You've got enough acid in your stomach to burn a hole in the carpet.'

In the 1971 film, Jack stops off for some quick trousers-on sex with 'Turnaround Betty' – 'Breakfast in bed' – while Stan eats his breakfast in the cab. The editing parallels these two 'meals', cutting at one point from Jack nuzzling a shoulder to Stan greedily biting into a juicy orange. The trio of bodily functions is completed by Blakey's unexpected arrival and Stan's claim that Jack is answering 'a call of nature':

Blakey: Do you mean to say he's been using that lady's facilities?
Stan: Well, you could say that.

This representation of women as perishable goods – eminently consumable but quick to turn rotten – has a chilling resemblance to Hitchcock's *Frenzy* (1972), a film which might appear to be a perverse presence in a chapter on comedy – only Peter Hutchings (1986) has commented on its affinity with low comedy. *Frenzy*, too, is an 'appetite' text, filled with grotesque gastronomic imagery – according to one critic, the film 'constantly alludes to the appetite of its audience, perhaps grown too large for anyone to satisfy' (Sgammato 1973: 135). The 'necktie murderer' Bob Rusk (Barry Foster) is as jauntily laddish in his pursuit of women as Jack, but we see the violence behind the charm. He eats an apple after the rape-murder of one victim, to whom he describes his sexual philosophy as 'Don't squeeze the goods until they're yours', and hides another's body in a potato truck.

Where does the carnivalesque stand in relation to the permissive, the increasingly official voice of the unofficial? In one sense, it doesn't – sitcoms aren't folk culture, regardless of the laugh track, 'the vestigial reminder of the music hall audience, the electronic substitute for collective experience' (Medhurst and Tuck 1982: 45). Stasis, nostalgia and change are all part of *On the Buses* – authority is mocked but accepted as inevitable (and, in mocking it, desirable), fried food, fag ends in the toilet and dirty nappies are as important as washing machines and family planning, 'liberation' is fine for separating clippies from their knickers but threatening if women become more than unskilled labour.

We need to look to a BBC sitcom to see carnival accommodate more radical changes in Britain's sexual culture, namely *Are You Being Served?* Murray Healy argues that the

Carry Ons 'opened up a space for a carnivalesque critique of dominant sexual discourse, and queers got in' (1995: 247), a coup cemented by *Served*. If Williams and Hawtrey were 'narratively straight but semiotically bent' (Medhurst 1992: 19), John Inman's Mr Humphreys was unambiguously out, 'not just homosexual', but '*gay* at a time when the word was still radically political' (Healy 1995: 253). And while he was still an 'eccentric' stereotype contained within the sitcom group, he was 'allowed to acknowledge some sort of gay scene, a network of other gay men (he even gets to have a drink with some transsexual friends in the ... (1977) film)' (ibid.: 255). Healy assesses the show: 'from a position and cultural perspective of queer confidence. It would have been hard for most contemporary gay viewers to read comfortably beyond the heterosexual imperative of these comedies' (ibid.: 256). But *Served* opens up a space – not found in the ITV sitcoms – within the reclaiming of 1970s smut. Catchphrases count for a lot in popular comedy, and 'I'm Free!' was a significant, if ambiguous, addition.

Angels and cherubic devils: Benny Hill

There's no fun in doing a gag with a girl's skirt blowing up and showing her knickers if she's showing them already, as they did with mini-skirts.
    With stockings, there's an element of embarrassment, and that's what the gag needs.

Benny Hill (*Daily Mirror*, 14 May 1979)

The sexual political battles fought over Benny Hill after his dismissal from Thames in 1989, and again after his death in 1992, indicate some of the limits and problems which accompany 'carnivalesque' defences of vulgar comedy. As early as 1980, he was singled out for criticism at the TUC Women's Conference in Brighton, although still voted ITV Personality of the Year in 1982. In 1986, Ben Elton articulated a growing liberal consensus when he told Q magazine, 'You have Benny Hill in the late Eighties chasing half-naked women around a park when we know in Britain women can't even walk safe in a park any more. That, for me, is worrying.' Two years later, the newly formed Broadcasting Standards Council joined the anti-Hill lobby. Kay Lewis, writing in The Guardian after Hill's death, attributed his worldwide success to 'the international language of misogyny' (24 April 1992: 26), but Hill's defenders were far more resistible than crude effects theory models of his undoubted sexism could ever be.

John Casey's 'Why Society needs Benny Hill' in *The Evening Standard* (9 December 1991) is fairly representative of what Lewis calls 'middle class, middle aged white men whose own attitudes to sex and women were formed, like Hill's, in the immediate post war years before the sixties and seventies wave of feminist ideas'. According to Casey, Benny Hill 'reincarnates the sort of comedy that not only is disrespectful of taboos – moral, political, religious – but is also the embodiment of the life force' (9). Even people who like Hill, myself included, might wonder which taboos exactly he was transgressing. But it becomes apparent that there is a slippage in the 'taboos' Casey is talking about, and that 'we need anything that breaks wind in the direction of current pieties: women's rights, gay liberation, ethnic minorities, kindness to animals, the environment' (oh, those taboos!). Perhaps the least attractive legacy of a diversity of interests and lobbies being grouped together as 'political correctness' is the licence it grants gruesome, embittered reactionaries to re-imagine themselves as cultural mavericks and iconoclasts. 'Censorious' feminists lose out on both counts. On the one hand, they are clearly cast as 'the establishment' – which would come as news, I imagine – but also as transgressors against tradition, 'rejecting the oldest traditions of European comedy. The old comedy of the ancient Greeks, as exemplified in the plays of Aristophanes, was a mixture of Benny Hill and Ben Elton.' There seems to be some confusion about who is setting which agendas here. But the pathologising of Hill won't do either – with success on this scale, 'attacks' and 'defences' aren't entirely the point.

Hill's television career took off in the late 1950s at the BBC. His rise to power is often paralleled with that of television – 'Benny was really the first star comedian to be made entirely by television', according to Ken Carter (*The Observer Supplement*, 17 December 1967)[6] – the very embodiment of variety transfigured by technology and its cultural consequences. Since he was an anxious, apparently indifferent stage performer, television seemed the perfect vehicle for Hill's conspiratorial glances and anticipatory smirks (Carter called it 'eyelash comedy ... You know exactly what he's thinking', while Michael Caine described him as 'a cherub sent by the devil'), his mixture of variety and burlesque, his parody of television forms (multiplying himself to play all of the contestants on *Juke Box Jury*, parodying the 'panning and scanning' of widescreen films on television), his comic monologues and songs, his trademark 'silent' sketches and chases. When not dealing with the materiality of television, Hill's material was so old that the *Carry Ons* would have turned it down, and he recycled gags and their components like algebraic formulae. His innuendo was already a source of concern for the BBC in the 1950s, but his most contentious material evolved during the 1970s – he signed to Thames soon after its inception, producing four shows a year in which the smut became increasingly integrated into the visual spectacle. This was new to light entertainment – lots of suspenders, bikinis and bending over, contrasted with the 'dragons' played by Bella Emberg or Rita Webb. The lack of narrative intensified the gap between these two 'postcard' types, whereas a performer like Joan Sims created a space for a broader range of representations in the *Carry Ons*. What Hill *did* have in common with the *Carry Ons* was the way he responded to relaxations in censorship by looking to earlier combinations of smutty humour and voyeuristic spectacle:

> When I was a lad and crazy to get into showbiz I used to dream of being a comic in a touring revue. They were extraordinary, wonderful shows with names like *Naughty Girls of 1942*. There were jugglers and acrobats and singers and comics, and most important of all were the girl dancers. My shows are probably the nearest thing there is on TV to those old revues.
>
> (quoted in Kirkland and Bonner 1992: 145)

46

'Modern' sexuality, meanwhile, is terrifying in all its forms. In a wishing well sketch, Benny 'replaces' his 'battle axe' wife with a bikini-clad girl. She, in turn, summons up a muscular body builder who wishes her away and chases Benny. As in a number of sketches, lechery is a narrative with an uncertain conclusion. Masculinity, in Benny Hill, is past its prime, jaunty and game but frail – the randy old man clutching his chest and expiring at the moment of sexual success is a recurring image. His supporting cast are of some considerable importance to this scenario. Jack Wright is emaciated, toothless and bald – his treatment gives the term 'slaphead' a rather literal meaning. He is the 'cemetery gates' of the show. In a hospital sketch, he's slapped, kicked and has a match struck on his head – as he undresses, the doctors gather round to laugh at him. Bob Todd, the best of Hill's team, seems desiccated by unnameable depravity, like a vicar with a terrible secret: in the sex comedy *The Ups and Downs of a Handyman*, his spanking-obsessed Squire Bullsworthy is a memorably unsavoury creation, tracking St-Trinian's-clad girls with horses and hounds – the film ends with a Benny-Hill-style chase. The 'official' is represented by comparatively younger men – the effete Nicholas Parsons, the smug or pretentious Henry McGee. Getting older is a licence to be 'naughty', it increases sexual arousal but brings the randy adventurer closer to death. In 'The Lover', Hill plays Jamie, who's only Scottish so he can wear a kilt which resembles a miniskirt – Jack Wright pinches him in one scene, while two women leer up his 'skirt' in another. He spends most of the sketch trying to steal Jack Wright's young wife, masquerading variously as a series of handymen, butlers and gardeners. He narrowly avoids castration with a sword – there's an insert shot of a banana and two grapes at his feet – and tries again, in drag this time, as a maid. Inevitably, Wright takes a fancy to him and chases him, but things look up when further maids move into the house, and his bed. In the final scene, we see him doddering on a park bench, Wright walking past with his wife on his arm and a ridiculous toupée on his head. Hill's frequent rejoinder to his critics that men came off worst in his sketches hardly dispels the misogyny, but it does point to the instability of low comic masculinity.

Upstairs, downstairs: the flat-sharing sitcom

Rigsby: But you're a member of the Permissive Society. You're supposed to know where the erogenous regions are.
Alan: Look, I know where the Himalayas are, but I've never been up 'em!

Rising Damp

It *is* the permissive society, right? The swinging seventies, I mean, Andy Warhol, *Flesh*, *Trash*. I mean, anything goes today, doesn't it? Er, could you just turn round while I put my trousers on, please?

Robin (Richard O'Sullivan) *Man About the House*

It was the flat-sharing sitcom, above all, which attempted to inject signs of permissiveness into light entertainment. In *Rising Damp* (Yorkshire 1974–8) and, particularly, *Man About the House* (Thames 1973–6), 'old' and 'new' lifestyles are contrasted and allotted different floors in the same house. Upstairs, a group of younger, middle-class characters try to come to terms with the changing sexual climate; downstairs, older, working-class characters get left behind. For grimy landlord Rigsby (Leonard Rossiter) in *Rising Damp*, 'the Permissive Society stops at that door … We don't want any of it in here.' The house itself acts in support of such prohibitions – dirty and cold, with a prime view (and smell) of the local abattoir. Alan (Richard Beckinsale) and Philip (Don Warrington) embody the new values in an old house. Alan is the more awkward and inexperienced, as Beckinsale's characters usually are. In 'The Permissive Society', an early episode, he's preparing something suspiciously like a cosmetic regime for a blind date – a Soap Bunny and an unnamed 'Masculine Spray to Brighten Up Any Man's Bathroom'. 'What are you gonna wear,' mocks Rigsby, 'Your Donald Duck shirt or the jeans with "Come and Get Me" on the crutch?' Frances De La Tour's Miss Jones – a nuanced performance just the right side of patronising cruelty – is an intermediary figure, disqualified from the sexual revolution by her age but eager to join in.

Man About the House's 'swinging' image was sold on Robin (Richard O'Sullivan), Chrissie (Paula Wilcox) and Jo (Sally Thomsett), all afghan coats and 'sexy lingerie' aprons. One of the series's title sequences shows them on a day trip to the zoo in a vintage car, as though they were the 'bright young things' from *Genevieve* (Henry Cornelius, 1953) updated by twenty years. The mixed-gender flat-share was the middle-evening racy premise – the format was sold to American television as *Three's a Crowd* – and, while no sex ever took place, the implication was that there was plenty of it going on somewhere, and that their libidos were as flared as their trousers. These were modern, young people, and we all knew what they were like.

Downstairs are the Ropers, George (Brian Murphy) and Mildred (Yootha Joyce), Donald McGill drawings brought to life (sample marital abuse: 'George, those cigarettes are going to be the death of you. Have another one'/'It's a pity you don't live in India. You'd be sacred.'). Marriage would be the end of the story upstairs – the series concludes with Chrissie's wedding to Robin's brother Norman – but downstairs it's the sitcom 'trap': 'When two people love each other, George, does it really matter if they like each other?' Desire has fled, at least from George:

Mildred (*watching TV*):   Ooh, you know when that wolfman ripped the blouse off that helpless maiden – ooh, it sent a shiver right down my spine. Coming to bed, George?
George: Er, no, not just yet. I'm going to make myself a cheese and onion sandwich.
Mildred: I'll wait for you.
George: Er, no, don't bother because I've got to go and tell them upstairs about the meeting tomorrow night.

Man About the House is arguably the first lifestyle sitcom, as flat-sharing sitcoms often are; rotas for bringing home boy/girlfriends, post-party debris and morning-after dissections, sexual banter, Robin's prurient acquisitions (*Naked Be My Nympho, The Sex Maniac's Cookbook*, a bedside lamp which 'undresses' a flamenco dancer when lit), the riot of purpleness which is the local pub, The Mucky Duck ('the beer's flat, but the barmaid isn't') – this, I must admit, was the sitcom I most wanted to live in as a teenager. But George and Mildred are required for contrast, as well as increasingly hijacking large sections of the show. The 'bright young things' aren't exactly swingers – Chrissie was brought up on a farm and 'wouldn't know an orgy if I fell over one'; Robin's Southampton origins place him at one remove from the metropolitan utopia. 'How Does Your Garden Grow' focuses on their panic when they think that cannabis is growing in their garden – they blame it on the squatters at number 12. 'Love and Let Love' is fairly representative of the show's contrasts. Upstairs, they're arguing over the sexual rota. Downstairs, George is in trouble for waiting until Mildred is asleep before going to bed – 'I've been sharpening my pencil collection,' he offers lamely. It's ultimatum time – either George 'performs' or Mildred leaves. In the Mucky Duck, he asks for some circuitous advice by way of a bizarre DIY metaphor:

George: It's Mildred, you see. She's a very demanding woman ... She keeps getting on at me to do things, like, er, like, well, you know ...

Robin: Putting up shelves?

George: Yes! She's never satisfied, you see. I mean, it's not as though I've never put up a shelf. Well, I may not put up shelves as often as some husbands do. But I do put up shelves. Sometimes. I don't know how often is what you'd call normal?

3 Prime-time permissiveness: Chrissie (Paula Wilcox), Robin (Richard O'Sullivan) and Jo (Sally Thomsett) in *Man About the House*. (© Thames Television.)

Robin: For putting up shelves? Well, there hasn't been a lot of research on that subject.

George: Well, the thing is, she's waiting for me.

Robin: That is awkward, isn't it. Well, you see, Mr Roper, I've got to go back to, er, *put up a shelf.*

This updates Orwell/McGill within different trappings; it 'takes it as a matter of course that youth and adventure – almost, indeed, individual life – end with marriage' (Orwell 1941: 149). George arrives home from the pub, well tanked up, as Mildred reads *Once is Not Enough.* 'George, you've been drinking too much,' Mildred complains. 'No,' he assures her, 'I've had just enough.' He has 'one little job to do' – 'Be gentle with me, Mildred' – just as the cistern upstairs bursts, drenching them. 'Leave it,' Mildred insists, pulling him on to the bed, 'Let's drown!'

Like Miss Jones in *Rising Damp*, Mildred is an ambivalent figure rendered more sympathetic by a towering performance. More importantly, Mildred is a bearer-of-wit in the series (she has great lines), which complicates the fact that we are meant to find her frustrated desires comic and occasionally mawkishly affecting. Her aspirations are linked to both class and generation – the extravagance of her clothes matches anything worn by the 'upstairs' characters – an impressive array of leopard-skin patterns and, above all, her 'wildly Freudian banana-print trousers' (Medhurst and Tuck 1982: 46) – locating her somewhere between the low comic 'dragon' and sexploitation's suburban wife.

While George and Mildred are mocked for their sexual desert of a marriage, and he for his provinicial 'obsession' with class, there's a sense that audiences developed a different sense of who the series's stars were. *Man About the House*'s 'youthfulness' was always precarious, as one *TV Times* reader's description of Richard O'Sullivan suggests; the 'saucy sex appeal of Leslie Crowther, with perhaps a dash of Des O'Connor' (February 1974). When the programme subdivided its traditional and 'permissive' components, *George and Mildred* achieved higher ratings than either its predecessor or its insipid rival, *Robin's Nest*.

Light entertainment/white entertainment

> A sitcom came on called *My Neighbour is a Darkie.* I suppose that wasn't its actual title, but that was the gist of it – that there was something richly comic in the notion of having black people living next door. It was full of lines like 'Good Lord, Gran, there's a coloured chappie in your cupboard!' and 'Well, I couldn't see him in the *dark*, could I?' It was hopelessly moronic.
>
> Bill Bryson (1995: 23)

> The names we call each other are almost terms of endearment.
>
> Jack Smethurst (*Daily Express*, 9 May 1975)

While it might appear to signal a thematic shift, it would be misleading to omit considerations of race from any discussion of 1970s comedy. The recruitment and naturalisation of 'race' and racism into prime-time entertainment stands in contrast to its perceived volatility in political discourse. The late 1960s witnessed what Jim Pines calls a 'new racism' (1992: 12), most publicly associated with Enoch Powell's inflammatory 'rivers of blood' speech in 1968. Powell was dismissed from Heath's (then shadow) cabinet, but commanded huge populist support. He was far from a pathological exception to British 'tolerance' – A. Sivanandan of the Institute of Race Relations later suggested that 'What Powell says today, the Tories say tomorrow and Labour legislates on the day after' (quoted in Whitehead 1985: 221). The 1971 Immigration Act supported the suspicion that Powell was a political pariah in principle but xenophobic pioneer in practice; the physical and media attacks on Malawi Asians in 1976, for example, suggested a pinnacle of anti-immigration fervour (see Braham 1982).

Light entertainment's handling of race grew out of two traditions, an old and a comparatively new one. On the one hand, unreflexive racist jokes could be found on programmes like Granada's The Comedians (1971-85), definitely not to be confused with the Trevor Griffiths play. The most vitriolic jokes came from white stand-ups like Bernard Manning, but the complex positioning of the black Yorkshireman Charlie Williams was indicated by his threatening riposte to hecklers that he might move in next door to them.

Till Death Us Do Part initiated the second tradition. A crucial permissive text of the 1960s, it was everything Mary Whitehouse loathed about Greene's BBC – in 1968, she was considering a blasphemy prosecution against the programme. The ideological complexities of the bigoted Alf Garnett – did audiences laugh at or with his views? – have been extensively discussed elsewhere. Garnett's populist appeal is very similar to Powell's – the latter 'had chosen to speak out on a subject that everyone else of repute in politics had chosen to avoid' (Braham 1982: 281). Saying the unsayable – the unfashionable, the anti-consensual – underpins both comedy's power to shock and a populist racist dynamic. The sound of racism – the linguistic variations and abusive concoctions (racist wit) – became central to the comic effect of subsequent 'race' sitcoms. But the programme trickled down into two modernising initiatives – an attempt to 'naturalise' and broaden the range of representations of black characters in sitcom (something Till Death never attempted) and to follow Johnny Speight's pioneering attempt to turn racism itself into a subject for humour on television.

The limits of these initiatives – even Love Thy Neighbour had good intentions – are indicated by two discourses on race discerned by Lola Young (1996) as especially prevalent during the 1960s. On the one hand, there was the 're-emergence of racist scientific theory' with its 'notions of racial and cultural superiority' (Young 1996: 116) – in a sense, it's the trickle-down of these views which is satirised in Till Death and its offspring. But the dominant white liberal take on black immigration was problematic, too, hinging on notions of 'assimilation' and 'integration' which implied that 'black settlers should abandon their cultures ... and embrace an unproblematized notion of a homogenous British culture' (ibid.: 117).

Both strands of 'race humour' prioritised Britons of Afro-Caribbean origin – now sufficiently 'assimilated' into a populist 'Britishness' to be offered probationary membership of the big comic 'us' – at the expense of newer Asian citizens. It's instructive, for example, to contrast the comparatively non-stereotypical characters of Philip in *Rising Damp* and McLaren (Tony Osoba), a mixed-race Scottish prisoner in *Porridge*, with the grossly caricatured Asians (some of them 'blacked up') in *Curry and Chips*, *It Ain't Half Hot, Mum* and *Mind Your Language*. In an essay on anti-Asian violence, Geoff Pearson elaborates on the way the West Indian, unlike the Indian or Pakistani, could be seen as 'one of us':

> He speaks our language (or so we tell ourselves) and he is of our culture –
> or so we fool ourselves. 'Pakis' ... on the other hand are not like us at all,
> or so the distinction says: they speak a different language, they eat peculiar
> food which does not smell like our food, and they keep to themselves.
>
> (1976: 50)

On the Buses delineates this racial boundary particularly clearly. Afro-Caribbean drivers are unproblematically part of 'us', but the Indian drivers are exotically Other. In an early episode, one of their wives takes over the canteen – ethnicity, too, is mediated through the stomach, and curry has not yet been incorporated into the great British night out. There are jokes about 'Ghandi's revenge' and she has to go, but not before claiming National Insurance and severance pay – 'England is a wonderful country' are her first words in English.

The comedy of racism ostensibly contrasts a white working-class bigot – Rigsby, Eddie in *Love Thy Neighbour* – with a black character of superior intellect and, sometimes more codedly, class. Philip in *Rising Damp* is an interesting figure. Inscribed into the British class system by his voice and education, but also an African prince, he represents both modernity and 'nature', occupying a place in the British meritocracy but also a 'primitive' sovereignty which guarantees his authentic masculinity. It's Philip who brings permissiveness into the house, in contrast to the gauche Alan, but this sexual capital is also bound up with his 'natural' attributes and with supposedly having ten wives. In 'For the Man Who Has Everything', a Christmas episode from 1975, he brings his girlfriend Lucy to the house. Lucy is from Northampton, but her clothes and braided hair lead Alan and Rigsby to believe that she is (directly) from Africa. Rigsby thinks she's a present from Philip, misreading a comment about something 'fiery' from home, which turns out to be a bottle of 'Jungle Juice'. 'My father sent me half a dozen,' Philip tells him, and Rigsby thinks there's a 'wife' going spare. He patronisingly explains launderettes, running water and supermarkets to her and tells her she speaks English 'like a native'. We are always invited to laugh at Rigsby's bigotry, but the supposedly more enlightened Alan is equally shocked by Lucy's appearance and stutters over giving a name to her 'difference'. There's a revealing subtext here; Philip is so completely 'one of us' (more 'civilised', if anything) that surely he will want a white woman. Black female sexuality, as in *Love Thy Neighbour*, is an exotic journey 'downwards', 'forbidden fruit' for a voyeuristic white gaze.

Love Thy Neighbour (Thames 1972–6) was the most successful British sitcom from 1973 to 1975, but in 1972 it was already ahead of *Till Death Us Do Part* in the ratings, an interesting shift. Can this be attributed to the presence of regular black characters (for whatever reason) or to the jettisoning of the more contentious material about religion and royalty? Racism in *Neighbour* is ostensibly a question of neighbourly idiosyncrasies, 'as if Eddie's racist behaviour was of the same order as Terry Scott's arguing about the height of a garden fence' (Medhurst 1989a: 18). The premise is simple – the Afro-Caribbean Reynoldses, Bill (Rudolph Walker) and Barbie (Nina Baden Semper), move in next door to the white working-class Booths, bigoted Eddie (Jack Smethurst) and tolerant Joan (Kate Williams). Thames's Head of Light Entertainment, Philip Jones, articulated the show's most frequently offered *raison d'être* when he claimed that it should 'help take some of the heat out of race relations' (*Daily Express* 14 April 1972). The question of *who* exactly was meant to experience a comic lowering of the temperature is of some considerable importance. This was the epitome of the 1970s race sitcom, in so far as:

> the same old categories of racially-defined characteristics and qualities, and the same relations of superior and inferior, provide the pivots on which the jokes actually turn, the tension-points which move and motivate the situations in situation comedies.
>
> (Hall 1990: 17)

The 'comic register' of such comedy, according to Stuart Hall, 'protects and defends' (white) viewers 'from acknowledging their incipient racism' (ibid.: 17). *Neighbour* ostensibly does this in two ways. First, white racism is working-class – we rarely see middle-class racists, let alone institutionalised racism, in sitcom. Moreover, it is linked to the organised working classes, implicitly backward-looking and narrow-minded – Eddie is a Labour-voting, *Daily-Mirror*-reading union man, his mannerisms oddly reminiscent of some of Harold Wilson's.

Joan: I don't understand you, Eddie Booth. For years you've been shooting your mouth about socialism and equality, equal rights for all.

Eddie: Equal rights does not entitle nig-nogs to move in next door!

Of course, trade unionism did not preclude racism, and could easily sit alongside a defensive white chauvinism – London dockers and meat porters, 'hardly traditional supporters of Conservative politicians' (Braham 1982: 281), marched in support of Powell after his dismissal from Heath's cabinet. But there's a lot of ideological manoeuvring going on here to localise and neutralise Eddie's bigotry. Bill, meanwhile, is a composite representation of black masculinity. Promotional material for the 1973 film describes him as a 'happy go lucky Jamaican with strong Conservative views'. Bill's high, braying laugh reinforces a stereotype prevalent for some time – uncomplicated, simple-minded good-naturedness. But Bill is also given the trappings of upward mobility, despite working at the same factory as Eddie, as though moving into a working-class suburb constitutes a black equivalent of embourgeoisement. Bill and Barbie own a stereo, a major status symbol in 1972, and seem to enjoy a better standard of living than the Booths. Bill's unlikely support of Heath is implicitly linked to his embrace of modernity, his transcendence of the British class system, while Eddie's affiliations are signalled as static, archaic, stultifyingly provincial.

The second form of 'protection' comes via Bill's sporadic counter-racism, purely reactive but represented as equally 'silly', or, in terms of the show's ideological project, balancing and reassuring. This isn't just a question of his retaliatory 'honky' or, interestingly, 'big white poof' to Eddie's considerably larger arsenal of 'sambo', 'nignog' and 'chocolate drop'. Barbie – who gets on perfectly well with Joan, as wives of comedy neighbours usually do – tells him 'You're too sensitive.' Bill is expounding on a more institutionalised racism than Eddie's overt prejudices – 'You go into any chemist and ask for flesh-coloured plaster, and see what you get.' 'So?' replies Barbie, 'Use insulating tape.' Most damningly, he tells Barbie that he wouldn't want black neighbours because of their adverse affect on property value.

But if Barbie's 'assimilationist' outlook is embedded in aspiring to racial invisibility, her sexuality ensures her hyper-visibility. Like Philip in Rising Damp, the Reynoldses represent permissiveness and, again, it's a marriage of the modern and 'natural' uninhibitedness. Barbie's body – in hot pants or bikini, never in a bra – is both exotic and 'liberated', its construction belonging equally to Playboy and National Geographic. Eddie can't keep his eyes off her – although he's outraged when 'accused of ogling Mrs Sambo' – and the camera rarely strays from her breasts and bottom, either.[7] In 'Thou Shalt Not Covet ...', each man imagines that his wife is the subject of designs by the other. Bill overhears Eddie and his white workmates Arthur (Tommy Godfrey) and 'I'll 'ave 'alf!' Jacko (Keith Marsh) admiring Barbie's 'knockers', but the conversation later turns anxiously to black male sexuality – 'You know what they say about blackies,' says Arthur, 'well ... bigger.' If you wait long enough, every racist anxiety gets a voice in this show.[8]

What is most interesting, however, is Neighbour's failure to achieve the disavowal Hall attributes to such programmes. Its determination to see the 'funny side' of racism is a thin veil over a particularly combustible ideological concoction. Love Thy Neighbour insists on the inevitability of racism – that is what it naturalises – and, as a cataloguing of numerous racist enactments, it has considerable socio-historical interest. Critics in the 'quality' press commented on its naturalisation of racist abuse, although Barry Norman here seems to be making the same class assumptions as the programme:

> Eddie's mild little jokes about spades and sambos and nignogs have no shock value and indeed are so gentle and even comfortable that the words themselves acquire a sort of respectability. Anyone, listening to Eddie, who has ever thought of black men as spades or nignogs might well feel reassured that this is precisely how he ought to think of them.
>
> (The Times, 21 April 1972)

If one wonders who exactly finds these words 'gentle' and 'comfortable', one answer seems to be Norman's critical peers. For the middle-class critic, the show was 'quite bland' (Peter Knight, Daily Telegraph, 18 April 1972), 'All very nice and soft-centred and predictable' (Mary Holland, The Observer, 16 April 1972), not shocking enough. James Murray of The Daily Express, in a regular piece of would-be populist ethnography called 'A New Look At What People Look At' (9 May 1975), arrived at a particularly memorable conclusion: 'who can really take offence if kids in school playgrounds nowadays copy the epithets of Eddie and Bill and call each other "Choc ice" and "Snowflake"? It's got to be an improvement on "nigger".' The general consensus, however, seemed to be that racism was passé, old news. The Race Relations Board – a frequent dissenting voice – thought otherwise. 'I haven't met a black person who isn't offended to hell by it,' the Board's Tania Rose told Francis Bennion in New Society (31 July 1975). By 1975, the tide was turning and the Community Relations Committee warned the Annan Committe about Neighbour.

The Hammer-produced feature film (John Robins, 1973) is far from cosy, in spite of its frenetic determination to be so. It opens with a satirically lyrical montage of Britain as empire, 'A land where all men are equal, irrespective of race, creed or colour'. Cut to Eddie and Bill trading insults – 'You bloody black troublemaker!', 'You racialist poof!' The credits roll over a continuous take as the hostility snowballs into a chain reaction of white-on-black-on-white aggression. As a black woman comes out of her house, Eddie throws something at her. Her husband comes out, walks down a few houses and throws a bucket of water over a white woman; her husband knocks on the next door and has soot dropped onto him from a window. And so it goes on: bricks put through windows, flower boxes destroyed, axes taken to front doors. This is a truly astonishing sequence, a real return of the repressed, given the climate of the time. Usually, 'aggro' is shown to be natural but containable, not the dystopian apocalypse which seems to be developing here. In 'Operation Aggro', Eddie organises a petition to 'Keep Maple Terrace White'. In an earlier scene, he finds dog excrement from another (white) neighbour's alsatian in his garden – he picks it up with a trowel and drops it over the fence, narrowly missing Bill. This is a very loaded image – it speaks volumes that white, middle-class critics found the show 'bland'. The image of excrement through the letter box was one of Enoch Powell's demonising tableaux, while in reality it was not uncommon for Afro-Caribbean and Asian Britons to receive such 'gifts'.

There is more than a note of hysteria in Love Thy Neighbour – it can't begin to contain what it wants to see as harmless fun; its violent subtext constantly threatens to break through, and briefly does so in the film. This is clearly the most difficult component in 1970s nostalgia – how to 'frame' for retro-buffs the racial discourses of light entertainment, which don't lend themselves to the same ironic appropriation that gender representations appear to. Should audiences long for this 'innocent' time or feel the superiority of 1990s liberalism? Terrestrial television has steered clear of Neighbour and been cautiously selective in its repeats of Till Death Us Do Part. But this potentially bolsters the sense of the forbidden, the unsaid, the repressed; and, in any case, any 1970s film which seems to begin with a 'comic' suburban race riot is of considerable historical interest.

4

LADS AND LOUNGERS

Some 1970s masculinities

Everything goes in cycles. It will be in fashion to be 'Real Men' once
again somewhere down the road.

> Lewis Collins (Bodie in *The Professionals*)

I couldn't be camp if I tried, because my background is working
class and I'm tough at heart. Someone described me once as looking
like an off duty navvy from 2001.

> Dave Hill, Slade (Tremlett 1975: 49)

When did postwar British masculinity have its first 'crisis'? The consensus seems to
be that the 'New Man' was not a phenomenon of the 1980s but a belated response
to the 1970s, 'brought about, it was said, by the advances of feminism and the gay
movement allied to the economic upheavals of post-Fordism, the switch from "male"
heavy industries to "female" service industries' (Simpson 1994: 1). But Mark
Simpson suggests that a larger crisis has been evident in the 1990s, 'a crisis of
looking and looked-at-ness, a puncturing of "manly visions" in film, rock and roll,
pornography, advertising and sport' (ibid.: 6), most visible in the way that heterosexual masculinity no longer seems able to represent itself, either as subject or
object, as a segregated sexuality distinct from homoerotic drives and pleasures.

Andrew Tolson's tellingly titled *The Limits of Masculinity* (1977) confirms that middle-class liberal men were having a 'crisis' fairly early on in the 1970s, a crisis indicated by the 'consciousness-raising' of the men's liberation movement – not to be
confused with the 1990s 'reclaim the phallus' men's movement – an attempt to incorporate feminist ideas about patriarchy into a 'new' masculinity. Tolson himself
joined such a group after reading the following ad in *The Women's Liberation Newsletter* in
1973: 'The possibility of men's liberation ... rests upon an awareness by men of the
limitations imposed upon them by a sexist society' (Tolson 1977: 9). It seems safe
to assume that a larger section of heterosexual men were not losing much sleep over
patriarchy stunting the possibilities of their gender identity, but Tolson is insistent
that a larger crisis was going on:

> For all men, particularly within certain fractions of the middle classes,
> the post-war experience has been disturbing. There is a contemporary

'problem of masculinity', involving an adjustment to disintegrating images of 'self'.

(ibid.: 15)

He goes on:

> the sexual tensions of the 'sixties', effects of the 'permissive society', have
> undermined the masculine 'presence' ... sexuality is publicized, criticized,
> compared. It is not so easy for men to maintain the pretence of sexual
> bravado.

(ibid.: 16)

If this crisis was going on – and I agree with Tolson that it was – then it was clearly
operating through a process of disavowal and overcompensation. It is here particularly that we need to pay attention also to the place of the 1970s in the 1990s
imaginary, because 1970s nostalgia creates the impression that this was not yet a
crisis in and of representation – rather, the decade becomes the point from which
the thread of 'real' masculinity can be picked up after the consciousness-raising
fads of New Man. It's the presence or absence of this representational crisis that is
really the starting point of this chapter.

The 1970s, as I've already suggested, seem to offer a nostalgic evocation of the
'masculine presence', evident not only in the 'heroes' of the era but in an almost
unprecedented empowering of the male gaze. This is the era of *Top of the Pops*' scantily
clad dance team Pan's People, (Benny) Hill's Angels, tobacco ads featuring a bikini-
clad Caroline Munro amidst promises of 'sheer enjoyment'. But Murray Healy suggests that the often hysterical displays of 'hard' straight masculinity could be seen
as a masquerade concealing larger uncertainties about male identity. He points to
the cautious and limited decriminalisation of homosexuality in 1967, the emergence
in 1969 of the toughest British postwar subculture, the skinheads, and the formation of the Gay Liberation Front in 1970 as events which 'signalled changes in the
way people thought about masculinity' (1996: 38).

In the early part of the decade, glam was the most obvious popular articulation
of the codes of masculinity in a limited state of flux – I say 'limited', because pop's
gender games are often swiftly recuperated; according to Iain Chambers, it 'confronted male youth cultures with what to it was most disturbing: the shifting, slid-
ing, but material, signs ... of an uncertain "maleness" ' (1985: 133). This gender
play long remained a boy privilege in pop, but Chambers rightly acknowledges that
androgyny was an important component in permissiveness, 'a display that was intent on demonstrating that the assumed "privacy" of sexual matters, then being so
fervently insisted upon by Mrs Whitehouse, was an illusion' (ibid.: 135). Frith and
Murray both extend this play with masculinity to the 'Bowie boys' of the early 1970s:
'the "sissiness" of the Bowie-boys became a comment on the usual signs of teenage
sexuality' (Frith 1989: 137), and the star 'provided the impetus for kids to dye their
hair fantasy colours like blue, green, scarlet and purple ... to wear clothes based on

Flash Gordon comics and thirties movies', to look to 'visions of other planets and metallic cybernetic futures' (Murray 1991: 223). But Bowie did something else – he articulated the subtext of these pleasures in his much-publicised (and subsequently retracted) coming out:

> David's present image is to come on like a swishy queen, a *gorgeously effeminate boy*. He's as camp as a row of tents, with his limp hand and trolling vocabulary. 'I'm gay,' he says, 'and always have been, even when I was David Jones.' But there's a *sly jollity* about how he says it, a secret smile at the corners of his mouth. He knows that in these times *it's permissible to act like a male tart*, and that to shock and outrage, *which pop has always striven to do throughout its history*, is a *balls-breaking process*. And if he's not an outrage, *he is, at the least, an amusement*. (my emphases)
> (*Melody Maker*, 2 January 1972, quoted by Tremlett 1974a: 93)

This is an interesting passage – in all but its syntax, it anticipates the sort of writing inspired by 1990s bands like Suede and Placebo. There's a lot of recuperating going on – Bowie's sexuality is a joke, an exotic diversion, the sort of publicity scam which has a long history in pop but with a permissive twist, evidence that he's 'man' enough to do it (it takes 'balls' to act the tart) – but we mustn't miss that fleeting submission to how gorgeous he is. George Tremlett's Bowie biography constructs this entirely as his edge over his glam rivals – 'this gave pop music a long-awaited new dimension, thought the hard-drinking journalists of the music press in their worn jeans and faded jackets' (*ibid.*: 94).

'High glam' had four central components – androgynous/bisexual chic; a mix of 1950s retro and SF-futurism (Roxy Music's 'art school vision of Eddie Cochran in the year 2001', Murray 1991: 224); the star as work of art (Warhol's influence on Bowie, the creation of Ziggy Stardust, Bolan's reinvention as Electric Warrior, what Frith calls 'art as the invention of self', 1989: 132); and theatre (Bowie, Alice Cooper). The ultimate high glam text, however, was arguably not Bowie – indeed, not a star or band at all – but *The Rocky Horror (Picture) Show* (stage show 1973, film 1975), admittedly a text whose impact was felt over a longer period of time. Bowie might have put suburban boys in outfits suitable for the Planet Mongo, but Frank N. Furter had them in fishnets and suspenders (even if For One Night Only), sold polymorphous perversity as positively compulsory and implored audiences, 'Don't dream it, *be it*.' He might live only in a theatre, but in no way was he going to demystify his sexual agenda as theatre. *Rocky Horror* is arguably the most enduring legacy of glam, and perhaps the most interesting in its impact.

Further down the spandex hierarchy, where Slade, The Sweet and Gary Glitter 'skipped the heavy raps about Theatre of Cruelty/Theatre of The Absurd/Everyone Is Bisexual, Maaaan and all the rest of it and simply concentrated on entertainment' (Murray 1991: 224), gender codes were equally conflicting in their way. Musically and visually, Slade were a collision of images and agendas, less straightforward than their 'good time' reputation might have suggested. Dave Hill wore women's boots and spoke longingly of marketing a range of Superyob fashions, but came over as an extraordinary failure of camp. The cover of *Slayed?* (1972) depicts the boys with the band's name 'tattooed' on their knuckles in biro to offset Hill's tight silver trousers and naked upper torso and Jim Lea's Amazing-Technicolor-Dreamcoat jacket. *Slade Alive!* (1972), recorded in 1971, finds them poised on the eve of glamdom – no longer skins but not yet encased in glitter and Man-at-Superyob. An impassioned rendition of John Sebastian's 'Darling Be Home Soon' is interrupted by Noddy burping (to the audience's noisy approval), while the guitar-torturing racket in the middle of a storming cover of 'Born to be Wild' wouldn't sound out of place on a Velvet Underground or Sonic Youth art-rock album. A review from the *Bradford Telegraph*, re-produced on the inner sleeve, describes 'A gentleman with a voice like a cut-throat razor urging people to join his fun' – 'Born' is introduced as 'another leaper' – and characterises their appeal as 'Pier-end-entertainment brought up to date'.

The Sweet were a bit less of a Lads' band, the Heavy Metal leanings on their dreadful B-sides notwithstanding (they were producers Nicky Chinn and Mike Chapman's most perfect creation). Frith characterises low glam as primarily 'a laugh (though I never was sure that Sweet got the joke)' (1989: 135), but I'm less convinced. The only people I knew with Brian Connolly's hairstyle were girls, and bass player Steve Priest was as prepared to play the game as Bowie, talking about donning a bikini for the summer in the pages of *Jackie*. Less naturally blessed than Bowie in the cheekbone department, The Sweet were convincing enough to suggest an *achievable* glamming-up.

Gary Glitter, perhaps most of all, represented an excessive hyper-masculinity col-lapsing into camp. On the one hand, the 'furry torso and spare tyre' (Murray 1991: 226) and gang imagery seemed to reinforce the big, big sound he evolved with Mike Leander, 'based around distant distorted guitars, an omni-present electronically com-pressed drum sound playing a metronomic jackbeat tempo and grunting call-and-response vocals based around catch-phrases and ... simple-minded nursery porn' (ibid.: 226). *Let it Rock* described 'Rock and Roll Parts 1 and 2' as 'a castration op where you throw away the patient and keep the balls' (quoted by Oldfield 1985: n.p.). He was 'the man who put the bang in gang', but the film *Remember Me This Way* (1973) includes a photo shoot in which he poses with a dummy leopard on a lead, like a model on a Roxy Music LP cover. One of The Glitter Band remembered him, on Channel 4's *Glam Top Ten* (8 May 1995), as 'a showbiz personality in the Joan Collins/ Liz Taylor ... style ... He'd throw wobblers if he didn't get the biggest suite in the dressing room, all that old rubbish that these people seem to go in for.' In a rare and interesting attempt to re-evaluate Glitter, Paul Oldfield discerns a kind of impossi-ble masculinity which collapses before our eyes:

> Glitter created an impossible star when his clothes were simply too con-trived to be recreated outside publicity photos and could not even be worn on stage. The silver suits, slashed to the waist, emanated from nowhere, or even from that imaginary place we now know as Boystown.
>
> (Oldfield 1985: n.p.)

The confusion over what Glitter might have *meant* was illustrated by a spectacle I witnessed on a train in the early 1990s – fans of his revivalist show were squeezed incongruously into the same carriages as those of Morrissey, performing in an adjacent venue on the same night. What followed played like a vocal battle between competing notions of camp, as rival fans tried to shout each other down. 'Lea-der! Lea-der!' chanted the retro glam fans in between casting aspersions on Stephen Patrick's masculinity. What *did* they think they'd just seen?

Glam was not, of course, the whole story of 1970s masculinity, even during its heyday. I want to focus, in particular, on two currently recirculated male figures – the Lad and what I shall call 'Safari Suit Man', the middle-aged swinger celebrated in television shows like *Jason King* and *The Persuaders!* and an important mythical reference point in the recent easy listening/'loungecore' scene (see Jones 1997). But first, I want to talk about underpants and aftershave.

The man who does have to try too hard

In the Name of the Father (Jim Sheridan, Eire/GB/US 1993), the film about the wrongful imprisonment of Gerry Conlon (played by Daniel Day-Lewis), for the 1974 Guildford pub bombing, ostensibly proceeds as a liberal humanist drama about legal and political injustice. But the film's period means that its early scenes also push it into the realm of the costume picture, and never more so than in a scene where Conlon/Lewis is threatened with a knee-capping by the IRA. He lowers his trousers to reveal extraordinarily brief, leopard-skin-patterned underpants, pants which sent a ripple of horror and/or recognition through the audience when I first saw the film. At the time of its release, an outfitter's in Shaftesbury Avenue displayed the outfits worn by its characters, a spectacle which suggested Merchant and Ivory turning their annoying period fastidiousness to an NEL pulp novel.

Pants like Day-Lewis's are a central component in 1970s masculinity. Andy Medhurst summarises Robin Askwith's similarly garish and arse-cleavage-enhancing pants – Dyer likens Y-Fronts to the bra in terms of uplift, streamlining and support (1993: 125) – as the 'gormless embodiment of laddish permissiveness and condom-free bravado' (1995: 16). 'Bring a little colour to your cheeks,' suggests a full-page magazine ad for Lyle and Scott Y-Fronts from 1971, accompanied by a persuasively large close-up of fire-engine-red briefs:

> You may be forced to wear pin-stripes on the outside. But you've surely got more room to manouevre on the inside ... there's a mass of different colours and patterns in 9 styles, so you'll never have a dull moment.

If that didn't sound exciting enough, for the more daring there were the briefer Undercover-Masters, which, as the name suggests, were sending out conflicting signals. On the one hand, they were less coy about their colours, which included Sugar Pink and Flame Red, but they also came with the promise of 'Masterful, masculine styling', in spite of their derivation from women's knickers. Dyer (1993)

60

notes that bikini briefs for men were first aimed implicitly at the gay market, but these ads are from *Penthouse*. Being 'colourful' and daring under your pinstripes; being 'masterful' in sugar pink – clearly a mild revolution was going on in 1970s man's (terylene) trousers. At the same time, however, Joe Hawkins, anti-hero of pulp novel *Skinhead*, is as semiotically literate about his drawers as James Bond is about cigarettes and claret, and, in *Skinhead Escapes*, he's having nothing to do with girly pants:

> Walter smiled, and discreetly turned to remove his briefs. Joe wanted to point and cackle. He'd seen Marks and Sparks latest creations – those multi-coloured shorts for men that had no fly and looked like a bloke had borrowed his sister's knickers. He didn't go for them. Unisex may be fine for some but he still clung to his jockey shorts for manly loo-ing.
>
> (*The Complete Richard Allen Volume One*: 268)

These renegotiations of the masculine coincided with the more concerted targeting of male consumers in advertising, and consequently the evolution of a new language for constructing men as conspicuous consumers. This had not yet evolved into the soft-focus narcissism and 'body maintenance' of the 1980s, but products like briefs and aftershaves indicated that changes were under way. The images used to sell such products worked in conjunction with those designed for more traditionally masculine products – beer and tobacco, the latter still a permissible part of television advertising.

The 'classic' masculinity used to sell Old Spice cologne or aftershave is a useful starting point. Old Spice Man is a surfer – 'rugged, outdoors and able to tame nature' (Simpson 1994: 124) – and the product itself is equated with the 'masculine freshness' of the ocean, so that its use is both 'natural' and, as the 1975 campaign insisted, 'The mark of a man'. Simpson captures the essence of the ad's initiative, 'to persuade men that buying something traditionally "feminine" – a cologne – is in fact the very summit of masculinity' (*ibid.*: 125). Old Spice Man opened a door, but he was already a little nostalgic even at the time of his appearance, while Brut Man was a more quintessentially 1970s figure. Judging by the ads' language, Brut *smells* in a way that Old Spice initially doesn't (it's just 'fresh'), but it smells of masculinity itself. Brut Man is The Lad – he inhabits the space between pop and sport. He's not afraid to incorporate 'feminine' smells and clothes into an otherwise hyper-masculine persona, thus the importance of Henry Cooper exhorting us to 'Splash it all over'. Simpson interprets this as a distrust of 'sissy, economic sprinkling' (1994: 125), but it also suggests an ecstatic wastefulness.

Three other ad types are important here – I'm going to call them Bitter Man, Tobacco Man and Hairspray Man (alternatively, Terylene Man).[1] Bitter Man is a working-class version of Old Spice Man – usually northern in ads themselves, but the archetype need not be. Bitter Man exists, thrives, as part of a rowdy, slightly dog-eared, male group. In a 1974 ad for Tetley Bittermen, we see a hysterical caricature of male camaraderie – men in a pub share a joke we never hear (there is no diegetic sound), their faces contorted by racking laughter in huge close-ups. The ad resembles the sort of 'boozer' which often turns up in the grittily violent cop show *The Sweeney* (Thames 1974-8). The 'boozer' in the crime show offers an escape from the 'feminine' for villains and coppers alike, the emasculating domesticity that Regan and Carter have to be liberated from (by divorce for the former, the death of his left-liberal wife for the latter). Inhabiting the same spaces as criminals and sharing a similar social backgound is an important part of the 1970s 'rogue cop's' authentic masculinity – Regan embodies a carefully contained transgressiveness congruent with his belief in law over rule (see Hurd 1981), 'moderately permissive but heterosexual … a moderately heavy drinker but not an alcoholic' (Clarke 1992: 246). 'Why don't you go back to your strip club,' scoffs a rival inspector, 'or wherever else you masquerade as policemen.'[2] By the time of *The Professionals* (1977-83), Law-and-Order Man was more receptive to fashion, and Martin Shaw's Doyle had a terrifying bubble-perm to prove it. But behind the Laddish banter and Lewis Collins's leather-blousoned insouciance lay a more survivalist conception of the now paramilitary dispenser of justice. Some of this anticipated the SAS fetishism of the early 1980s, following the siege of the Iranian Embassy, but Bodie, in 'Wild Justice', also points to the out-of-control soldier hero that Hollywood was soon to explore in films like *Rambo: First Blood Part II* (1985); taking revenge on a motorbike gang for the death of a former colleague, he starts to resemble a malfunctioning combat machine (his boss, Cowley, threatens to kill him like a wild dog). Bodie and Doyle spilled over into the 1980s, by which time they were widely mocked for their excessive testosterone – feminist critiques were built into the show in an attempt to defuse them. But their disciplined bodies, embracing mystical martial arts as well as military reconstruction, were easily incorporated into the discourse of 'body maintenance' which ran through fashion-and-fitness culture in the 1980s, embodying what Featherstone (1982) calls a 'calculating hedonism':

> Discipline and hedonism are no longer seen as incompatible, indeed the subjugation of the body through body maintenance routines is presented within consumer culture as a precondition for the achievement of an acceptable appearance and the release of the body's expressive capacity.
>
> (*ibid*.: 18)

In the 1970s, hedonism was still wasteful and undisciplined, splashing aftershave all over the shop, squandering talent like the footballer George Best or overindulging rock stars. Regan and Carter's unflattering anoraks and bedraggled demeanour, the former's prematurely grey hair and caffeine-flared nostrils never deterred young women from finding 'real men' irresistibly attractive.

Tobacco Man, meanwhile, represents an ultra-masculine potency which spills over into high camp, his pipe or cigar hysterically phallic ('*Man. Man. Manikin* – the cigar with the big flavour', 'A pipe does something for a man'). Tobacco Man is irresistibly attractive to women, but, like the man who uses Denim aftershave and 'doesn't need to try too hard', he is more likely to repel them – Denim Man grabs a pair of female hands just as they are about to plunge down his unbuttoned shirt. A 1973 Benson and Hedges ad shows a man with a Jason King moustache ignoring an attentive female companion as he smokes his cigar. One year earlier, Benson and Hedges Man walks through a railway station, seemingly behind the Iron Curtain (like the 1980s Levi Boy who smuggles in denim and The Face as emblems of freedom), wearing a suede coat and a black peaked leather cap, pipe full of 'flake or rough cut' (which is he?), accompanied by a huge, bald manservant ('Size is everything,' Jason King insists of his cigars in one memorable episode). A group of women coded generically as 'dolly birds' trail behind him, groupie fashion – he points to one of them and baldie sweeps her up in his arms and deposits her in St Bruno Man's compartment, where he promptly ignores her.

Hair Spray Man is too old or 'straight' to be inserted unproblematically into 'the permissive society', but dips a cautious toe in its waters, through longer hair, terylene flares or the spectacular floral shirts offered by Double Two International's That Shirt! – 'That shirt is something else! Tailored to fit your body like skin.' The That Shirt! ad finds the middle-aged swinger at a discotheque, cravat reassuringly present, suggesting that the product is the Undercover-Masters of overwear. A 1973 ad shows two youngish men in suits – evidently something in the City – coming to terms with the implications of longer hair. Brylcreem, by now, could offer only the dubious benefits of a 'bounce', but the untreated hair of the first man is entirely at the mercy of the elements. With the aid of The Natural Way, not only is his friend's hair staying put, but it will probably never move again. Some of this imagery translates into the world of aftershaves, often encoded as bestowing an unprecedented and terrifying attractiveness on the wearer – Valerie Leon's pursuit of the ineffectual Hai Karate man, trying to defend himself with karate chops, has become a quintessential image of 1970s advertising, while Tabac's wearer muses, 'I sometimes ask myself, Is it me?'

Lads

Charlie George! Superstar!
Walks like a woman and he wears a bra!
football chant (quoted by Hornby 1992: 72)

The 1970s Lad embodies a slightly more fluid masculinity than contemporaneous ads suggest – one need look only to football, pop, even sitcoms. He is also a less confident figure than his 'New' 1990s counterpart, less certain of having negotiated fashion and feminism, a 'coming to terms' figure. He might be awkward, comic and a little bit stupid – Robin Askwith or Adam Faith's Budgie (LWT 1971–2) with his 'two-tone jackets, throttled collie hair' and 'quintessential early Seventies workplace, the Soho porno bookshop' (Penman 1988: 62). It's worth mentioning that his manipulative pornocrat boss, Charlie Endell (Iain Cuthbertson), is an equally resonant figure.

The football–pop interface is central to Lad mythology, as is evident in accounts of Rod Stewart and Arsenal striker Charlie George. Stewart is almost the prototype for the 1990s New Lad, a middle-class boy made over with a working-class image

– his parents owned a small newsagent's. Nick Hornby's 'Sparing the Rod' (1994) insists that 'Rod wasn't a mere recording artist, he was a lifestyle ... He *resonated*' (26). This 'resonance' resides partly in soccer blokishness – 'At school, the sight of him kicking balls into the "Top of the Pops" audience excited a great deal of favourable comment' (ibid.: 27) – and role model accessibility: 'it was much easier to *be* Rod Stewart than it was to be Hendrix or Jagger or Jim Morrison ... all you needed to do to acquire Rodness was drink, sing, pick up girls and like football' (ibid.: 27).[3] But Stewart inscribed these everybloke qualities – 'Rodness', if you like – on to an AristRockratic lifestyle. He 'picked up' beauty queens or Britt Eckland and, asks George Tremlett, 'Who but Rod Stewart would fly from the States to Dublin just to see a football match on TV?' (1976: 7). But Hornby also wants to find the emotional vulnerability behind the feather-cut-and-tartan swagger and sees the 'booze-and-football photos' or the microphone-sharing camaraderie of performances with The Faces as compensation for the 'rampant sissiness' of his ballads (1994: 28), as though sentimentality and muscle-flexing were ever far from one another.

Similar motifs turn up in both Hornby's and Pete Fowler's accounts of Charlie George as a figure emblematic of 'a time when football was beginning to resemble pop music in both its presentation and its consumption' (Hornby 1992: 56). Fowler reverses the 'Rodness' formula when he suggests that Skins watching Charlie were enjoying the same relationship with their idol as Mods watching The Who, 'watching their equals acting out their fantasies' (1972/1996: 165). His shoulder-length hair notwithstanding, Fowler is adamant that Charlie was a 'skinhead's dream', a 'skinhead who's made it' (ibid.: 165) rather than a glam idol – he wasn't to know that George would go on to make a record as Charlie Gorgeous – and Hornby concurs when he observes that an earlier hairstyle 'looked suspiciously as if he were trying to grow out a number one crop' (1992: 57). Fowler also reverses Taylor and Wall's account of the respective fortunes of pop and football. He prioritises the Skin consumer, and suggests that the major 'faces' of the 1970s were footballers not musicians. More interestingly, he compares Charlie George with George Best, five years his senior. Best's stardom, he argues, was moulded entirely by pop discourses – the public made sense of him in relation to Swinging London, clubs, boutiques and 'birds', as much as anything he did on the field. Best was a Mod hero, 'his mode of living ... decided by pop' (1972/1996: 164), a larger-than-life figure whose 'focal point' was Carnaby Street (ibid.: 165). Charlie George, on the other hand, appeared to have no public life off the field – he was inarticulate in interviews according to Hornby and 'looked and behaved as if running around on the the pitch dressed as a player were the simplest way to avoid ejection from the stadium' (1992: 57). But if George looked androgynous enough to incur the sort of chants cited above, he also exuded a 'hard man menace' (ibid.: 57) – his name is dropped in the opening paragraph of Richard Allen's *Boot Boys* as though he were synonymous with aggro. Hornby remembers him lifting a Newcastle player by the throat, and he capped a provocative equaliser against Derby County with 'an unambiguous take-that-you-provincial-fuckers V-sign' which earned him boos, an early bath and a fine (ibid.: 58). For Fowler, this, too, was a significant shift from Best – even bad behaviour was confined to the field.

You might not know if Charlie was 'a boy or a girl', but he might kick your head in while you were deciding.

Meanwhile, Lads were everywhere in 1970s sitcoms – the medical pranks and competitive 'pulling' of the *Doctor* series, the hard-bitten sagacity of Peter Cleall's Duffy in *Please Sir!* But the most interesting figure can be found in *Man About the House*. Robin is a cookery student and sitcom's major model for 1970s male fashion.[4] When we are reminded so many times in the early episodes that he is *not* gay, it seems safe to surmise that we are in the presence of some kind of New Masculinity. He spends most of the first episode in a yellow, fur-trimmed chiffon gown when his own clothes are soaked and has to pretend to be gay for the Ropers to allow him to stay in the flat with Chrissie and Jo – 'Look, dear,' Mildred advises Chrissie, 'I don't want to worry you, but I think that's a man dressed up.' His new flatmates make some insinuations about his cooking ability – he'll make someone a 'lovely wife', they tease – and his only alternative to sharing with them is a gay flatmate:

Robin (*on the phone*): Am I what, sorry? Gay? Well, I'm a reasonably happy sort of chap … (*realisation dawns*) Oh, sorry, *that* gay? No, er Douglas (*voice starts to deepen*), I don't think we'd get on very well together …

But the key signifier of Robin's Lad–Fop is not the cycle of girlfriends and doomed attempts to get off with Chrissie, but rather the sexy-lingerie-printed apron – such aprons were available in the shops and men *did* wear them. Here was an item which spoke volumes about the wearer's perception of gender codes – modern enough to play around (jokily) with 'manliness', *man* enough to get away with it (as *Melody Maker* implausibly believed Bowie to be).

Even so, when promiscuous laddishness became a more enduring part of *Man*, it was displaced on to another character, Robin's disreputable friend Larry (Doug Fisher) and his parade of stereotypical don't-fancy-yours-much girlfriends – 'I'm a decent girl!' protests one of them, 'You can't be!' he retorts, horrified at the thought. When Larry later moves into the attic flat, filling it with softcore motorbike posters and discarded knickers, there is a sense of him taking up a lease in Robin's unconscious, bolstering up heterosexual profligacy while also providing a comic disavowal of its worst manifestations. His function as low alter ego is confirmed in 'Never Give Your Real Name', where he has given Robin's name to an ex-girlfriend who now believes she's pregnant. Nice sitcom boys don't do things like this, but their sidekicks can do it for them.

Safari Suit Man: *The Persuaders!* and *Jason King*

[*Jason King*] involved a ridiculous rake in a poofy kaftan whom women unaccountably appeared to find alluring … though I saw it only once more than twenty years ago, I have never lost the desire to work the fellow over with a baseball bat studded with nails.

Bill Bryson (1995: 22)

When they showed the pilot episode [of The Persuaders!] as part of 'TV
Heaven', someone walked into my lounge and accused me of
watching some ancient gay-porn film, such was the puffed-up body
language and dramatic glances they sparred with.
                            Laura Lee Davies, Time Out (August 1993)

Safari Suit Man – in his fictional incarnation, a kind of vigilante tourist – combines
elements of Tobacco Man (an exaggerated sexual magnetism) and Hair Spray Man
(he's middle-aged, but fashion-conscious). But he has important generic determinants, too, in the thriller tradition of the gentleman amateur from the 'leisured
ruling classes' (Bennett and Woollacott 1987: 111) and in the 'pop' discourses of
the 1960s.

The glossy adventurer series – usually made in Britain, but with international sales
in mind – includes as its most notable 1960s examples The Avengers, Danger Man, The Prisoner and, to include an American example, The Man From U.N.C.L.E. David Buxton characterises such programmes as examples of 'the pop series', embracing pop's 'new world
of total design' (1990: 73), its rejection of 'depth', which 'can only detract from the
display of designed surfaces which are themselves rich in meaning' (ibid.: 97). Pop
elicited a new way of looking, 'learning to concentrate one's gaze on surfaces in a world
in which fetishism had been extended to almost all objects (and to people themselves)'
(99). This was evident not only in the glamorous surfaces of The Avengers' mise-en-scène or
the jokey treatment of death popularised in the Bond movies, but in the conception of
character: 'Characters in series were no longer social archetypes representing various
facets of "human nature" but designed to double as fashion models' (ibid.: 74). Thus
the first Diana Rigg/Emma Peel series of The Avengers was also a vehicle for 'The Avengers Collection', the op-art outfits designed by John Bates at the Jean Varon fashion house
which could actually be purchased by the series's wealthier viewers. Danger Man, meanwhile, included a weekly credit for the 'Fashion House Group of London'. The safari
suit series dispensed with the pop-art designs – its overall look hinged on the Mediterranean travelogue that the later Bond films also embraced – but the character-as-
wardrobe principle became even more central:

> The series has sartorial elegance. Danny Wilde and Brett Sinclair have the
> money to buy only the (most) expensive clothes. Ultra-modern but not
> Carnaby Street. Modes for the modern man. And Roger Moore has de-
> signed his own clothes for the series.
>
>   (publicity for The Persuaders!)

Not only did Moore design his own clothes, he had a regular credit for it, suggesting that this was a more important sign of authorship than the handful of episodes
he directed. The clothes tended to look as though they had been provided by Double Two International of That Shirt! fame – orange silk shirts and pink polka-dot
ties amidst the more sober beiges of his jackets and tuxedos (beige was Roger's
colour from The Saint to his incarnation, from 1973, of James Bond).

Jason King was equally less than the sum of his wardrobe, the contents of which, with his penchant for lavender hues, made Moore/Sinclair's look distinctly cautious by comparison. Everything about his appearance was excessive – *The Sunday Times* referred to the 'lavish use of highly superfluous hair' at the time of *Department 'S'* (12 January 1969), blissfully unaware that it would evolve further into a spectacular grey-highlighted bouffant. In 'Flamingoes Only Fly on Tuesdays', Jason suffers a kind of sartorial violation as intimidation. When three hoodlums break into his hotel room, they try to frighten him off by mutilating his beloved (self-designed) suits – 'You've just destroyed a work of art!' he protests in dismay, 'I've only worn that once – I must sit down!' Before leaving, one of them stands behind him and slowly slits his jacket open up the back, prompting a facial expression which suggests a much more intimate kind of violation. Jason's foppery has a price – there's a sadistic streak in the programme, which can't resist puncturing his elaborate peacockery. According to the programme's co-creator Dennis Spooner, 'He was designed to be a total eccentric ... He was the only hero you did the most extraordinary things to' (quoted in Tibballs 1994: 58). He recalls the plot of 'A Thin Band of Air', in which Jason infiltrates the villains' hideout in a packing crate, surrounded by pillows and supplied with an oxygen mask. Once he arrives, the FRAGILE/THIS WAY UP warnings are rudely ignored, and Jason is deposited upside down, whereupon his pillows burst and the oxygen mask covers him in feathers. Hitchcock's 'Torture the Heroine' maxim seems to have been re-written here as 'Torture the Fop' – 'There was no other hero on television you could do that with because although he always had the answer right, it never quite worked for him!' (ibid.: 58).

In *White Hero Black Beast*, Paul Hoch conceptualises the cyclical history of competitive masculinity as an oscillation between two types – the Puritan, 'hard-working, hard-fighting', adhering to 'a production ethic of duty before pleasure' (1979: 118) and the Playboy, 'who lives according to an ethic of leisure and sensual indulgence', often reflected in his flamboyant clothes 'with bright colours characteristic of the leading class in playboy periods' (ibid.: 118). This oscillation is determined by changes in patterns of work and economic surplus – 'The playboy style requires a sufficient economic surplus, and a sufficient class polarisation, so that the necessary wealth to pursue the life of leisure can exist at the top of society' (118) – but it also involves changing conceptions of what masculinity actually is:

> For the new 'leisure class', work and warfare no longer connote manly status, but inferiority: its battles for masculinity are fought not with swords, but in terms of an ethic of wealth and conspicuous leisure, emphasising upper class etiquette and elaborate playboy rituals of extra-marital dalliance.
>
> (ibid.: 118)

This is not to say that 'manliness' was uncontested during such Playboy periods as the Roman Empire or Renaissance England.[5] The 'perfumed dandyism' of the Enlightenment gallant prompted an unambiguous reading from Puritan quarters: 'they thought these strutting peacocks must be homosexuals (and, in many cases, they were certainly not wrong)' (ibid.: 137), and an 1849 essay on 'Reasons for the Growth of Sodomy' asked why 'the young fops don't just put on petticoats and have done with it' (138). But from the lace and ruffles of the courtier to Bowie's dresses and Jason King's 'poofy kaftan', there doesn't seem to have been a clear consensus on the dandy's sexuality – an Australian poll voted the latter as the man most women would like to lose their virginity to. Alan Sinfield notes that in the late nineteenth century, 'effeminacy was associated with the idle aristocracy, objectionable on the grounds that it was a symptom of excessive cross-gender attachment which re-sulted in the disorder of men's "natural" mastery over women' (quoted by Healy 1996: 55). But even Oscar Wilde's 'effeminate, dandy manner did not signify queer-ness ... effeminacy and same-sex passion might be aligned, but not exclusively, or even particularly' (ibid.: 55).

The 1970s Playboy hero has to leave economically depressed Britain – or not be British, like Tony Curtis's rags-to-riches oil tycoon, Danny Wilde – in order to sus-tain his economic privilege and hedonistic, leisured lifestyle. Jason is a tax exile – 'I'm only allowed in England for 36 hours' – and Brett and Danny are on a perma-nent Mediterranean holiday. This is why these series are never very exciting as ad-venture shows – The Avengers and The Prisoner did have some narrative drive – because they are predominantly about leisure and lifestyle. This doesn't make them any less pleasurable or interesting, but did lead The Daily Telegraph's critic to complain of The Persuaders!: 'The two men spent so much time last night zooming round Monte Carlo in their brightly coloured sports cars that the play seemed like a prolonged com-mercial for high-performance petrol' (18 September 1971).

There's another important difference from the 1960s spy adventure, where con-spicuous consumption could carry narrative and ideological weight. Bond, Steed and Emma Peel, Solo and Kuryakin were Playboys and Puritans (or simply Puritans, as in Danger Man and The Prisoner), enlisted by the 'free world' and all employed in order to enjoy their material pleasures. Safari Suit Man works only reluctantly. Brett and Danny are blackmailed into their vigilante roles by the retired Judge Fulton (Laurence Naismith), who wants to dispense private justice – they either work for him or serve three months in prison for a particularly boisterous hotel fight. Jason's only 'boss' is his editor, Nicola, but he has to assuage the wrath of the tax man – in 'A Deadly Line in Digits', an unnamed secret service organisation adopts the Inland Revenue as a cover in order to enlist his services forcibly. In some respects, these heroes hark back to an earlier prototype, the pre-Bond gentleman amateur with a private income – Buchan's Richard Hannay and 'Sapper's' (McNeile's) Bulldog Drummond – whereas 'Bond belongs not to the Breed but to a new elite – international rather than paro-chially English in its orientation – committed to new values (professionalism) and lifestyles (martini)' (Bennett and Woollacott 1987: 112). The myth of 'meritocracy' in the 1960s gave Bond a further dimension as part of his membership in a new elite, a twist cemented by the casting of the working-class Connery. That Moore went straight from being Lord Brett Sinclair to the 1970s Safari Suit Bond indicates that class polarisations were widening again in the conception of the playboy hero.

The motif of travel carried over, however, the 'narrative code of tourism through which the strange and exotic locations of peripheral societies are represented as the object of Bond's Western, metropolitan look' (ibid.: 247). But 'exotic' terrain doesn't just include other countries and cultures in the Safari Suit narrative – it includes the landscape of permissiveness itself, conceived as the equivalent of 'the leisure and prostitute centred assertions of masculinity of the Roman Empire' (Hoch 1979: 120). Thus the safari suit itself is an icon of middle-aged 1970s masculinity, connoting its wearer as permanently on holiday, a tourist of permissiveness, a gender imperialist in search of liberated 'big game'.

In this respect, Roger Moore was more Hair Spray Man than Tobacco Man – he wasn't camp enough for the latter. He played two interesting film roles in between *The Saint* and *The Persuaders!*, the latter making him the highest-paid British television star up to that point. In *Crossplot* (Alvin Rakoff, 1969), he plays an advertising executive drawn, *North By Northwest* fashion, into an espionage plot. In *The Man Who Haunted Himself* (Basil Dearden, 1970), he plays a dull suburban businessman who is haunted by a flamboyant, permissive *doppelgänger* wearing the sort of clothes Moore was soon designing for Brett Sinclair. The sense of a *Daily Mail*-reading stockbroker who 'uncannily' becomes a debonair action man hangs over Moore during this period. In *Roger Moore as James Bond 007* (1973), a 'diary' of the making of *Live and Let Die*, his first stab at Bond, he sulks with his wife, talks about his kidney stones and tries to convince his sceptical children that yes, he is James Bond now – he remains the most parodic incarnation of 007, as though Suburban Man could never quite believe in this new 'licence' and his implausible good luck.

The elaborate title sequence of *The Persuaders!* (ATV 1971–2) encapsulates its 'real' story – the story of how Britain and America, respectively, produce the Playboy type through the English class system and the 'American Dream'. Two files appear on the screen, giving way to contrasting life-story montages – from the slums to oil tycoon for Danny, Harrow, Oxford, Ascot and motor-racing for Brett, but the two narratives converge in images of bikinis and diamond necklaces, roulette wheels and wads of money. Even sexual capital is acquired differently – in the opening scenes of the pilot 'Overture', Danny is chatting up air hostesses and Brett has a sports car full of rotating women. This 'opposites attract' dynamic is explored most engagingly in 'Chain of Events', where the two go camping together (in more than one sense of the term). Danny 'roughs it' in frontier garb, starting a fire with sticks and catching his own fish – Wilde by name and wild by nature. An alarm bell goes off and the camera pans to a gigantic tent equipped with a shower, cooker, freezer and a chandelier hanging from the awning. Brett emerges in a velvet dressing gown, having watched television until about eleven o'clock the previous night and nodded off under his electric blanket – 'I must admit, I rather like roughing it, but I miss the morning papers.'

The Judge's role is to attempt to impose a puritan masculinity on these two workshy reprobates – 'You're both facile and foolish, and a useless waste of humanity, but you like to fight.' Brett, at least, concurs in principle with Fulton's law-and-order rhetoric – 'I think you're the sanest man I ever met' – but the Judge doesn't appear

4 Safari Suit Man (1), an adventurer-hero defined by leisure and conspicuous consumption: Danny (Tony Curtis) and Brett (Roger Moore) in the thick of the action in *The Persuaders!* (Courtesy of Polygram/Pictorial Press.)

5 Safari Suit Man (2): Peter Wyngarde tends to his battle wounds in *Jason King*. (Courtesy of Polygram/Pictorial Press.)

in every episode.[6] As often as not, foiling dastardly schemes constitutes an amusing diversion in between gambling and sunbathing.

It's scarcely unprecedented for 'buddy' narratives to trip over the homosocial into the homoerotic, and Laura Lee Davies's visitor might have found further ammunition in the narrative of 'Overture'.[7] Initially competitive – sufficiently so to fight – Brett and Danny have a race in their sports cars, a scene filled with split-screen glances and a Tony Hatch/Jackie Trent love song on the soundtrack: 'When the sun shines down on love ... / We can find the sun together / Come away.' The fight is prompted by an argument over cocktails, not least the image of two olives 'gently bouncing against each other'. Danny is ecstatic when he discovers the identity of his opponent – 'Lord Sinclair! I never did it to a Lord before!' They frequently compete in their pursuit of women, but only a man ever comes between them, Danny's childhood friend turned bad in 'Angie ... Angie' (even the title underscores the sense of wistful romance). Brett tells his friend that 'You can't go back to the way things were, because they were never like that in the first place', but Danny has to learn the hard way. Angie is killed, and the two heroes enjoy a slightly awkward reunion:

Danny: I'll tell you something, your Lordship. You've got style.
Brett: Mm, you're not so bad yourself, but let's not get maudlin.

The final joke concerns Danny's use of Brett's lucky number as a secret code during a shootout – it turns out he got it wrong, like calling out the wrong person's name at an inopportune moment.

Jason King, meanwhile, bonds only with himself – 'I am my own favourite subject,' he declares grandiloquently, and is often seen reading his own books (which are, after all, about his own idealised self, Mark Caine). *Jason King* (ATV 1971–2) was a spin-off from *Department 'S'* (ITC/ATV 1969–70), a pre-emptive version of *The X-Files* about a branch of Interpol formed to investigate 'unsolvable' incidents (the disappearance of a town's inhabitants, a man in a spacesuit in Soho). Jason's colleagues were computer expert Annabelle Hurst (Rosemary Nicols) and the more conventionally heroic Stewart Sullivan (Joel Fabiani) – Mr King was that generic standby, the 'professional' crime writer who operates as 'amateur' detective, the bestselling author of books with titles like *Index Finger Left Hand* and *The Lady is Ready*. It was Jason's 'Carnaby Street masculinity' (*Daily Telegraph*, 18 January 1969) and 'warm brown gravy voice' (*Daily Mirror*, 14 April 1969) which seemed to guarantee him his own star vehicle, where the snakeskin jackets, Oscar Wilde quotations and fey womanising became even more extravagant.

Andy Medhurst takes the show's popularity as 'conclusive proof' that 'camp had stopped being primarily a subcultural guerrilla code and became big mainstream business' (1994: 3), but his insistence that it was 'patently a huge send-up of heterosexuality's ridiculous contortions' doesn't entirely guide us past its spectacular misogyny:

Jason: You've been yapping all day about women's liberation and the equality of the sexes ... What contribution has your sex made, apart from the obvious, to, say, photosynthesis?

Lee (a photographer):   None.

Jason: The new drugs on schizophrenia, probably the greatest contribution since Pasteur – *a man*.

Lee: Just give me a drink, will you?

Jason: Navigation?

Lee: I bet I know more about navigation than you do.

Jason: Well, then you can find your own stumpy way to the drinks table.

Stumpy way? 'Camp' doesn't quite get at the twitching disgust condensed into this phrase. Where it is consistent and revealing is in the representation of a pathologically solipsistic masculinity, like Tobacco Man with his pipe or cigar, an impossible male fiction collapsing into itself.

'Well done, Mark Caine,' Stewart Sullivan would mock Jason every so often in *Department 'S'*, and the sense of Jason as his own preposterous creation is embedded implicitly in *Jason King's* title sequence. As our hero sits at a typewriter, his 'exploits' move across the screen as the page moves back and forth on the bail bar – from the beginning of each episode, he is 'writing' himself. In 'Wanna Buy a Television Series?', Jason attempts to sell Mark Caine to a television producer, and narrates a typical story in which he 'plays' Mark. But in any case, the most frequent plot device is the slippage from fiction to 'real life' – criminals basing schemes on Mark Caine plots, Jason finding mystifying parallels between the diegetic mystery and his latest novel. 'Mark Caine has completely taken over,' observes Ingrid Pitt's Nadine in the episode of the same name – 'Yes, he's inclined to do that,' Jason acknowledges. Publicity added a further layer in this collapsing of King into Caine – both were extensions of Peter Wyngarde, an idea he still promotes in recent interviews: 'I decided Jason King was going to be an extension of me ... I was not going to have a superimposed personality. I was inclined to be a bit of a dandy, used to go to the tailor with my designs' (*The Observer Magazine*, 19 December 1993: 8). An ITC publicity piece fleshes out this elaborate masquerade in which 'Jason is undoubtedly a combination of fiction and fact ... if Jason King is Peter Wyngarde, he is also Mark Caine':

> Mark Caine is the detective character created by novelist Jason King, and he sees himself as this fictional character which, in turn, is a combination of imagination and Jason King himself ... Jason King was born in Dangeeking, India. Illegitimate son of a Glasgow engineer and a little-known French countess.
>
> That's fiction. Peter Wyngarde was born in Marseilles, though he is of Anglo-French parentage. He is the perfectly legitimate son of a British diplomat and a French mother ...
>
> 'Jason King' is therefore a fascinating combination of fact and fantasy. Wyngarde himself developed the character considerably from the original outline. He suggested the name. He also suggested the name of Mark Caine.

But somewhere along the way, the originating source of Wyngarde/King/Caine, the ur-fantasy of male potency which seems to operate on a loop, disappears. On a notorious and long-withdrawn LP, Wyngarde 'becomes' King as though he didn't exist before his creation. And this might go some way to explaining why Jason is presented to us as both ridiculous – he loses fights not only to the villains but to jealous husbands and boyfriends ('I'm gonna show this pretty boy just what I think of him') – and representative of 'what every man wishes he could be, and is in his own secret dreams – and what every woman wishes every man was!' (ITC Publicity). If nothing else, he gives us one or two clues as to what Manikin Man might have had on his mind – his own fascination, his own obsolescence.

By the end of the 1970s, an intellectual agenda was taking shape that would start to 'make strange' the 'known quantity' of masculinity. The notion of masculinity as social role, as 'construction', as something which men learned (or were 'burdened' with) rather than simply embodying is evident in both Andrew Tolson's and Paul Hoch's books. What remains surprising, looking at Richard O'Sullivan in his apron, Jason King in his lavender kaftan or even Charlie George's glam hooliganism, is the implication in contemporary popular memory that the rest of the decade was a reassuring haven of uncomplicated straightness. Whenever masculinity's 'crisis' actually started, it certainly seems to have been in place by the 1970s, and the signs of it were everywhere.

5

'KNUCKLE CRAZY'

'Youthsploitation' fiction

> this conflict between the young and the state was, in fact, all-out war. A war threatening the authority that a country needed to keep it stable.
>
> Richard Allen, *Skinhead* (1970)

> he felt that the country was being run down by the old and reactionary ... It had reached the stage where people had forgotten what it meant to do something on one's own – to take an individual decision – to spit in the eye of conformist society. They both thought that there had been something in the ideals of the old Angry Brigade, but that was long over ... the country badly needed a force like the Angels that would help to purge it of its complacency and would raze the shibboleths of conformity.
>
> Mick Norman, *Angels from Hell* (1973)

The dominant themes of 1970s British fiction have been characterised by Bart Moore-Gilbert as 'Industrial confrontations, class warfare, terrorism, regional tensions, conflict between the races and genders ... giving the impression of a society on the brink of disintegration, or even civil war' (1994b: 152). Moore-Gilbert is thinking of writers like Lessing, Ballard and Amis (Kingsley *and* Martin), of hardback, 'serious' novels, but he could just as easily be speaking of the cheap paperbacks one would have found on revolving racks outside newsagents or lying in wait, like pulp hooligans, for 'the peaceful citizen browsing through W. H. Smith' (Chambers 1985: 247). The *kulturgeist* of what *Policing the Crisis* calls the 'exceptional state' was visible in the titles and belligerent covers of books like *Skinhead* ('The savage story of Britain's newest teenage cult of violence') and *Suedehead, Guerrilla Girls* and *Knuckle Girls* ('The Horrifying Story of a "Bother Girl"'), *Demo, The Degenerates, Hitch-Hiker, Freaks, Chopper, Wheels of Rage* and *Rogue Angels*. In his introduction to the reissued omnibus of Mick Norman's *Angels from Hell* series, Stewart Home discerns 'the atmosphere of a country reeling under the blows of unemployment and economic decline' (*Angels from Hell – The Angel Chronicles*: n.p.).

Written in brutal and visibly hasty prose styles – the same phrases, even paragraphs, recur in different books – these tales of violent youth cults running amok are as evocative of the period's upheavals as any texts you could find. Politically, they come across as a diverse (if confused) range of texts, but the right and left populism, respectively, of Richard Allen's and Mick Norman's novels seem agreed on an impending, irreversible chaos, and that all that's left to hold on to is the hard, unyielding male army; the 'terrace patrol' of ex-skinheads which polices the football terraces in Allen's *Terrace Terrors*, the 'Last Heroes' biker gang fighting the repressive state (and, importantly, 'conformity') in *Angels from Hell* and its three sequels. While Allen aims for tabloid timeliness – he was impressively responsive to the shifts from Skins to suedeheads to smoothies – Norman crosses over into dystopian science fiction. *A Clockwork Orange* was an important reference point for many of the youth cult novels, but *Angels from Hell* also anticipates the post-apocalyptic survivalism of films like *Mad Max* as well as evoking the Orwell-meets-Marvel-Comics conceits of records like Bowie's *Diamond Dogs* (1974) and Thin Lizzy's *Jailbreak* (1976). *Angels from Hell* projects the 1970s into an imagined 1990s of oppressive social control, compulsory repatriation, the outlawing of youth cults set against a landscape of surviving subcultures fighting each other as well as a very 'exceptional' state.

'Behind the school desk' fiction

If the nostalgic gaze associated with *Dr Who* is positioned for ever behind the sofa, popular memory has cast the consumption of youth cult fiction, too, as taking place behind a piece of furniture – in this case, the school desk. If the former evokes pleasurable, childish fears, the latter summons up images of counter-education, of subcultural capital smuggled into the classroom:

> For any kid attending a comprehensive school between 1971 and 1977, Richard Allen's books were required reading ... it was New English Library's *Skinhead* wot provided your sex'n'violence education.
>
> (Steven Wells, quoted by Healy 1996: 88)

On *Bookmark*'s tribute to New English Library, *Skinhead Farewell* (BBC2 23 March 1996), Stewart Home recalls reading Richard Allen's books 'under the desk', while ex-Skin Steve remembers *Skinhead* as 'the first book I ever read at school without being bullied into it by a teacher': 'they were factual, they were about football ... violence and ... sex. That's what we wanted at 13, 14 years old – we were right on it.' On the same programme, a well-meaning liberal English teacher in Bethnal Green talks about using *Skinhead* in place of C. S. Forrester's *The Gun* to catch the attention of his 'disaffected and alienated' pupils. While the book's racism was troubling, it was the first novel he had seen them read 'of their own volition'. This ambiguous populism is inseparable from any account of the genre.

While some of the (usually pseudonymous) writers have been preserved for cult posterity – Allen, above all (in STP's six-volume *Complete Richard Allen* series), Norman and Peter Cave, it's New English Library itself which emerges as the prime mover in the genre, the most prolific and successful publisher of 'aggro' fiction. According to then managing director Bob Tanner, speaking on *Bookmark*, the turn to a youth market reversed a fifteen-year decline in profits. The success of Skinhead in 1970 – it sold over a million copies – initiated a major boom period for NEL. Editor Peter Haining has described the process whereby 'this youth market ... who were interested in contemporary things that were happening ... not just about literary, faraway worlds; what was happening on the streets' was targeted; a process, not too surprisingly, which sounds very much like assembling issues of a tabloid newspaper:

> We used to have these brainstorming sessions ... when we would see what was making the headlines in the newspapers, what people were discussing, where the young people were going, where their interests lay and just ... use that as the background and the basis for commissioning books on those subjects, which we needed to get out quickly and get on sale and catch these markets, because trends, even then ... were changing very quickly.
>
> (Bookmark – Skinhead Farewell)

Bookmark's programme gives the impression of a creative team which recalls David Thompson's description of Hammer's personnel as 'decent men who did the garden at weekends' (quoted in Hutchings 1993: 96). Sandra Shulman, author of Daughter of Satan ('Their beautiful bodies belonged to the devil – A novel in the tradition of Rosemary's Baby') and The Degenerates wrote orgy scenes as 'a shopping list of perversions' and claims not to have known what 'shafting' or 'going down' meant. 'Richard Allen', whom many readers believed to be a skinhead himself, was, in fact, James Moffatt, already in his fifties.[1] Moffatt's prodigious output included horror as Etienne Aubin (Terror of the Seven Crypts, Dracula and the Virgins of the Undead), crime as Hank Jansen (Pattern of Rape, The Dish Ran Away, Abomination), sexploitation as J. J. More (The Massage Girls, The Set-Up Girls, The Walk-On Girls) and SS-ploitation as Leslie McManus (Jackboot Girls, the Churchill's Vixens series). But 'Richard Allen' was the real bestseller, and eighteen novels were published by NEL under his name – Skinhead (1970), Demo (1971), Suedehead (1971), Boot Boys (1972), Skinhead Escapes (1972), Skinhead Girls (1972), Trouble for Skinhead (1973), Teeny Bopper Idol (1973), Glam (1973), Smoothies (1973), Sorts (1973), Top-Gear Skin (1974), Skinhead Farewell (1974), Dragon Skins (1975),[2] Terrace Terrors (1975), Knuckle Girls (1977), Punk Rock (1977) and Mod Rule (1980). George Marshall describes Allen-land as:

> A seedy world where barmaids are always spilling out of their low-cut tops, everyone and his dog are on the fiddle and arguments are settled with a swift kick to the balls. A world where Clockwork Orange meets Sid James and the Carry On team, to produce a page-turning cocktail of sex, violence and teenage mayhem.
>
> (The Complete Richard Allen Volume Three: 6)

Plaistow knuckle boy Joe Hawkins – West Ham hooligan, cop killer, a little bundle of deviance waiting for subcultural shifts to give him new life – was the popular anti-hero of Skinhead, Suedehead, Skinhead Escapes, Trouble for Skinhead and Skinhead Farewell, the latter killing him off in a plane crash; even so, Allen/Moffatt was planning a resurrection at the time of the writer's death in 1993. Joe is often talked about in novels in which he doesn't appear – his illegitimate son (by rape, inevitably) is the hero of Mod Rule – but by the time of the elegaic Dragon Skins and Terrace Terrors Allen had created a new hero to allow for a more sentimental depiction of skinheads – ex-Skin Steve Penn, settling into 'respectable' life and trying to recuperate his aggro days as law-abiding transferable skills.

If the theoretical discourses of the 1970s spoke of the 'death of the author', NEL's authors were often protean, excessive presences. In Allen/Moffatt's case, this often took the form of multiple disguises – not only the multitude of pseudonyms, but veiled appearances in his own books; as James Mowatt in Skinhead or Steve Penn's 'favourite author' in Terrace Terrors who helps put him on the straight and narrow. In the same book, Reg Peterson, a 'one-time pimp and friend of everybody who screamed "Police brutality" … A pervert and acid-tongued bastard' (The Complete Richard Allen Volume Four: 264) seems to become 'Allen' via his contact with Steve. Significantly, this involves not only a turn to the right, to law and order, but also an embrace of literary populism – 'He knew, now, what an author's duty was – provide material for the people to read. Never again would he make the mistake of writing for critics' (ibid., 268). Characters in both Allen's and Mick Norman's books refer to their novels and those of other NEL authors: 'I bought paperbacks too. My favourites were Richard Allen's Skinhead and Justice for a Dead Spy by James Moffatt' (Skinhead Girls, in The Complete Richard Allen Volume Two: 70). But 'Allen's' 'voice', in any case, is a fairly overdetermined one, all too alive and present. Healy identifies what sounds like a parody of the classic realist text's 'hierarchy of discourses' in Allen's 'fairly literal use of the authorial mode sometimes referred to as the voice of God' (1996: 91) – 'He plays epistemological games with his characters, countering their thoughts with that which exceeds their limited knowledge' (ibid.: 90). Allen's notorious treatment of race is a case in point. In Skinhead, we are treated to Joe's feelings about black immigrants, views which need not necessarily be those of the book's 'metalanguage':[3]

> The stink of the blacks made him sick. He hated spades – wished they'd wash more often or get the hell back where they came from. This was his London – not somewhere for London Transport's African troops to live. He enjoyed the occasional aggro in Brixton. Smashing a few wog heads open always gave him greater satisfaction than bashing those bleeding Chelsea supporters.
>
> (The Complete Richard Allen Volume One: 18.)

Joe starts to needle one of the black men in the pub, and his gang is likened to 'a gang of Nazi S.S. men' (ibid.: 20). But the (interiorised) response of his projected victim has to contend with a great deal of authorial 'noise':

> Mentally, he rejected these white savages – and all Englishmen – as inferiors striving to prove their right to subjugate black peoples. He didn't stop

to think about the poverty and superstition that made his homeland a place to avoid, or leave, nor the debt each of his people owed to the British administrators, the British tax-payer, the British sense of fair-play. He forgot these things because he wanted a job, a decent home – even if, after occupation, he turned it into a slum-dwelling – and a right to stand on his own feet without having a witch-doctor, a tribal chieftain, or an arrogant headman telling him what to do, when to do it, how to do it. He remembered his rights in England – the right to protest and call the British bastards and exploiters.

(*ibid.*: 20-1)

It's this 'excess', if not the accompanying politics, which attract the deconstructive, avant-garde attention of Stewart Home, who has plundered NEL fiction for cut-up experimental novels. But for Healy, it is unambiguously in the service of propaganda 'as it allows space only for the reader's acceptance or rejection, but not critique, of that which is proposed' (1996: 91). Allen's style is most frequently likened to that of tabloid newspapers, where, as Peter Braham has suggested, one can identify conflicting messages expressed in 'two voices' – editorials which ostensibly give us 'news as we would like it to be' versus the news itself which presents 'news as it is' (1982: 270). Focusing on the handling of race, Braham argues that 'While the news pages seem to be full of conflict and tension, editorials are likely to emphasize harmony and the need for good race relations' (ibid.: 269). These discourses do not enjoy equal force, however – the 'news as we would like it to be' identifies itself as speech, whereas the 'invisibility' of 'news as it is' confirms the unchanging nature of 'reality'. Allen reverses this. The narrative and dialogue seem to express 'responsible' outrage at Joe's lawless racism, while the 'editorializing' allies itself with his prejudices, indeed bolstering them up with an authoritativeness beyond his discursive reach. But it comes out of the shadows in order to do so – later books often start with an almost literal 'editorial' by Allen – and I'm less convinced than Healy that its effect is quite so direct unless it reflects prejudices already shared by the reader.

Mick Norman's narrative 'voice' is equally self-conscious:[4]

Creep into the black cave inside Priest's head. Listen at the corners of his mind to the dark, unspeakable thoughts that lurk there. Thoughts of blood, rending flesh and cutting … Death. Death. Death. Death.

(*Angels from Hell – The Angels Chronicles*: 33)

Had you forgotten Kafka? Admit it. Be honest. You thought he was with Gerry? Look a bit back and you'll see Gerry and *two* Last Heroes. That's Gerry, Brenda and Bard. Not Kafka.

(*Angel Challenge*, in *The Angel Chronicles*: 158)

But this is not Allen's tabloid voice; if anything, it's closer to the music press, or even the underground press. The narration makes much use of fragments of texts that strive to make sense of sub- and counter-cultural activity – press reports, music press interviews and sociological texts, the latter reflecting the 1970s' flourishing of sub-cultural studies. Chapters in between the 'action' consist of 'extracts' from such imaginary texts as *Hell's Angels – A Key to Unlock the Head of an Uptight Society* (Hunter Thompson?), *An Ogre for Society – An Investigation of Incidences of Delusional Psychoses Inspired by Youth Cults* (Stan Cohen?), *Telescopic Knife* (a British rock magazine) and *Think it's Good and it Ain't – A Study in Popular Sociology*, which describes the Angels as a 'phantasmagoria of fantastic flickering figures to dim and dazzle the eyes of Mr and Mrs Middle-Class in their semi-detached suburban little boxes' (*Angels on My Mind*, in *The Angel Chronicles*: 293).

'Aggro Britain'[5]

The hooligan narratives of NEL's youth cult fiction are perhaps best understood against three contextual backgrounds: the 'exceptional state', *A Clockwork Orange* and subcultural theory.

For the authors of *Policing the Crisis*, the moment of the 'exceptional state' is marked not only by a crisis in hegemony 'when the whole basis of political leadership and cultural authority becomes exposed and contested', but by a shift towards an 'authoritarian consensus' (Hall *et al.* 1978: 217). This involves a process of 'unmasking', and the revelation of coercive political intervention is a key element in the youth cult novel. Allen's novels both reveal and speak from this authoritarian discourse, a discourse that even his villains accept as the 'truth'. *Sorts* takes place in what is clearly meant to be the very centre of the counter-culture – a folk festival, which is represented as a hotbed of subversion ('MIGHT IS RIGHT – YOUTH FREEDOM MOVEMENT'), perversion and explicitly Manson-like cultishness:

> The Manson image burned deep in his breast. The Manson curse hovered above him.
>   ... He had his 'family', the drugs, the free-loving, babes showing signs of pregnancy, the stealing, the mugging, the total disregard for suffering on the part of their victims ... when he issued an edict he did have this weird sort of hold over them.
>
> (*The Complete Richard Allen Volume Two*: 167)

When deranged hippy Jock commits murder, he's confident that a soft, permissive state will let him off:

> *God preserve do-gooders, he thought. In them we trust! Without their Bible-carrying long-faced righteousness, hippies, drop-outs and the like would have long ago been put down, abolished and totally erased from the scene ...*
>   He sweated. God, if they swung convicted killers today, he wouldn't be on the run. Even his drug-infested mind would have stopped short of murder. Another praise for do-gooders rushed into his muddled mind. Without them his kind couldn't exist. Nohow. Nowhere. Never.
>
> (ibid.: 173–4)

Jock's mind may be 'muddled', but the message isn't. Only Skins, Suedes and Smoothies – Joe Hawkins apart – get special dispensation to go on the rampage – 'at least
they worked and socialised to an extent' (129). Increasingly, youthful hooliganism
becomes an acceptable 'phase'. Steve, in Terrace Terrors, is reassured that there's 'not a
damned thing wrong having your fling as a kid' (The Complete Richard Allen Volume Four:
190). This view was not confined to fiction. A West Ham Labour MP claimed that
'The Bovver Boys of 30 years ago were the Battle of Britain pilots' (quoted by Healy,
1996: 51), while a psychology professor, writing in The Sun, characterised 'Paki-
bashing' as harmless, timeless teenage rebellion:

> although the skinheads are creating a potentially explosive situation now
> that they have moved into the racial field. If Paki-bashing was happening
> in the States, it would be a turbulent situation. Fortunately the Pakistanis,
> unlike the negroes, like a quiet life.
>
> (ibid.: 43)

Subtext: don't worry, 'they' won't hit back. Clearly, there were bigger fish to fry –
'immigrants' being one of them – and a bit of racist aggro was containable.

In Angel Challenge, one of the Angels draws our attention pointedly to a recurring
intertextual reference.

> Greetings, oh my droogs. Welcome am I my brothers ... We went to a
> Classic this p.m. to viddy a screening of the mighty Clocky O. Wondrous
> still, my brothers.
>
> (The Angel Chronicles)

While the years have not been kind to Stanley Kubrick's smug, portentous film – its
withdrawal from distribution in Britain has given it a cult appeal that its visibility would
be less likely to sustain – it would be a mistake to underestimate its importance. In A
Clockwork Orange, Alex (Malcolm McDowell) leads 'ultra-violent' gang the Droogs through
a series of beatings and rapes until he is captured and brutally reprogrammed (at least
temporarily) – never before had violent youth cults been packaged in such a glamorous
form. It was number 11 at the box office in 1972 (the BBFC's causes célèbres usually made
money). During the Ziggy Stardust tour, Bowie came on to the film's theme, and Murray
Healy detects a connection with early 1970s youth cults:

> In all but their Smoothie hair, Alex and his 'droogs' were realized as skinheads
> in their suedehead incarnation, dressed in Sta-press-like rolled-up trousers
> hitched up with braces, accessorized with bowler hats and walking sticks.
>
> (1996: 87)

The Angels from Hell series makes more conscious reference to the film. A victim's beating is
accompanied by a rendition of 'Singin' in the Rain', while, in Angels on My Mind, the Angels'
leader Gerry is captured and subjected to experiments resembling Alex's treatment:

Her ideas, as far as I can understand them, involve digging back into the
past adventures of young criminals to try and determine a pattern ...
Once the clues to their past have been located, they can be used to change
their present and make them useful members of the world.

(The Angel Chronicles: 275)

But it's the film's apparent moral paradox – oppressive state versus violent youth –
that seems to really take hold. The Last Heroes have few redeeming features – 'You
think we're some kind of alternative salvation or something? It's us who are trying
to fuck it up even more' (Angels from Hell: 20) – but it's significant that Gerry is a
disillusioned arts student. Just as Alex's 'heroic' status hinges on a modish rebel
misogyny, the Angels start to resemble a guerrilla force as art school statement, a
situationist prank timed to coincide with Britain's slide into anarchy.

   Third, youth cult fiction emerges as the low counterpart of the blossoming British
subcultural theory; the context for both was, as Stan Cohen puts it 'a sour, post welfare
state Britain which had patently not delivered the goods; the cracking of all those interdependent myths of classlessness, embourgeoisement, consumerism and pluralism'
(1972/1980: iii). The 1970s sees the publication of such influential books from Birmingham's Centre for Contemporary Cultural Studies (CCCS) as Cohen's Folk Devils and
Moral Panics (1972), Hall and Jefferson's et al.'s Resistance Through Rituals (1975), Mungham
and Pearson's Working Class Youth Culture (1976), Willis's Learning to Labour (1977) and Profane
Culture (1978) and Hebdige's Subculture: The Meaning of Style (1979). Following Raymond
Williams's initiative, they ostensibly examined culture as 'everyday life', but, in fact,
favoured 'spectacularity', the 'expressive fringe delinquency' (Cohen 1972/1980: 180)
or style pioneers celebrated by Hebdige. From Gramsci, they reworked notions of
hegemony and 'spectacular', if doomed, resistance – as Gelder and Thornton put it,
there is 'a familiar narrative at the Birmingham Centre, that subcultural empowerment
is empowerment without a future' (1997: 87). It isn't difficult to see how such a 'narrative' translates into generic fiction. By the time of Hebdige, Barthes had joined the
mix, and subcultures were analysed in terms of signs, codes and signifying practices,
although Cohen's 1980 Foreword to the revised Folk Devils and Moral Panics offers an interesting critique of such developments. Healy notes that while Richard Allen is overtly
hostile to sociology, he in fact 'concords with many of their findings':

   The generic requirement, a passage showing the hero assembling the elements of his subcultural style before the mirror, explains those elements
   in the same way as the academic studies explain an articulation of
   working-class identity.

(1996: 95)

In Suedehead, Joe reads a magazine article on the new 'cult' – the piece is 'a mag-
net he could not fight against' (The Complete Richard Allen Volume One: 133) and he
starts to reassemble himself, adding a sharpened umbrella tip to his repertoire.
This book, most of all, suggests subcultural expression as a state of semiotic

flux and mobile identity – Healy calls it 'a far more open text [than *Skinhead*] where Joe's identity becomes more fluid' (1996: 98). Joe rejects the skinheads for their 'strict limitations on what to think, what to do – and how to do it' (ibid.: 170). As a suedehead, on the other hand, he is liberatingly unaffiliated, does not 'belong to any classifiable fraternity, good or bad ... A genuine suedehead had neither creed nor association' (170). Taken to prison (again) at the end of the book, he wonders what new 'vogue' will await him when he gets out, what possibilities for self-re-invention.

Subcultural theory coincided with a specific subculture, one which was also to sell a lot of paperbacks – the skinheads. Skins and pre-Hebdige subculturalists were seemingly made for each other. It was all here – a strong sense of class identity (although the suedehead incarnation complicates this with the appropriation of 'city gent' trappings), a spectacular dead-end of resistance, a sense of 'authenticity'. Before punk's foregrounding of the art school input into British subcultures, the following statement by Phil Cohen is fairly representative of an assumption made by early CCCS writers: 'I do not think the middle class produces subcultures, for subcultures are produced by a dominated culture, not by a dominant culture' (1972: 97). But how 'authentic' could Skin style be, given that subcultures, by definition, functioned to 'express and resolve, albeit "magically", the contradictions which remain hidden or unresolved in the parent culture' (ibid.: 94)? Mungham and Pearson describe the image as 'both a caricature and a re-assertion of solid, male, working class toughness' (1976: 7), and Phil Cohen identifies a 'contradiction ... between traditional working-class puritanism and the new hedonism of consumption' (1972: 94), which also sounds like one of the cruxes of permissive populism. Allen's Skins are anti-permissive in their hatred of hippies and 'layabouts':

> One thing Joe really detested was a hippie. For a start, they didn't wash ...
> Mostly, though, he hated them for not working. He had to work; if he didn't there'd be no cash in pocket ... The bleedin' Welfare State took care of them – grants if they were students (and that was a big laugh!), hand-outs from Social Security to pay fines for demonstrating and pot-taking ... Christ, what a rotten way to treat tax-payers, he thought!
>
> (*Skinhead*, in *The Complete Richard Allen Volume One*: 38)

But while they can, to a certain extent, speak for a middle-class (Powellite) conservative like Allen/Moffatt, they are also a product of an over-stimulated, permissive culture:

> [Joe's] was a senseless world of violence for the sake of violence, his ideal devised by those wishing the end of civilised behaviour patterns; his the starstruck era of pop and pot and the belief that might is right even if might has to play games and call itself right.
>
> (*ibid.*: 97)

Pete Fowler's 'Skins Rule' (1972/1996) is written from outside academic debates, yet converges with such accounts of the skinheads as John Clarke's, where they are located as part of 'the young's sense of exclusion from the existing "youth subculture" (dominated in the public arena by the music and styles derived from the "underground")' (1976: 99). For Fowler, the Skins were an explicit reaction against '1967', the cultural capital accumulating around rock, and a more general, drippy 'niceness'. He focuses on their activities at The Rolling Stones' Hyde Park concert, billed as 'A Nice Day in The Park'; as they put the boot into loved-up hippies, they start to look like a small-scale symbolic Altamont, a belated rainstorm on the Summer of Love: 'It was things "nice" that the skins objected to. John Peel and the other beautiful people saw everything as being "really nice" – the skins wanted others to see them as really horrible' (1972/1996: 162). 'It was an auspicious debut,' he adds in a later Afterword (ibid.: 169).

There is, of course, another issue which problematises the Skins' 'authenticity', which taxes would-be sympathetic subculturalists and clearly concerns pulp writers in the 1970s – race. When the Skin returned in the late 1970s, the dominant stereotype amongst left-liberals was of an NF-supporting, swastika-tattooed Rottweiler, knuckle-boy-turned-Nazi-knucklehead. 'Ethnicity,' Hebdige suggests, 'is also an option for whites who feel neglected or excluded' (1982: 31). This is consistent with his argument that white British youth subcultures traditionally defined themselves in relation to Afro-Caribbean immigrants – neo-Skins, like British Rastas, were making 'bids for some kind of dignity' (ibid.: 32). What got 'purged' amongst many late-1970s Skins was the debt to black culture – the original cohort drew heavily from Jamaican Rude Boy style: 'Their cool, disdainful attitude to strangers and their style and exuberance in the dance hall made them respected and admired by their white contemporaries' (Knight 1982: 10). Most commentators agree that this was a precarious dialogue, but there were black Skin crews such as The Kilburn Blacks and both white skins and black rudies listened to much the same (black) music. Taylor and Wall (1976) point to 1972 as a key year in the end of this honeymoon, marked by Skins attacking second-generation blacks in Toxteth, the 'end of interracial Reggae' (108), the growth of British Rastafarianism; Knight implies that Rastas might have seemed a little too close to black hippies, with their drugs and spirituality (1982: 15). Skins and young West Indians were semi-criminalised by their very appearance, the former virtually policed out of existence, rounded up at football matches or placed in enclosures like the 'Arsenal cage': 'There was no point in being a skin if you simply got nicked by the police wherever you went' (ibid.: 20).

Early Skins cautiously extended the boundaries of 'us' in much the same way as the comedy discussed in Chapter 3. Afro-Caribbeans could be offered probationary membership, but 'Pakis' (not just Pakistanis, but any Asian British citizens) were another matter: 'Asian immigrants had a different, closed way of life and did not blend with traditional working-class or East End ways of living' (Knight 1982: 20). Fowler cites Des, a Skin who beat up an Asian man. His crime? When Des asked him for a light, he bought him a box of matches. Fowler suggests that Asians were perceived both as failing to mix and trying too hard at the same time – 'They dress in carefully tailored suits, they are polite, they are nice' (1972/1996: 163). In other words they are 'Ear 'oles', while some West Indians have some potential as 'Lads'; they 'are more "normal" in the skins' eyes. They get drunk, they like dancing, they like dressing up in skin gear' (ibid.: 163). The stereotype of Asian passivity – in comedy, in 'Paki-bashing' and its media interpretations – was arguably destroyed when the Hamborough Tavern was burnt to the ground by the Southall Asian Youth Movement in 1981 to prevent the planned appearance of Oi! band The 4-Skins. But there were signs that enough was enough as early as 1976: when a white gang murdered Gurdip Singh Chaggar, an eighteen-year-old Punjabi, also in Southall, the community responded with a storm of protest and the 'siege' of Southall police headquarters.

Such nuances of ethnicity don't really register in Richard Allen's books, although the Ugandan Asians had clearly become more 'acceptable' between Smoothies in 1973, where they are fair game for a kicking, and Top Gear Skin in 1974, where we learn that 'now they had arrived, the government seemed to be coping with the situation quite successfully' (The Complete Richard Allen Volume Three: 210), hero Roy is not in favour of attacking them and the accompanying aggro scene is pointedly lacklustre. Clearly, the 'Amin factor' counted for something. But Allen's Skins are an ethnically cleansed community. There are no Rude Boys, and racial boundaries are non-negotiable. However, publisher Dotun Adebayo, speaking about Allen on Bookmark, remembers feeling distanced from the books' racism: 'I hate to say this today, but ... because a lot of the racism was focused on people of Asian origin, as a 12-year old Afro-Caribbean boy in London, I didn't feel as uncomfortable with it.' Peter Cave's Mama (1972/1995) plays most visibly on such divided sympathies through the character of Winston, who wants to be the first black British Hell's Angel. Initially told that 'We don't have no bloody coons in the Angels' (30), he proves himself, is initiated and given a new name – Superspade. There soon follows an uncomfortable moment when the gang go 'Paki-bashing' – Cave's books are essentially skinhead novels with biker trappings – stopping to look uncomfortably at their new member. But they needn't have worried – 'I hate them friggin' Pakis as much as you do,' he reassures them, 'Hell, man, they're bloody niggers ain't they?' (64–5). Like the 'good sports' in racist humour, his 'good humour' is 'infectious', everyone relaxes and he joins them in scalping a Pakistani teenager.

While their sub- (or counter-) cultural trappings are different, Allen's and Cave's novels tell much the same story – individuals and gangs pose a problem for law and order, while also 'policing the deviants, and preserving the given definitions, for the dominant' (Healy 1996: 46). Joe's position outside the boundaries of acceptability also allows him to operate as a border guard against more worrying permissive hordes – blacks, 'Pakis', 'queers' and hippies. Even as Allen progressively recuperates the Skins as a social grouping, Joe remains 'out there' as a reminder of the limits placed on white masculine aggression as well as its usefulness in suppressing other deviants. But he also becomes a receptacle for values and qualities displaced from those other groups. His rebellion against the parent culture has its negative reflection in the hippy counter-culture. Pearson (1976), quoting Jeremy Seabrook, suggests that

84

qualities associated with the Asian community were close to those celebrated in nostalgic evocations of white working-class life – community, duty to kinsfolk, the extended family – 'as though the working class were confronted by a spectre of their own past, which they were anxious to banish' (67). Joe's 'excessive' masculinity, often expressed through rape, is likened to a caricature of black masculinity in *Suedehead*: the 'unleashing of jungle emotions did something for his savagery-starved system', and his 'partner' spells out the comparison: 'You're like all those Jamaicans I've ever met. A woman is a receptacle for their lust – nothing more' (*The Complete Richard Allen Volume One*: 180). The same book is the youth-cult novel most concerned with queer-bashing, which, Healy argues, concomitantly 'queers' Joe himself. He emerges from prison, where he has been the 'special target for every queer in the Scrubs' (ibid.: 104). Outside, he can't keep away from gay men – he 'learns to "do" queer – but only in order to gain access to the homes of rich gay men' (Healy 1996: 98). As he plans his pick-ups, he starts to sound more hustler than queer-basher, prowling the underground 'trying to separate the wolves from the ewes' (*The Complete Richard Allen Volume One*: 134) – spotting a likely target, he thinks, '*If he wasn't in such an exposed position I'd kick his sexy-ass*' (ibid.: 136). Not all of this is lost on Joe himself – in *Skinhead Escapes*, he recalls how he 'had taken it upon himself to rise above his station in life and gone queer-suedehead' (ibid.: 257).

Healy suggests that 'there's something queer about all teen cults – just like dirty homosexuals, they're dangerous, delinquent and demonized by the press ... Both act as conspicuous reminders of what men should not be' (1996: 27).[6] There's a scene which recurs in both Allen's and Norman's books – a central character is forced into same-sex(ual) contact, recoils and then finds, to their alarm, an involuntary physical stirring. In *Angels from Hell*, it takes place during that most loaded of Angel scenes, the initiation, where the Angel-to-be is daubed in the collective vomit, urine and excrement of the gang.[7] If this scenario isn't loaded enough, Gerry is forced to kiss the leader he will replace, Vincent, and is shocked by the response it provokes. It is to this precarious maintenance of the male body and the male group that I now want to turn.

The boys are back in town

> DIMENSION 5 was now in the hands of the Overmaster, whose lust for ultimate power had become an obsession. Religion and the media were all under his control ... Many were arrested and jailed.
>
> ... The Warrior had become weary and disillusioned with war, but seeing how the people struggled to be free he knew once again he must raise up his sword ...
>
> sleevenotes, Thin Lizzy's *Jailbreak*

It's 1997; that is, a 1997 of the 1970s imagination. All youth cults have been out-lawed. In America, the Wallace–Nixon coalition has appointed a Secretary of State with Special Responsibilities for Social Hygiene, 'someone who would rid the Land of the Free of the free-loaders, the hippies, peaceniks, deviants, long-haired students, black militants, communists and – Hell's Angels ... Reagan did the job in just fifteen months' (*Angels from Hell*: 18).[8] Britain, meanwhile, has been cleaned up by hardline Home Secretary George Hayes, a process which involves compulsory repatriation and, with the entry of Whitehouse and Longford into politics, the purging of the sex industries. As a result, 'sex crimes had rocketed' (*ibid.*: 53) – the Danes were right, it seems! There are only five gangs left, with a total membership of four hundred. Consequently, the Angels are 'the first true Underground in Britain for centuries. For the dilettante scribblers of the early seventies the name had been a collective affectation – for the bikers it was a necessity of existence' (*ibid.*: 15).

This is the impressive canvas across which Mick Norman's 'Last Heroes' ride in *Angels from Hell, Angel Challenge, Guardian Angels* and *Angels on My Mind*. But even more telling than this fantasy of disintegration and authoritarianism is the survivalist figure of Gerry Vinson, 'Wolf', the Heroes' leader. An arts graduate, whose degree proved to be 'useless', he has flirted with the Young Anarchists and the Angry Brigade, before settling for the army, where, serving in Ireland, he is reinvented as the proverbial 'human killing machine' by his tough sergeant. It's this mixed heritage which allows him, in turn, to reinvent the Angels for the hard time ahead: 'Gave the boys that bit of discipline. Toughened them up in the right way ... A guerrilla army, fast and mobile' (*Angels from Hell*: 32).

If the political nature of this scenario seems ambiguous, it's worth considering how Hall *et al.* characterise the 'vanguardism' of the Angry Brigade, as well as such international contemporaries as Baader–Meinhof and the Weathermen, as suggesting 'a single-minded determination to drive the logic of struggle through to its most extreme conclusion ... produced by isolation from any kind of mass struggle – and frustration at the snail's pace of reform' (1978: 291). While the bombings were linked to 'key class issues' – Ireland, the Industrial Relations Act, the closure of Rolls Royce and the Ford strike – what seemed equally significant was the desire for tangible enemies and a plan of action. In the case of the Angry Brigade, this 'arose from a deep conviction of the manifest human injustices of the system; and since, in the libertarian cast of thought, the oppression of the state is always direct and unmediated, it could only be met by direct and unmediated means' (*ibid.*: 292). The fundamental need for a proactive agenda, however, was scarcely specific to the left, any more so than at the time of any crisis. Klaus Theweleit's study of the German Freikorps, the 'White Terror', marks out a fantasy which can be found in fascism, left terrorism, the survivalist fantasies of pulp fiction and rock'n'roll rebellion.

Given the 1970s fascination with fascism, both modish (Roxy Music's Nazi uniforms, Bowie's notorious 'dictator' speech in 1976, punk's swastikas) and otherwise (the NF's populist support, the appearance of private armies), Theweleit's extraordinary, if eccentric, psychoanalytic reading of the Freikorps exercises a particular pull here. The Freikorps 'policed' Germany after the First World War in both official and unofficial capacities – hired by the the socialist chancellor to bring order, but also pursuing revenge campaigns against those who they felt had betrayed them (communists and other 'subversive' types). Analysing their letters and novels, Theweleit constructs a fascist type, a 'psychotic' whose ego has never been properly formed.

These ideas draw on the psychoanalytic theories of writers like Margaret Mahler and Jacques Lacan. In its earliest years, the argument goes, the child perceives no boundaries between itself and, in particular, its mother. In order to imagine itself as 'I', a subject, it must first recognise itself as an object, as distinct from the mother. Theweleit's argument is that the fascist type never achieves this state, that he is 'not-yet-fully-born' (1989: 243) and cannot form object relations. His sense of his own peripheral boundaries is therefore precarious, constantly under threat. He counters this threat first through aggressive differentiation: 'the man holds himself together as an entity, a body with fixed boundaries ... He defends himself with a kind of sustained erection of the whole body, of whole cities, of whole troop units' (Theweleit 1987: 244). The threat to this armoured self is often represented in the imagery of floods and oceans, 'inundating and engulfing' (ibid.: 229) – 'floods of papers, political, literary, intellectual currents, influences ... They want whatever floods may come to rebound against them; they want to stop, and dam up those floods' (230). Floods loom similarly large in sections of the 1970s' political imaginary – the tide of permissiveness itself, the immigrants, 'queers' and dirty hippies who threaten the solid masculine identity of Allen's Skins, the pervasive fear of 'softness'. The hippie, in several Allen books, has submitted to, even embraced, an all-pervasive filth; Joan, the heroine in Sorts, recoils from 'the hippie desire to walk around in soiled clothing, to stay unwashed, to have their long hair matted with lice and dirt' (The Complete Richard Allen Volume Two: 14). But the 'not-yet-fully-born' also desires fusion, which manifests itself in two ways. First, violence often takes the form of the dissolution of the boundaries between attacker and victim, not least in the rape and murder of 'Red Women': 'the victim loses her outlines as an object. The same thing happens here to the perceiving subject. He, too, finds himself in a state of dissolution' (Theweleit 1987: 203–4). We are told that Ina, in Knuckle Girls, suffers from 'brain-flooding', an explanatory term 'for the adrenalin rise which occurred when pain and pleasure were inseparably linked in the subject's mind' (The Complete Richard Allen Volume Two: 236–7). This engorgement suggests a phallicising of Ina's body – she's the most 'masculine' of Allen's female characters – and her fantasies of violence resemble Theweleit's boundary-dissolving 'bloody mass': 'She lay on her bed, letting the mental pictures form, reform, and melt into a beautiful crimson blob that moved and shifted and grew ugly in its terrible agony' (ibid.: 260). But the more important form of fusion is the reconstruction of the body through military drill, the insertion into the troop as 'totality-machine': 'Under fascism, the most common form of the "I" is as a component within a larger totality-ego – the "I" as "we"' (Theweleit 1989: 243).

Mick Norman's novels usually end with the Angels having to go back 'underground', that is to say, dissolving into fragments, disempowered by being so much less than the sum of their parts. According to Hunter S. Thompson, the Angels' 'desperate sense of unity is crucial to the outlaw mystique ... When somebody punches a lone Angel every one of them feels threatened' (1967: 83). While Gerry is established as the hardest of hard men, he is easily overpowered when separated from the Last Heroes in Angels on My Mind. Tellingly, he is reduced to childlike dependence on a powerful 'mother', Dr Angela Wells, whose Clockwork Orange deprogramming of his violent 'nature' involves taking him back to childhood. Steve, in *Terrace Terrors*, is similarly emasculated when separated from army and 'uniform'. The 'terrace patrol' is worryingly close both to the Freikorps and to the NF's later fantasies of using skinheads as a force to 'police' the boundaries of the nation. This is how Steve addresses his 'force':

> Look boys ... We're legal now ... Think of yourselves as fuzz without the uniform. We don't act as skins or boot boys. We try to bring decency back onto the terraces ... If it's little bleeders getting thrills by causing mayhem, break 'em up. Anyway you want. The skin way ... no aggro for the sake of aggro. Only as a chastisement.
>
> (*The Complete Richard Allen Volume Four*: 202)

The Last Heroes perform much the same function at teeny-pop concerts in *Guardian Angels*, a fantasy at least qualified by the self-conscious references to Altamont:

> WARNING!
> The show is for you to enjoy. Do that, and nobody will get hurt. Step out of line, and you'll imagine the WORLD HAS ENDED.
> So, just COOL IT.
>
> (*The Angel Chronicles*: 230)

It's the 'feminine' itself which is being policed here, and which threatens the Angels' collective 'body' from without and within. The teeny and 'middie' fans (imagine Barry Manilow fans armed to the teeth) generate serious casualties amongst the Angels, while a 'militant' offshoot threatens the group from the inside. Holly and Lady, we are told, are 'lethal. Totally ruthless against men. Cripplingly effective' (*ibid.*: 205), and Gerry can (temporarily) subdue them only with the aid of his 'lady' Brenda, who plans to split herself – the narrative contrives to kill her instead. When Gerry pledges the Heroes' allegiance to another group, he adds 'What's left of us' (248), and finally, inevitably, 'The Last Heroes would, yet again, have to go underground' (261).

I want to sound a note of caution here. First, there is, as Marek Kohn puts it, 'a danger, when surveying popular imagery, of seeing fascism in every corner' (1981/1989: 143). As I've suggested, this distaste for 'softness' and desire for disciplined action is not exclusive to the right – Home believes that his own appropriation of NEL-pulp imagery reveals that '"left" and "right" wing doctrines are distorted reflections of each other. This is hardly surprising given that communism and fascism ultimately spring from a single source – Hegel' (1995: 111). In any case, I'm not certain that it is fascism, as such, that Theweleit is describing, so much as a kind of warrior-masculinity that can be appropriated by fascism. For one thing, one has to take a gigantic leap of faith to accept one of Theweleit's central premises, namely that a 'psychotic' psychic type 'may have been the norm in Germany' (1989: 213). Simon Reynolds and Joy Press discern similar imagery in what they call 'combat rock', a formation which includes the guerrilla chic of The Clash and the apocalyptic Black Panther imagery of

Public Enemy and which offers 'the bliss of boyish camaraderie, the potency of a strength-in-numbers that falls midway between the teenage gang and a military formation' (1995: 67). The Clash's album *Combat Rock* suggests 'that it would be exciting to live in a society where to play or even listen to rock'n'roll was a crime against the state' (*ibid.*: 72), but it's Thin Lizzy's *Jailbreak* which brings us even closer to the Angels from Hell, with its 'mix of renegade mythos and mid-'70s fear of totalitarianism' (68). *Jailbreak* evokes different kinds of 'rebellion' – homosocial exuberance ('The Boys Are Back in Town'), Irish history ('Emerald') and generic self-reliance ('Cowboy Song') – but the organising rubric of 'rock'n'roll' tends to unify them into one glorious lads-against-the-world struggle. 'We're a dying breed,' Phil Lynott is quoted as saying in Stuart Baillie's CD liner notes, 'All we got is rock and roll and the road. We got no wives, no family, no homes, just this.' This is very much in the same idiom as Norman, who seems to address a more 'hip' audience than Allen, thus the in-jokes about Roger Corman and *Cahiers du Cinéma*. This is the point where pulp SF collides with a formative heavy metal imaginary, its sexual politics ransacked from motorbike magazines and the casual misogyny of rock culture.

In *Angels from Hell*, the Angels fight the law, and the law (temporarily) loses. Subsequently, the Angels' enemies are indicative of a more general threat to the male group – the twin threat of feminism and scream-age hysteria in *Guardian Angels*, for example. In *Angel Challenge*, the second in the series, the 'new spirit of freedom' following the government's defeat opens the door for the return of other youth cults. The Skulls, for example, are a modified version of old friends: 'Mix in the old skinheads of the late seventies and add a dash of "Clockwork Orange". Work in a bizarre dress sense, odd rules and season well with incredible viciousness' (*The Angel Chronicles*: 101). But the real villains of *Challenge* are the Ghouls, an outfit of glam bikers led by the flamboyant Evel Winter. Decked out in satin, sequins, eye liner and perfume, they don't take a lot of decoding – Evel's penchant for calling people 'Duckie' confirms that this isn't Slade we're talking about here. But the Ghouls' sexuality is presented in conflicting terms. They are identified by an 'absence of sexual activity' (122) and do grievous bodily harm to anyone foolish enough to call them 'queer'. Their contempt for women empowers them as a unit – 'they emphasise their top-ness by not messing around with women. At all ... Just each other and their hogs' (113) – and their public fellatio suggests something closer to high-glam's gender rebellion, recuperable as 'theatre', rather than homosexuality-as-desire.[9] But this blurring of the homosocial and the homosexual rather problematises the Angels' overall image.[10] Homosexuality is an ambiguous presence in the 'Last Heroes' books. Rupert Colt, assistant director turned entrepenreurial dilettante, is a recurring character who establishes an uneasy friendship with the Angels. Rupert is stereotypically limp-wristed and devious, but also credited with genuine subcultural status, which counts for a lot in these books – he's on the deviates list of George Hayes's Social Offences Branch. But the Ghouls are a different matter, and another contemporaneous 'Hell's Angel' is worth citing here. Wrestler Adrian Street was the very epitome of Evel Winter, a hard man in 'poof's clothing'. In Simon Garfield's invaluable book about the downmarket, beer-bellies-and-bruisers world of British wrestling, Street explains his image:

Up until then almost all the wrestlers had been hard, and if they weren't they pretended. But here was this 'poof' in their midst, and it threw them. The fans hated it, but you could see they were a bit intrigued and I think the women were maybe a bit turned on. Nobody was doing that before me.

(quoted in Garfield 1996: 72)

Street claims to have arrived at his fifth-member-of-The-Sweet look by accident, rejecting the image of American wrestler Gorgeous George but drawn to silver lamé, velvet, blonde 'mullet' hair and sequins. His colleagues appear to have been more semiotically attuned – 'Wooo Mary!' they said, and bent their wrists mockingly at him. 'I was really pissed off,' he claims endearingly, 'I'd spent all that money' (ibid.: 71). So Adrian decides to extract low camp revenge – he 'plays the poof' in the ring, skips around his enraged opponents, invariably minces to victory and leaves working-class audiences foaming at the mouth. Was this low culture's first uneasy acknowledgement both of the (partial) legalisation of homosexuality and of the newly visible gay political power, a bonecrushing glam rocker in spandex and eyeliner? When Street formed a tag team with 'Bad' Bobby Barnes, they became the Hell's Angels, not with bikers in mind but 'angels who had turned bad. We came on like two choirboys in white satin capes, and our initials in silver sequins, and our silver hair over the top' (ibid.: 74.) But Street's sexuality, like the Ghouls', could never be spelled out – he didn't represent a specific sexuality; rather, a 'nancy boy' who was tougher than he had any right to be, a confusing spanner in the works of masculinity. Mick McManus, British wrestling's most popular bad guy, did not, for all his villainy, behave or dress like that.

Clearly, quite a lot was going on behind the school desk – quite what teenage boys made of Mick Norman is anybody's guess. It's striking, however, that, of all the 'low' texts discussed in this book, novels such as Richard Allen's come closest to possessing cultural capital – in the high prices they command (Confessions novels, by contrast, are easily obtained for less than £1), in Stewart Home's insertion of them into art practices, in pop culture's references to them (Morrissey's 'Suedehead'). Leaving aside the racism (usually the sticking point in nostalgia), homophobia and brutal sexual violence (rape, Angel women 'pulling the train', that is, being fucked by the entire gang), what also stands out is the nostalgia for a time when there really seemed to be no future.

6

CAN YOU KEEP IT UP FOR A DECADE?

British sexploitation

Film studies has not, to say the least, concerned itself very much with what John Walker calls 'the cinema of J. Arthur Wank' (1985: 67). David McGillivray's groundbreaking *Doing Rude Things* first indicated the extent of this 'lost continent', and it remains a valuable account of British sexploitation's development and its prime movers. But one of the book's greatest strengths is also a limitation – McGillivray was part of this narrative, writing horror and sex films during the 1970s. He offers little analysis beyond some familiar comments on the undying inhibitions of the British, and never gets to grips with his own ambiguous investment in the films. His own involvement helps to smooth over this evasiveness, but there is a sense of the films being both an important part of cultural history and of no importance whatsoever. Their status as something like an epoch-defining genre suggests more of the former than the latter, but McGillivray wants to make it clear that he knows what 'quality' is. 'Other countries may have produced classics of movie erotica; Britain hasn't,' he insists. But 'as pointers to the obsessions and hypocrisies of an age which influenced many of the film-makers at work today, these films have at last acquired true value ... what made the British public flock to see such rubbish?' (1992: 19). A gap opens up here – 'we', ironic and amused, look not only at a body of films beyond/beneath discussion but at the low 'they' who went to see them. One of the aims of this chapter is to narrow that gap.

I want to say something here about the relationship between sexploitation and pornography. The two categories obviously converge and overlap, but there are also important differences between their respective historical developments and aesthetic aims. This is not simply a question of differentiating between softcore and hardcore, a distinction which, as Andy Moye has pointed out, 'is not fixed and definite' (1985: 45), determined as it is by shifts in what is legally permissible and by the 'specialist codification' (*ibid.*: 45) more typical of hardcore. Pornography pre-dates photography, while sexploitation evolved out of the 'glamour' pin-up. Pornography is bound up with *seeing* and *knowing*, a 'low' manifestation of a larger process of sexual surveillance. Both Stephen Marcus (1966) and Linda Williams (1990) observe the way its history parallels the development of the sexual sciences, so that both endeavoured to record and describe sexuality, to (literally) penetrate the secrets of, in particular, the female body. Sexploitation, on the other hand, isn't just retarded pornography, held back by censorship – its cultural affiliations and modes of looking are significantly different. Arguably, it can be identified as the convergence of two aesthetic/cultural traditions – the dubious 'respectability' of art photography and forms of lowbrow popular entertainment. 'Art' magazines featuring nude pin-ups can be traced as far back as the 1920s, and their cultural pretensions were as consistent as they were transparent – '"art" has been the single most exploited guise for the presentation of full nudes' (Gabor 1996: 65). These were ostensibly produced for art and photography students, the captions spoke of composition and lighting, but the images conformed to the conventions (poses, framing, the model's gaze) of the 'glamour' pin-up, found fully clothed (or in bathing costumes) in its movie star equivalents – Marilyn Monroe brought the two types of pin-up together most publicly and notoriously. An issue of Contours from 1955 features a model nearly bursting out of a black lace bra, looking at the camera with what is generically coded as an 'inviting' look; but the caption is speaking a very different language:

> A pensive mood is projected in this shot of a mediatating [sic] model in a semi-relaxed pose. The design on the hip and the lace of the bra invite added attention and interest. The forms are sharp.
>
> (quoted in Gabor 1996: 72)

There's an evocative phrase which sums up the agenda of the 'art' pin-up – 'admiring the female form' – capturing as it does the reduction of its models to matters of line and shade and its construction of the consumer as sophisticated man-of-the-world. These are the conventions which pass into calendars and upmarket 'men's magazines'. The latter replaced artistic pretensions with 'lifestyle' – 'the indoor, sophisticated, city-bred man' (Gabor 1996: 78), most influentially in Playboy (1953–), and subsequently in Penthouse (1965–), Mayfair (1966–) and the relaunched Men Only (1971–), originally a pocket-sized celebration of cars, clothes, food and travel with some star-related 'glamour'. George Harrison Marks's Kamera and Solo (both 1958–) belong to the 'art' tradition, but Marks's background also tied him to the other formative strand – music hall and burlesque, striptease, the Windmill Theatre's menu of nudes and comedy, the construction of 'girlie' magazines as Forces entertainment, with an emphasis on exotic sexuality found abroad (especially with a 'French' theme). There are obviously very different class constructions implicit in the appeal of these two modes, but that didn't necessarily translate into actual consumption – people who claim to buy Playboy for the articles have traditionally been met with a sceptical raised eyebrow. When this translated into British cinema, it was invariably the burlesque tradition that was the dominant one.

An important component of the 'sexploitation gaze' is suggested by Nuttall and Carmichael's description of 1950s glamour magazines Spick and Span:

> The thighs oozing over stocking-tops, the elaborate inelegance of the clothing, the glimpse of council-estate front rooms and motorway lay-bys behind the girls, the air of archness and callow self-consciousness which many of the models have, as though they feared for the cleanliness of their underwear, all add to the impression that these girls don't normally pose

for photographs or lie around in their knickers ... Consequently the stocking-tops, suspenders, G-strings, high heels and so on ... actually have the appearance of something not meant to be seen.

(1977: 51-2)[1]

This is not the full medical examination of the pornographic gaze, which, say, David Sullivan's softcore-by-necessity aspires to; rather, 'that swift and secret erection that occurred when the girl in the full skirt ran down the bus stairs too fast' (ibid.: 52). The not-meant-to-be-seen gives us the line from Harrison Marks to Benny Hill and illuminates the paradox of the Confessions films which baffled 'quality' critics: how they could combine presumably permissive nudity and sex with a level of innuendo which suggested that both remained 'forbidden'. Another distinction is worth making. Pornography aspires to the abstract, a virtual absence not only of narrative but of the body as anything but a mathematically determined fucking machine. Sexploitation, on the other hand, has a penchant for story and context; Spick and Span's quintessential front rooms and lay-bys, the mini-narratives The Sun supplies with its Page 3 girls.[2]

British sexploitation films took off in the late 1950s; theatrically with nudist films like Nudist Paradise (Charles Saunders, 1957), but also in the 8mm silent 'glamour' films which could be obtained from newsagents' and electrical shops, or through the post. These softcore loops were the British equivalent of the burlesque films made in America after the war (see Schaefer 1997) and offer us further clues to why sexploitation's dominant allegiance has been to comedy in Britain. McGillivray outlines the music-hall/stand-up backgrounds of Harrison Marks and Pete Walker (son of Band Waggon's Syd Walker), but this affinity is visible in the films themselves. Glamour films were a return to 'primitive' cinema both stylistically and in their interrelationship with forms of live entertainment. Tom Gunning has called such a mode a 'cinema of attractions', an 'exhibitionist cinema' distinguished not only by the virtual absence of linear narrative but by a particular relationship with the audience – 'a cinema that displays its visibility, willing to rupture a self-enclosed fictional world for a chance to solicit the attention of the spectator' (1990: 57). The most frequent sign of this address in pre-1906 cinema was the look at the camera – in the 1950s/ 60s glamour film, it's the wink that's important.

Harrison Marks was the British glamour king, although he made an uneasy transition to features. Xcitement! (1960) is 'cinema of attractions' via the world of Peeping Tom. As Pamela Green strips for the camera in an apartment set, she maintains eye contact with the camera, handing a drink and a cigarette to Marks/the spectator – a hand enters the frame to take both. The Fourposter plays like a cross between a Benny Hill 'silent' sketch and a Carry On costume film with added sex. Part of the film shows a traveller being progressively worn out by what turn out to be identical twins. Meanwhile, 'Vicki Kennedy' (Carry On regular Margaret Nolan) is menaced by Marks (as a hunchback) and his former comedy partner Stuart Samuels. In the final scene, Marks, Nolan and Samuels take a bow; when the shot is held, Marks holds up a sign which reads 'What do you want, blood?'; cut to 'The End' printed on Nolan's bottom.

A remark by Stephen Marcus points to another kinship between sexploitation and comedy. Marcus is talking about the relationship between pornography and 'official' morality, a relationship founded equally on opposition and mutual dependence: '[pornography] reveals the discrepancy which exists in society between openly professed ideals and secretly harboured wishes or secretly practised vices – it may act indirectly to "unmask" society's official version of itself' (1966: 233). This account of the base desires of the body at war with and constantly giving the lie to the high ideals of the 'soul' is familiar – George Orwell says much the same thing about the smutty milieu of Donald McGill's seaside postcards, a sensibility taken much further in the 'boss-eyed cock-artists and buxom crumpet' of later postcard artists like Fitzpatrick and Taylor, 'a world of alcoholic commercial travellers on a perpetual headlong course of lechery' (Nuttall and Carmichael 1977: 37). This subversion is limited in aim as well as effect – as Marcus suggests, it offers no alternative vision and is, if anything, 'perfectly and happily at home with hypocrisy, cant, injustice and all kinds of social malevolence' (1966: 233). Little wonder, then, that Marks and *Carry on Camping* are so contemptuous of 'free love' – better a sexual economy of petty theft than welfare state benevolence.

Sexploitation cycles of the 1960s were determined partly by censorship, but some of the formulas persisted into the 1970s. A cycle of social problem films which includes *Beat Girl* (Edmond T. Greville, 1960), *The Yellow Teddybears* (Robert Hartford-Davis, 1963) and *That Kind of Girl* (Gerald O'Hara, 1963) continued with films like *A Smashing Bird I Used to Know* (Hartford-Davis, 1969), *Groupie Girl* (Derek Ford, 1970), *Permissive* (Lindsay Shonteff, 1970), *Cool it Carol!* (Pete Walker, 1970) and the belated *Home Before Midnight* (Walker, 1979). A series of pseudo-documentaries owed less to John Grierson than they did to the Italian 'mondo' or 'sexy' films – *West End Jungle* (Arnold Louis Miller, 1961), *London in the Raw* (Miller, 1964), *Primitive London* (Miller, 1965), *The Wife Swappers* (Derek Ford, 1970) and *Naughty!* (Stanley Long, 1971). The latter crossed over into what I've chosen to call the 'suburban report' films[3] – *The Wife Swappers* again, *A Promise of Bed* (Derek Ford, 1970), *Monique* (John Bown, 1970), *Suburban Wives* (Ford, 1971), *Commuter Husbands* (Ford, 1972), *The Love Box* (Billy and Teddy White, 1972), *Au Pair Girls* (Val Guest, 1972) and *Escort Girls* (Donovan Winter, 1974). The 'suburban report' films paved the way for the mid-1970s sexcoms, which I shall look at in the next chapter, but what most of them have in common is a multiple narrative anchored by some kind of thematic focus (wifeswapping, adultery, an escort agency) and/or a narrator, storyteller or 'expert' to guide us through. The impression of a tabloid exposé is reinforced by the proliferation, in Derek Ford's films in particular, of narration and voices – usually at least one narrator, the voice-over of the participants in the stories (like the 'accessed voices' in a news story) and, in *The Wife Swappers*, an 'expert' psychologist. The storyteller in *Suburban Wives* is a local reporter who, like her equivalent in *Commuter Husbands*, is also a character in one of the stories.

Prior to 1974, sex is largely addressed as a 'problem' or an 'issue'. *The Wife Swappers*, made in 1969 but released in 1970, is a transitional film – it combines pseudo-documentary, social problem discourses and the prurience of the suburban exposé. Its hyperbolic disapproval of the 'swinging scene' veers close to self-parody – 'it had to be that way,' producer Stanley Long told McGillivray, 'This was just to get the film through the censor because it was all right providing you didn't approve of what you were showing' (McGillivray 1992: 57). But of course titillation and disapproval are by no means mutually exclusive, and a number of the film's sexual ideologies recur in other films.

Pornography/permissiveness/repression: *Naughty!*

Living two lives must have been a bit of a strain. All that moral indignity on the one hand, and all this naughty behaviour on the other.

Narrator, Naughty!

The central characters in *Eskimo Nell* (Martin Campbell, 1974) endeavour to film three versions of the famous dirty poem to satisfy different backers – a hardcore version, a kung fu musical and a gay Western. When shifty producer Roy Kinnear absconds with the money, they turn to a fourth backer, the Society for Moral Reform led by Lady Longhorne – 'I represent a vast minority of people in this country who are clamouring for a total ban on anything but nice, wholesome stories.' They endeavour to make a fourth, 'wholesome' version in order to fund the other three secretly. The 'Festival of Light' version is selected for a Royal Gala Performance, but, inevitably, the hardcore version is accidentally shown instead. These are the two versions which really matter, the film's two comic Others. On the one hand, there's the thinly veiled hypocrisy of moral reformers – 'I've studied pornography over the years, and I know what effect it can have on you,' proclaims Lord Coltwind, twitching like a vision of Bob Todd depravity. Equally untenable, though, is the pornucopia demanded by their American backer 'Big Dick' – 'I want to see girls being whipped, plenty of flagellation, bondage, rubber appliances, leatherwear, chains, lesbianism, kinky gadgets, and you can throw in a bit of bestiality at the same time. Then, in the second scene ...'

This interrelationship between repression and uninhibited abandon informs *Naughty!* 'A Report on Pornography and Erotica'. As its title suggests, the film is most comfortable with a saucy, by implication nationally specific, middle ground. The film is a mixture of historical recreation, vox-pop interviews of questionable veracity, found footage and a kind of docu-drama. But it really breaks down into a contrast between Victorian repression and early 1970s Britain about to be engulfed by commercial sex. Early in the film, we are introduced to Horace, 'an ordinary kind of fellow ... Mr Average, you might say, or is he?' We see him, in London for the day, stray from Piccadilly Circus to Soho, a pre-Indecent-Displays-Control-Act Soho with windows full of magazines and marital aids and cinemas offering *Swedish Language of Love* and *Anatomy of Love*. Horace is located between two polar opposites – his nagging, sexually uninterested wife whom we hear in a sound flashback ('I don't know what's the matter with you ... It's all those books you've been reading') and the cinema club doorman who lures him in to see 'the same old stuff' – 'He's not going to see anything new – it's still not legal here.' Sex is 'somewhere else' – 'In Sweden, it is legal,' muses Horace, 'and I bet the girls throw themselves at you.' Horace functions as a kind of cultural gauge for what follows.

It's worth speculating on the influence of Stephen Marcus's *The Other Victorians* on the film's Victorian sections. Marcus's book had been available in paperback since 1969 and highlighted as an important book by *Nova*. *Naughty!* received slightly better reviews than its generic peers, and David Robinson in *The Financial Times* and Arthur Thirkell in *The Daily Mirror* commended it for signs of 'research'. It draws on some of Marcus's cast of characters – Henry Ashbee's extensive porn collection, the dubious dealings of John Hotten, Henry Hayler's 'dirty pictures' (reclaimed for the sex comedy lineage through the use of speeded-up photography), the English penchant for flagellation. It demonstrates a comparable accumulation of primary material – 'primitive' silent porn, the diverse material at the Amsterdam 'Wet Dream' Film Festival, footage of John Lindsay shooting hardcore in a suburban front room, explaining the 'come shot' to his leading man and insisting that 'it's got to be sexy'.

Marcus's account of pornography's coexistence with prohibitive decorum is a complex one. He describes porn and Victorian morality as 'reversals, mirror images, negative analogues of one another' (1966: 286), discourses in which the 'same set of anxieties are at work' (ibid.: 287). In pornography and the sexology of William Acton, one finds:

> worlds without psychology; they are worlds of organs and physiology in which everything is convertible into matter ... both represent a primitive form of materialism. In pornography, this fantasy purports to be subversive and liberating. In Acton's work it represents itself as grimly scientific and ineluctably tragic.
>
> (ibid.: 33)

An example would be the opposition between prohibitive masturbation myths – the life-sapping, growth-stunting effects of self-abuse – and the pornotopian incitement to 'spend' in every way possible and at every opportunity. Both condense essentially the same economic metaphor on to the body, simply opposing a logic of 'scarcity' and 'plenty'.

Foucault develops similar ideas in his account of sex and power. Rather than 'revolution' granting the sexual power withheld by 'repression', it simply re-channels and re-orders it. Moreover, notions of repression are 'gratifying' because of what he calls 'the speaker's benefit': 'If sex is repressed, that is, condemned to prohibition, non-existence, and silence, then the mere fact that one is speaking about it has the appearance of a deliberate transgression' (1976/1981: 6). The 'repressive' Victorian practices of the medical examination, psychiatric investigation and ascribing of 'perversions' actually brought pleasure and power together:

> The pleasure that comes of exercising a power that questions, monitors, watches, spies, searches out, palpates, brings to light; and on the other hand, the pleasure that kindles at having to evade this power, flee from it,

fool it, or travesty it. The power that lets itself be invaded by the pleasure it is pursuing; and opposite it, power asserting itself in the pleasure of showing off, scandalizing, or resisting. Capture and seduction, confrontation and mutual reinforcement.

(ibid.: 45)

The populist version of repression is the 'hypocrisy' model – the Victorians who practised virtue in principle and vice in practice; even better, virtue and vice of an exceptionally refined sort. In Hammer's *Taste the Blood of Dracula* (Peter Sasdy, 1969), three Victorian fathers rule their children with proverbial rods of iron but their nightlife escalates from brothel-visits to a particularly ill-advised blood-drinking ritual. *Naughty!* takes the masturbation prohibition by the scruff of the neck in one of its comic highpoints. The stern Victorian patriarch catches his son in the act and trots out all the tales of degeneration and madness. But the avuncular narrator interjects – 'It's all rubbish ... Ask him if *he* did.' Finally, he delivers the *coup de grâce* – 'Well, now you know. But don't take any notice, because your dad's off to the brothel now.' Self-abuse figures prominently in the film's natural, uninhibited sexuality – the strenuous activities of a monkey in the zoo shocks the same Victorian mother who chiselled off a statue's genitals in the previous scene. 'Oh dear, Auntie, don't be so shocked!' chides the narrator – extreme repression is feminine and castrating, 'natural' sexuality masculine, infantile, in short, 'naughty'.

Eskimo Nell's 'Big Dick' finds his counterpart in *Naughty!* in the figure of Al Goldstein, editor of *Screw*. 'If I haven't got a hard-on by the end of the first reel, I'll want to know the reason why,' warns Dick, while Goldstein declares that one film at the Wet Dream Festival gets 100 points 'because I got about eighteen hard-ons'. For Goldstein, liberation is largely a question of tumescence – anti-porn legislators are 'people whose hard-ons are memories from thirty years ago ... Catholics and homosexuals who don't want to admit what they are ... frightened, impotent people'. The Wet Dream Festival is presented as the 'libertarian' discourse on sex, and the panellists include *Oz*'s Richard Neville and Germaine Greer 'representing the feminine angle' (probably not how she was introduced on the day). One of the editors of *Suck* distils the logic of this model of freedom, one which Foucault and low comedy alike would make short work of:

> When we are unafraid and free from possessiveness, it will make little difference what kind of social organisation we choose to live under, because we will be open, kind and generous. It is sexual frustration, sexual envy, sexual fear which permeates all our human relationships and which perverts it.

Significantly, John Lindsay has learned to speak this language, too – war is the real pornography, he tells us, and talks wistfully of an Action Man doll with a 'nice penis which gets hard' and an 'Action Girl with a nice wee pussy'.

Naughty! constructs suburban Horace as a comic figure, but, like him, seems to wonder 'where it will all lead'. Finally, it settles on the image of the three Victorian

men who translated pornography and the concomitant representation of an industry 'forever at work to deceive the public'. There, definitively, is an agenda which
pornography and sexploitation can agree on.

Lost girls: the social problem film leaves home

The original cycle of British social problem films coincides with the period covered
by John Hill's *Sex, Class and Realism* (1986) – 1956 to 1963. The films of Basil Dearden
and Michael Relph (*Sapphire, Victim*) or those written by Ted Willis (*Woman in a Dressing
Gown*) constitute a kind of 'public service' genre cinema, setting out to entertain and
to educate, to tackle controversial subject matter within popular narratives. But Hill
acknowledges the existence of a more prurient strain, recognisable not only by more
sensational subjects but by their more titillating treatment. Exploitation and the social
problem films were not, in any case, absolutely distinct categories, John Trevelyan's
efforts notwithstanding. A 'controversial, bizarre, or timely subject matter amenable
to wild promotion' is one of the three defining properties of 1950s exploitation
outlined by Thomas Doherty (1988: 8), the other two being a low budget and a
teenage audience.

Hill observes that youth was the hot topic of the problem film, and that this was
often a way of dealing with a sexual culture in transition. Three of the films men-
tioned by Hill – *Beat Girl, The Yellow Teddybears* and *That Kind of Girl* – are closely linked
with sexploitation; the last two were made by Compton-Cameo. In *Beat Girl*, Soho
beatnik club The Offbeat is pointedly adjacent to Christopher Lee's raffishly glamorous strip club. Gillian Hills's Jennifer is doubly deviant – a jailbait delinquent with
a broken family and a 'bad crowd' ('hopeless and soapless'), but also irresistibly
attracted to the world of commercial sex. 'It's Legal,' proclaims Shirley Anne Field's
unforgettable solo number, but what's on Christopher Lee's mind isn't. *The Yellow Teddybears*
was based on a news story about schoolgirls wearing gollywog brooches to signal
the loss of their virginity. If the 'legitimate' social problem film fizzled out in 1963,
for sexploitation it was more like a beginning, leading to the more explicit softcore
films of the late 1960s and early 1970s.

Groupie Girl, Permissive and *Cool it Carol!* all feature characters who travel to London from
their provincial homes in search of a piece of 'permissive' action. – 'it's so boring up
here,' complains the heroine of *Groupie Girl*, 'People are boring and there's nothing to
do.' All three were released in the same year (1970), and there is a sense of looking
backwards at the 1960s as well as acknowledging that this is no longer the 'Swinging'
London of films like *Blow Up* (1966) or *Smashing Time* (1967). *Groupie Girl* contains its
own version of The Rolling Stones' Redlands drug bust, while *Cool it Carol!* throws in
references to 'London bus' movies, photographer David Bailey and the 1963 scandal
linking call girl Christine Keeler to Conservative War Secretary John Profumo (Carol is
even photographed in the most famous Keeler pose, naked astride a chair). These 'cau-
tionary' tales focus on innocents abroad, disillusioned or damaged by their experiences in the big city. But their 'social problem' credentials are most tellingly represented
by the following statement from *Groupie Girl*'s musical director, Ashley Kozac:

If there is one way to draw the attention of society to the sick minds of the groupies then this film is the answer. I think it will deter many young teenagers from becoming groupies.

We kept the sex scenes in the film because we want to get it home to parents that these things actually happen.

(*Daily Mirror*, 6 June 1970)

This is not only a little disingenuous about the film's projected audience; its shrill disapproval isn't entirely registered in the finished product. British film critics didn't buy into such claims – 'the tone is, if anything, amoral and the sexploitation blatant,' judged *Monthly Film Bulletin* (September 1970: 186), while *Cool it Carol!* was described as 'a thoroughly nasty bit of pornography' (Felix Barker, *Evening News*, 19 November 1970), 'a depressingly sleazy film' (Dick Richards, *Daily Mirror*, 19 November 1970) and, best of all, 'a patch of untreated effluent' (Dilys Powell, *Sunday Times*, 22 November 1970). Less typically, Paul Joannides found *Carol!* 'beguilingly good-humoured ... quintessentially English, unconcerned and pragmatic' (*Monthly Film Bulletin*, January 1971: 6), but this did not lead him to make any great claims for it.

Groupie Girl and *Permissive* both deal with the groupie 'scene', in effect forming a hybrid of sexploitation and the British pop film. *Permissive* is the one with pretensions, full of *Easy Rider* flash-forward inserts and hippy pontificating, but it's also the more conservative of the two. Suzy (Maggie Stride) joins her more experienced friend Fiona in London, already attached to a sub-Jethro-Tull folk rock group, Forever More. The real focus is on the groupie community itself, characterised by its mutual distrust and ruthless treachery – hair-pulling, knicker-flashing fights are de rigueur in both films. Suzy claws her way into the affections of lead singer Lee, a gnome in a polo neck who seems to have escaped from Mike Leigh's *Bleak Moments*. This involves replacing and displacing Fiona, whom she finds in a hotel bath, wrists slashed. Initially shy and vulnerable, Suzy leaves her friend to die and joins the band on the bus.

Groupie Girl is more prurient, but also more interesting. It was co-written by Suzanne Mercer, also the co-writer of *Naughty!* Mercer was married to the drummer of prog-rockers Juicy Lucy, which might explain why the film's evocation of the music scene is more interesting than *Permissive*'s. Not only is there the distinction between 'blanket-covered mattresses, fag-filled saucers and draughty transit vans' (Chibnall and Hunter 1995: 12), of on-the-road sloggers and the country houses of the emerging AristRockracy, but also the pleasure of trying to guess who 'Orange Butterfly' and 'The Sweaty Betty' are meant to be.

Sally (Esme Johns) stows away in a band's transit van because pop music (and its much-publicised sexual profligacy) 'doesn't really get to where I live'. We see her putting her money in her bra and her Post Office savings book in her knickers. At one level, this is used to emphasise her provincial naivety, but it's also a singularly blunt image of how she takes on exchange value. Sally's function as an object of exchange is brutally hammered home during the film's most disturbing scene – she is passed between two moving transit vans when Orange Butterfly tire of her and literally pass her on to The Sweaty Betty. This time we get some glimpses of rock's masculine codes, reminiscent of a male homosocial economy described by Mark Simpson:

> Girls are a currency of esteem between them, goods to be exchanged, a *sign* of their masculine prowess. The value of these goods, their currency, is determined entirely by what they fetch in the male market, their use value in the competition between males.
>
> (1994: 47)

'If you leave your chicks lying about my room, what do you expect?' one member of the band says defensively after appropriating someone's 'property'. Compared to pop, rock was as yet comparatively short on female stars – on the touring scene, women were (and frequently still are) 'a thing, an activity ... something to share, exchange and collect' (Simpson 1994: 47). Sally's transference is prompted by an argument over ownership, which must be asserted without there being any hint of emotional attachment. Steve, Orange Butterfly's vocalist, makes a possessive lapse in relation to Sally and, in effect, immediately devalues her – 'We don't want your bloody scrubbers!' someone shouts from The Sweaty Betty's van, despite assurances that 'she's in great nick'. Symbolic violence towards the 'feminine' realm of domesticity and attachment is, according to Reynolds and Press, 'the defining mark of all classic instances of rock rebellion' (1995: 3). The rock rebel continuously re-enacts separation from the mother – 'women figure as both victims and agents of castrating conformity', they argue in a phrase which captures the construction of the groupie particularly well. 'Women represent everything the rebel is not (passivity, inhibition) and everything that threatens to shackle him (domesticity, social norms') (ibid.: 3).

By the end of the film, Sally seems to have sexually encountered the full spectrum of pre-glam rock masculinity, finally meeting folk singer Wes, who tells her, 'You're a groupie, and groupies get used; and then they get thrown away.' But the scene's sexual economy is bigger than he is, and his manipulative manager pressurises him into dumping her. 'When you go home to your mother, girl, tell her where you've been,' intones the song over the final credits, reinforcing this gendering of social space. In fact, none of these films invests a great deal in 'home' – it is a place which has to be abandoned. But if patriarchy feels just fine in flares and sideburns, where is someone like Sally supposed to go? If this makes *Groupie Girl* sound unusually right-on, then it also gets a lot of mileage out of Sally's exploitation and she is, as a character, an absolute blank space. But its depiction of rock misogyny is singularly unflinching, even if it regards that as the natural way of things.

Near the beginning of *Cool it Carol!*, the eponymous heroine (Janet Lynn) is asked an important question by her father; obtaining permission to travel to London clearly depends on her answering correctly. 'Is your maidenhead intact?' he enquires bluntly. Apparently, it isn't. 'Oh, well, you can go then,' he decides, taken aback only for a moment, and gives her some money ('Pragmatism,' concluded Paul Joannides in

Monthly Film Bulletin). The film pulls off the boldest hybridisation of all – the social problem film and the sex comedy, navigating some unexpected shifts in tone. This scene implies not only that at least some permissiveness would need to have pervaded Shropshire in preparation for London but that 'the assumption of a sexual norm and corresponding concern with regulation' (Hill 1986: 124) is clearly under re-negotiation.

Cool it Carol! contrasts two images of London belonging to two different generic representations – the 'Swinging' London of 1960s British cinema ('This is what I thought it would be like,' says Carol as they nearly get run over by a London bus) and the vice-ridden London of sexploitation. Carol and Joe (Robin Askwith) travel to London in search of the former and, instead, find the latter. 'It's groovy of you to take me with you, Joe,' says Carol, underlining the world she expects to find. She wants to be a model, but, in this film, modelling means *Mayfair* and being discovered for the movies means hardcore pornography. 'I don't mind people looking at me,' she tells Joe on the train as he tries to concentrate on his *Penthouse*, 'matter of fact, I quite enjoy it.' But her parents' neighbour puts it more succinctly – 'That arse will be the making of your Carol.' Carol embodies a Page 3 conception of female sexuality – a nice, ordinary girl, unashamed of her body, untainted by others' consumption of her.

Like Suzy and Sally, Joe and Carol dream of escape. She's the daughter of a funeral director and works at a petrol station, her one glimpse of glamour a local beauty contest she once won. He works at a butcher's, where the boss's son has just severed his finger in a bizarre comic accident – it turns out to be significant that the film begins with a gag about male impairment. Their relationship is one of convenience – it seems to end amicably as soon as they return home – and mutual protectiveness. They have unsuccessful sex on the train – 'I wasn't any good, was I?' grumbles Joe, but Carol reassures him that the object of the exercise was that 'we know each other better now'. His inability to perform recurs during the first half of the film.

They drift into turning tricks through a combination of hunger and curiosity. But Joe's curiosity, considered alongside his sexual reticence, blossoms into an interesting subtext. He remarks that it 'must be a very sexy thing', to which Carol replies, 'It turns you on, doesn't it?' The narrative seems to support her observation, but Joe's investment in her experiences goes beyond the voyeuristic – her seduction by Chelsea Potter smoothie Jonathan (Jess Conrad) has already been paralleled with Joe's humiliating loss at roulette. As Carol turns her first trick, Joe makes tea for all three of them – he is the most domesticated of pimps ('Couldn't find the biscuits,' he says apologetically). This leads to a return engagement with the same taciturn kerbcrawler, a married man who 'just can't get enough of it'. This time, he invites four additional 'customers' to be serviced in succession for a total of £25, taking a cut himself. As the scene unfolds, the camera remains largely on Joe, emphasising his reactions as Carol encounters each member of an increasingly unsavoury group. There is more at stake here than coyness. The decision to focus on Joe while only hinting at what is happening to Carol underlines his identification with her – the scene is depicted primarily as *his* experience. Undoubtedly this downplays what happens to Carol, but this shifting sense of who exactly is being fucked here is underscored by Joe's subsequent beating at the hands of the kerbcrawler (A Child is Being Beaten, it seems). 'What's the matter, ponce,' sneers his assailant after Joe's ineffectual assault, 'not enough jam on your bread?' Immediately afterwards, Joe is able to have 'successful' sex with Carol for the first time. 'Those men ... what they did to you ...' he begins to say, but the impression is not of a voyeuristic turn-on. Joe doesn't want to control Carol, he wants to be her. During both of the scenes in the kerbcrawler's flat, he hangs after her as though he is going either to join in or to take her place. Unable or unwilling to adopt an 'active' sexual role, Joe only performs by positioning himself in relation to Carol's humiliation.

Carol is never allowed this degree of complexity, and the film doesn't do much to counter the idea that it is her arse which is the making of her and that her 'innocence' is eminently exploitable. Joe's naivety is presented as more of a liability, but the film doesn't want to explore how else he might survive in viceland, except for a throwaway joke. Two gay shop assistants early in the film donate a neck scarf to him 'compliments of Roger and Barry' and he is soon posing in front of his hotel room mirror, admiring his sartorial acquisition. Like every other character in the film, they turn up at the party thrown by Joe and Carol at the end of the film, referring to him as 'Prince Charming'.

The final section of Cool it Carol! doesn't quite know where to go, dissolving in a sea of jokey Keeler/Profumo references and retreating from its extraordinary middle section. Carol operates as an expensive call girl and models for 'David Thing', a fashion photographer. Disillusioned, they return home, neither damaged nor chastened by their experience. This lack of a punitive or morally educative ending annoyed The Daily Mirror's Dick Richards: 'Mr Walker, do you really believe that this "happy" ending pays off for all the nudity, sex and trashy innuendo in your film? Who are you trying to kid?' (19 November 1970). Interestingly, the film was loosely based on a story in News of the World, and Joe's real-life counterpart ended up in prison. Whatever else this fairy tale in viceland suggested, the apologetic tone of the social problem sexploitation film was clearly on the way out.

Suburban report

Let's have kicks, Pat. Life gets boring.

'Jim', Naughty!

If you want a story, why don't you think on the Suburban Wife? I'll even give you a title – 'The Sexual Desert' ... But, even in the worst desert, if you look hard enough, sometimes you can find some water.

'Irene', Suburban Wives

Suburbia figures prominently in a broader range of texts than sexploitation alone. It takes on a particular resonance in the 1970s and is worth considering in a bit more detail.

Jim and Pat, 'a suburban couple involved in the making of blue films', appear towards the end of Naughty! As they cautiously dip their toes in permissive waters, they might have strayed from a Kinks song or from Blur's 'Stereotypes'. Jim is very enthusiastic about spanking, Pat considerably less so. As a compromise, they look for other kinds of 'kicks' – a bit of wifeswapping and some amateur pornography. Suburbia, here, is a kind of last outpost, a measure of how far the 'sexual revolution' has travelled. The 'suburban report' films, too, are ever insistent on the 'normality' of their protagonists – 'who are these sexual adventurers?' asks the press synopsis for *The Wife Swappers*. 'Not the homosexuals, perverts and dropouts openly accepted by the Permissive Society, but normal, respectable married couples from all social levels, operating through secret and highly organised clubs.'

Suburbia, as Roger Silverstone puts it, 'has remained curiously invisible in the accounts of modernity' (1997: 4), partly because its image suggests something defined by absence, 'by what it lacks – culture, variety, surprise – not by what it offers – safety, privacy, convenience' (Frith 1997: 276). John Carey's *The Intellectuals and the Masses* contains a useful account of the literary animus against 'clerk life' in the early part of the twentieth century, an account especially striking for how many of the prejudices it recounts have both persisted and trickled down. This hostility wasn't necessarily unanimous – the suburbs could be represented as a garden (by John Betjeman, for example) or a desert (C. E. M. Joad recoiled at the 'purulent beastliness' of Worthing). More accurately, the suburbs were a garden which had been transformed into a desert, 'the hidden underbelly of modernity in all its tortured, clichéd glory' (Silverstone 1997: 3). The original 'garden suburbs' were built at the turn of the century; green, middle-class districts where people like Graham Greene and Evelyn Waugh grew up. But as it became necessary to build new ones, this was perceived as a 'spoiling of the suburbs': 'the process by which established and largely green middle-class suburbs were engulfed by new development, with rows of houses being fitted on to adjacent meadow land, and the gardens of old mansions being bought by speculative builders' (Carey 1992: 47). Nevertheless, the notion of suburb-as-garden has never entirely gone away. One finds a version of it in certain Ealing films (*Passport to Pimlico*, in particular) or, lower down and by implication, in the 'suffocatingly normative contentedness' of sitcoms like *Terry and June* (Medhurst 1997: 252).

The 'desert' invited two types of critique. The first was environmental, the 'ugliness of suburban sprawl' (ibid.: 49).[1] Booker's description of Milton Keynes as the ultimate symbol of the new towns policy – 'hundreds of grim little misshapen boxes, in brick or corrugated metal, turned out by machine' (1980: 146) – updates the intellectual's contempt for what seemed to be a kind of hyper-suburbia, a 'schizoid science-fiction dream' (ibid.: 147). But then Booker is the sort of person who starts quoting Aldous Huxley at the first sight of a leisure centre. In the second critique, the suburbs became synonymous with the high-culture-deficient 'clerks', seen as the epitome of (particularly lower) middle-class philistinism and banality. Somewhere along the way, the distinction between environmental and cultural deterioration evaporated – the expansion of the suburbs 'exacerbated the intellectual's feeling of isolation from what he conceived of as philistine hordes, variously designated the middle classes or the bourgeoisie, whose dullness and small-mindedness the intellectual delights in portraying (that is, inventing)' (Carey 1992: 50).

One or two more specific prejudices bring us closer to the suburbia of 1970s sex films. One was the designation of suburban life as one of 'specifically female triviality' (ibid.: 52) – The Daily Mail, with its fashion sections and home hints, was designed specifically for clerk culture. And, as early as 1922, Arthur Machen, in The Secret Glory, was imagining illicit suburban sex involving commercial travellers – the OMO Wives were already in place.

In sitcom, suburbia is often a way of talking about mobility, class and gender. The image of characterless, jerry-built boxes is epitomised by Bob's new housing estate in Whatever Happened to the Likely Lads? (BBC 1973–4). 'We haven't got a name for it yet,' he tells Terry in 'Home is the Hero', pointing out his home-to-be. 'Well, you'll certainly need one, won't you,' smirks Terry, 'or you'll never find it again.' He expounds further, painting a familiar picture, but from a different class perspective:

> There's something depressing about these estates. It's the thought of you all getting up at the same time, all eating the same kind of low calorie breakfast cereal, all coming home at half past six, switching on the same programme at the same time and having it off the same two nights of the week.

Suburbia, here, is more than dehumanising; it's emasculating, too. This is very much the site of 'specifically female triviality' – suburbia is the finishing line of Thelma's cultural trajectory, the epitome of her pretentious snobbery. While Terry is gently mocked for his archaic masculinity, his geographical affiliation – emasculation is displaced on to recurring images of slum-demolition – guarantees him some licence to pass judgement on 'feminine' housing estates. In George and Mildred (Thames 1976–80), it's Mildred who's keen to be assimilated into the commuter belt, while George is resistant to the showpiece front lawns and bidets of Hampton Wick. But the programme invests less in 'authentic' masculinity than Whatever ...? and offers us the pleasure of the Ropers invading the space of the ghastly Fourmiles who live next door. At the end of the first episode, 'Moving On', they destroy their front garden, an act of incredible symbolic violence. Suburbia is both garden and desert in George and Mildred – a sign of upward mobility for Mildred and a petty 'desert' of snobbery ripe for mild sitcom subversion.

Punk turned more aggressively on the suburb-as-desert. Malcolm MacLaren, Vivienne Westwood and Bernard Rhodes's 'You're gonna wake up one morning and know what side of the bed you've been lying on!' T-shirt listed 'The suburbs' as one of its 'hates'. In England's Dreaming, Jon Savage reproduces a diary entry from the end of 1975:

> London suburbia: sterility – cynicism – boredom ready to spill over into violence; incipient right-wing backlash. Fuck London for its dullness, the English people for their pusillanimity and the weather for its coldness and darkness.
>
> (1991: 107)[5]

But punk was more than a revenge on places like Bromley; it was as dependent on their boundary-setting complacency as *George and Mildred*. Punk was a lace-curtain-twitcher of a subculture if ever there was one. Frith, Lebeau and Medhurst (each in Silverstone 1997) talk about the importance of suburbia to British pop – not just punk, but the tradition of ironic suburban storytelling that can be traced from The Kinks to Blur. Frith's essay is particularly suggestive of how suburban dreariness can take on a perverse exoticism, how it operates as a space for fantasising within/about. 'The suburbs they are dreaming,' declare Blur in 'Stereotypes', a song about middle-aged wifeswappers, and Frith clearly agrees: 'the essential boredom of suburbia becomes, oddly, a kind of utopia, a place where there's nothing to do except dream of other places' (1997: 274). Pop is able to invest such daydreams with subcultural capital – 'Bohemia in a bedroom', Frith calls it, 'an alternative lifestyle practised at home, and displayed as a kind of performance art at the bus stop and railway station, in select club backrooms and parents-are-away-for-the-weekend parties' (ibid.: 272). 'Ordinariness' is what makes 'difference' more vivid, the fantasy of escape more deliciously intense. But this is a youthful fantasy – 'wifeswapping' is what the conformist parent generation does to spice up the tedium, a fantasy based not on escaping but on re-imagining the suburbs. Pop, too, is fond of finding 'kinky' sex(uality) here – transvestism is a particular favourite, from Pink Floyd's 'Arnold Layne' to Blur's 'Tracy Jacks'. But wifeswapping suggests a meeting of domesticated banality and middle-aged permissiveness – an orgiastic Tupperware party. The outlets for such fantasies, too, suggest their different constituencies – art school bohemia and pop lyrics versus tabloid mythologising and straight-to-paperback exposés – but the *mise-en-scène* for each narrative, and suburbia's highlighting of 'little transgressions', is essentially the same.

I want to look at three overlapping uses of suburbia. In the first, suburban 'swinging' condenses the infiltration of permissiveness into 'everyday life' – it is here, particularly, that the blandness and banality of the location offer a counterpoint to the activities going on there. Second, as a 'feminine' space, suburbia becomes a way of talking about female sexuality, or rather, specific types of female sexuality – thus the emphasis on the housewife rather than a bohemian swinger. The third use of suburbia is perhaps more evident in the sexcoms, but worth introducing here – suburbia as a male 'hunting ground', but for a specifically non-suburban masculinity. As the suburban housewife's libido intensifies, male sexuality has to be drafted in from somewhere else.

A comment by Nuttall and Carmichael points to a complementary uniformity and idiosyncrasy embedded in the suburb's distinction between front and back.[6] Its main emphasis is on the front, the only part of the house visible to the public gaze because of its proximity to the road plan. And yet, they argue, it is not the visible which conveys individuality here – the fronts are 'interchangeable ... a ludicrous attempt to mass-produce the unique' (1977: 16). Rather, it's the back garden which offers lifestyle clues, 'collar and tie discarded, cosmetics unapplied, hair uncombed' (ibid.: 17). The exposé then is precisely what its name suggests – a stripping of the 'front', an exposure of the sexual 'back garden' of suburbia, its kit fully off, as it

were. One of the genre's dynamics is a gleeful uncovering of the hypocrisy of su-
perficial respectability – 'Neatly trimmed lawns, tree-lined streets – smug affluence!'
sneers the press synopsis for *Suburban Wives*.

Over a montage of commuting in and to the 'city', *Wives* offers the following narration:

> Between 8 and 9 am, five days a week, an army marches – the commuter
> army. Monday to Friday, they invade then seize the city, they administer,
> account, finance, arrange, service and lubricate the great machine that is
> the economy. Behind them in the dormitory suburbs, this same army has
> left a great social phenomenon.

Leaving aside all this servicing and lubricating imagery, as these commuters appear
to be giving the economy a good seeing-to, we move to a contrasting sequence as
the camera travels through a landscape of unchanging 'boxes' and blocks. The soundtrack, on the other hand, suggests anything but drabness and uniformity. We're
treated to 'Real Live Woman', a sub-Tom-Jones belter of a song which moves from
images of 'closed minds behind closed doors with nothing new in view' to the
following advice:

> You're a real live woman with a lot to give,
> So open up your mind and live!

We'll come back to these 'Real Live Women', libidos throbbing behind the drab
exteriors of the dormitories. There's another sense of the 'suburban' sensibility as
last sexual outpost, one that brings us back to the notion of 'catching up', a sort of
sexual democracy. Hugh (David Dixon) in *Escort Girls* is literally a clerk, and
stereotypically Welsh, too, to distance him further from the sexual licence of the
metropolis. He's one of a selection of characters in the film marginalised by age,
region, looks and class who make use of an escort agency. The film opens with him
listening to two office girls on Christmas Eve, gossiping about male misbehaviour –
'Oh, no offence, Mr Lloyd,' one of them assures him, 'I didn't mean you, of course.'
As he finishes up, there is a tangible sense of lack, in more ways than one. He goes
to dinner with escort Susan (Maria O'Brien), and mispronounces 'pasta' while she
mocks her 'suburban and provincial' relatives – 'Watching telly every night, bingo
on Saturdays and polishing the car on Sundays – their idea of excitement.' Nevertheless, she helps him see off his virginity – 'I never expected this, you know,' he
stammers, 'It's very kind of you.' The final scene 'returns' to the opening – 'Nice
morning!' Hugh chirps laddishly to the office girls, slapping one of them across
her behind with his newspaper.

The figure of the suburban wife is represented as being both banal and voracious,
passive and rapacious, timid and uncontainable. *Suburban Wives*' two songs spell out
this paradox; in addition to the aforementioned 'Real Live Woman', there's also 'Nine
to Five O'Clock Widows', a mawkish, condescending folk song about 'sad ladies' in

106

6 Suburban sexuality awakes in Derek Ford's *Suburban Wives* (1972).

'house[s] of grey'. Both the 'Real Live Women' and the 'Nine to Five Widows' inhabit the 'sexual desert' investigated by local reporter Sarah (Eva Whishaw). This version of the 'desert' is related fairly early on to thirst, to appetite – the lifelessness of suburbia intensifies desire rather than diminishing it.

Stephen Marcus discerns an 'idiosyncratic, though familiar' model of Nature in Victorian pornography, one which also pertains here:

> It slumbers, but can be alarmed; and then it is 'too powerful'. It is implicitly opposed to moral and social feelings, yet it is somehow connected with the 'recesses' of the heart. It makes itself felt through the senses, through 'new and wild sensations', and it produces at first not pleasure but disorder, confusion, 'a complete tumult'.
>
> (1966: 208)

Marcus doesn't quite spell out the implicit gendering of 'Nature' here, especially given that it is the corollary of feminine 'virtue' in official Victorian discourses on sexuality. But this is the version of female sexuality one encounters in sexploitation and comedy, in arty porn like Borowczyk's La Bête and in the escapades of Benny Hill and Robin Askwith. Female sexuality 'slumbers', but once awake – especially with a new sexual political agenda – it's a libidinous leviathan (The Daily Mirror's critic described Suburban Wives' characters as a 'monstrous regiment of frustrated wives'). It sees off Borowczyk's eponymous hairy rapist (death by exhaustion) and constantly threatens the male body of low comedy with exhaustion, emasculation and engulfment. Later, it is re-articulated around the porn star's 'insatiability' – Linda Lovelace and Marilyn Chambers in America, Fiona Richmond and Mary Millington in Britain.

This is the crux of The Wife Swappers' talk of 'escalation', a word it uses so frequently that it would have made a pretty apposite title. The 'propensity for escalation', as the film's 'psychologist' puts it while giving his papers a reassuringly authoritative shuffle, ostensibly defines the pathology of an ungendered swinger, but one soon detects which way the wind is blowing. He even historicises escalation for us – 'Woman's drive for so-called equality means that if a husband finds such activity tempting, she will want to find it equally so.' Equality doesn't come into it, however, in the actual episodes. Paul and Ellen are our first couple; after seven years of marriage, they inhabit 'a slightly fractious relationship in which sexual interest [has] all but gone'. It's Paul who fancies a bit of a 'swing' at first and Ellen who's developing a tense, nervous headache at the thought. They get started with Leonard and his platinum blonde wife Jean, who immediately makes a play for Paul. Ellen seeks refuge in the kitchen, but is miraculously won over by the gap-toothed, hirsute Leonard, with his lime-green shirt, cravat and incongruously sensible cardigan, telling her to 'relax, darling'. Soon they're playing a bizarre 'strip' game involving handfuls of corks and before we know it, it's an organised party with a larger group, 'one stage further in the escalation of the pleasure seekers'. At the party, Paul starts to lose his nerve at precisely the moment that Ellen warms to the idea. 'I felt a growing sense of excitement,' she tells us, the focal point of everyone's gaze, and her 'initiation' is reflected in a pair of sunglasses.

'Man is a Hunter', insists *Commuter Husbands'* compensatory theme song with an audible lack of conviction. Nevertheless, the same predatory theme is affirmed in the press synopsis for this follow-up to *Suburban Wives*:

> Man, when off the leash, reverts to his natural role as the HUNTER, a predator with an appetite not for food, but for a more tasty dish called WOMAN. The prey exists in abundance and usually enjoys being caught; all he needs is Opportunity.

This is *Penthouse* talk: permissiveness intensifies the 'natural' relation between the 'sexes'. But *Commuter Husbands'* promotional mouth is bigger than its narrative trousers; strikingly, it can't come up with the stories to support its hunting metaphor.[7] Rather, it adopts a kind of anthropology of the 'sex wars' in which masculinity is a distinct casualty. The storyteller this time is Carol (Gabrielle Drake), whom we first meet, appropriately, at the Penthouse Club (and subsequently at other male fantasy locales – a sauna, a casino, the Cameo Moulin in Soho, where a double-bill of *Sweet and Sexy* and *The Lustful Vicar* is showing):

> To this haven of soft lights, sweet music and pretty girls, all of a cleavage, comes the male of the species, to restore and have soothed his wounded psyche. A psyche battered and bruised by that fiercest of all fights, the battle between the sexes. In that life or death struggle, this is one of the foremost battle casualty stations, a sort of field hospital really.

A fairly typical episode tells the story of Arnold, who has visited prostitute Lola every Thursday for the last twenty-five years. But he never has sex with her, preferring to spy on the couple next door through a two-way mirror in the bathroom. 'You're a dirty old man, Arnold,' Lola tells him when she discovers what he comes for, 'And after twenty-five years of thinking you were a harmless old sod with no one to talk to.' She sends him packing, and it transpires that his wife has been listening from a cupboard. She thanks Lola for her help and we learn that she overheard her with an earlier client, too; she found it 'quite exciting', suggesting that 'Nature' is about to awake once more. Most interesting, though, is the story of plumber Arthur, a Noddy Holder lookalike called to the house of German sex star Carla Berlin. 'Cor, I could do her plumbing a bit of good,' he speculates, not unreasonably given the generic circumstances. But it isn't the time for the working-class sexcom hero just yet, in spite of the sex party taking place at Carla's apartment. He kisses a naked woman, who gives him six out of ten – 'It's a pass rate, nothing more.' He ends up locked out of the house, looking longingly through the window and missing the party. Finally another girl invites him to give her a massage, but he does so only vengefully, relishing his oily hands. More than anyone else in the film, however, Arthur is a sign of things to come.[8]

Monique: from vampire lover to au pair girl

Monique, made in 1969 and released in 1970, departs from the other suburban sexploitation films in a number of ways. It eschews the multiple narrative and narration for three-handed drama. Like *Escort Girls*, it's a sexploitation film with more than a few pretensions to 'proper' cinema. More importantly, it suggests a more conscious 'coming to terms' with the impact of feminism than the other suburban films, which either address female sexual 'liberation' indirectly and anxiously through the notion of 'escalation' or buy into the fantasy typified by a comment from Claudine Beccarie, 'the French Linda Lovelace' – 'I'm not Lesbian. Nor bi-sexual. I believe in men. Sexually liberated is what I am!' (*Cinema X*, December 1975: 14). *Monique* offers a different kind of 'liberation'. *Sight and Sound* called it a 'slap-and-tickle version of *Theorem*' (October 1994: 62), one of those fatuous comments that inadvertently pinpoints the precise centre of interest. This is, after all, a Tigon film, and one which makes generically familiar use of suburbia – 'There is nothing unusual about the suburban household,' insists the synopsis – and the figures of the au pair and the 'frustrated housewife'.

Monique (Sybilla Kay) is the French au pair who goes to live with Jean (Joan Alcorn) and Bill (David Sumner), a married couple with two children. Jean is dissatisfied with both her life – 'I'm bored doing nothing!' – and her marriage. The title sequence intercuts Bill, flirting as he commutes, with Jean alone on a park bench, watching the children playing. Later, we hear her musing on the advantages of an au pair during some perfunctory sex with Bill – she's mentally designating the spare room as he goes down on her. The au pair is the figure who most frequently 'imports' sex and sexuality into British sexploitation, and Monique seems to bring permissiveness with her. She goes out for the evening in one of Jean's nighties, worn with knee-length boots, and this is initially played out as Bill's fantasy. Bill and Monique end up in bed together after he helps her off with her boots, but her attention soon shifts to Jean as she helps pin up her skirt. On Christmas Eve, they exchange significant looks and a kiss while Bill dresses up as Santa Claus. What follows takes place off screen, but Jean appears in Bill's room endowed with all the signifiers of 'sexual awakening' and they have what is clearly meant to be their first mutually satisfying sex.

Jean is transformed in more ways than one. We see her in *that* nightie, transformed by Monique's wearing of it. She starts to speak French, and they whisper to each other in the kitchen. This sense of speaking a new language is reinforced by Bill's inability to read what is being played out before him – he believes himself to be, as the synopsis puts it, 'the master of not one but two women'. Finally, he walks in on them and does a lot of nervous re-thinking of his marriage and his masculinity: 'I suppose really if I can do it, why shouldn't she? I mean, why one law for the man and another for the woman ... it's just that, why not another man? No, *not* another man. It's better like this, I suppose.' The film is very knowing about its sexual fantasies. During a conciliatory dinner, Monique suggests that Bill go to see a 'very sexy Swedish film – after all, that's what I'm here for'. And when Bill is invited to join in, the hetero-porn fantasy of the lesbian scenario seems about to be drafted in. But the spectacle of Bill smoking nervously and gulping from a wine bottle – 'I will, in a minute' – rather undercuts this heterosexual recuperation, an impression the denouement does little to dispel.

Whatever its limits, *Monique* is worth comparing with two contemporaneous British films about female same-sex desire. *The Killing of Sister George* was released in 1969, its vision of tweed-bound bitchiness probably not helped by placing it at the mercy of Robert Aldrich. *The Vampire Lovers*, Hammer's adaptation of J. Sheridan Le Fanu's *Carmilla*, was released in 1970 and shares the same producer, Michael Style, with *Monique*. Style, his partner Harry Fine and writer Tudor Gates had been brought to Hammer to inject elements of sexploitation into the so-called 'Karnstein trilogy' which also includes *Lust for a Vampire* (1970) and the impressively overripe *Twins of Evil* (1971). There's a growing body of writing on the figure of the lesbian vampire (see, for example, Zimmerman 1981; Krzywinska 1995), and Peter Hutchings characterises *The Vampire Lovers* 'ambivalence' thus: 'on the one hand, indeed a "vampire-rapist", a destroyer of young, innocent women; on the other, a sexual liberator of females trapped within patriarchal households and definitions of the feminine' (1993: 160).

But *Monique* rather blows away the idea that the latter needs to be somehow encoded in the former in popular cinema, an assumption also made by Bonnie Zimmerman – 'Lesbianism ... must be vampirism; elements of violence, compulsion, hypnosis, paralysis, and the supernatural must be present' (1981: 156). Zimmerman sees such images as being specific to the period 1970 to 1973 when 'feminism was not yet perceived as a fundamental threat ... The creators of those images – like the pornographic filmmakers who appeal to male fantasies with scenes of lesbianism – must have felt secure enough in their power and that of their primary male audience to flirt with lesbianism and female violence against men' (ibid.: 156). Of course, *Monique* is not a vampire story, and I'm not advocating that it should be read as one. But horror and sexploitation seemed to be exploring similar fantasies and anxieties here, and the comparison is worth making – what other popular cultural images might audiences have drawn on to make sense of the film?

Monthly Film Bulletin's anonymous reviewer seemed troubled by this 'sexual fairy tale', finding it 'lacking in any clear moral perspective' and objecting to 'the overly ambivalent title character – a mixture of shallow-minded teenager and worldly-wise sophisticate' (August 1970: 166). Monique is, indeed, a composite figure, equal parts Julie Christie and Ingrid Pitt. On the one hand, she's an uninhibited 1960s girl, with her leather mini and knee-length boots, her multiple boyfriends scattered around the world and her penchant for football and driving sports cars. Her transformation of Jean is initially cosmetic – clothes-swapping and a semiotic recoding of her nightie. But she's also a secular, liberating Carmilla, insinuating her way into the bourgeois home as a 'companion', partly in the guise of a male fantasy.

Like the permanently wide-eyed companion played by Madeleine Smith in *The Vampire Lovers*, Jean is represented as a sexual child – the synopsis describes her as 'sexually unawakened, almost to the point of frigidity'. More than once, she is framed next to her children's dolls; on Christmas Eve, we see her cradling one of them, a scene filmed from Monique's point of view. Her awakening ostensibly revitalises the heterosexual couple rather than transforming it, but this is only a partial recuperation. For one thing, it's marriage and the family themselves which have been constructed as the 'desert' to Monique's invigorating 'water'. While Bill and Jean stay together, the finale prioritises Monique and Jean. Monique invites her to Paris 'with Bill or on your own', and, while Jean replies that 'we' will, Bill stands uncomfortably to one side, distinctly marginalised in the frame as well as the narrative. While he might not be joining Massimo Girotti for some primal screaming in the wilderness, his restoration is invested with a singular lack of conviction.

Monique tackles all three of the suburban films' thematic tropes – the 'desert' as a counterpoint to and exacerbation of sexual licence, the foregrounding of female desire as an 'issue' or 'problem', and even the 'hunting ground' for a sexual subject who has to be drafted in from elsewhere.

Sexploitation goes mainstream

The year 1974 was a turning point for the sex film, as it gained an economic importance best gauged by the unprecedented success of *Emmanuelle*, which made over £200,000 in its first fifteen weeks at the Prince Charles. There was much talk in *CinemaTV Today* of a new age of 'quality' sexploitation. 'The day has definitely gone when you could show a bad sex film and get money back from it,' claimed Tim Evans of Miracle Films. 'People are now asking for sophistication. You see it boils down to what you can now see on television' (*CinemaTV Today*, 25 January 1975: 13). This 'sophistication' often took the form of 'historical' trappings, such as Italy's penchant for nun movies. But British sexploitation's 'mainstream' phase was marked by the dominance of comedy featuring stars largely familiar from television.

The episodic nature of *Can You Keep It Up For a Week?* (Jim Atkinson, 1974) underlines its descent from the suburban films – the end credits designate its characters according to narrative archetypes, 'The Office', 'The Hobson Apartment', 'The Babysitter', just as *Suburban Wives* specified 'The Husband', 'The Au Pair', 'The Photographer'. But these episodes are now anchored by a male hero and on the picaresque relationship between work and sex. Gil (Jeremy Bulloch) is given an ultimatum by his girlfriend – if he can't hold down a job for a week, it's all over between them. He joins the 'At Your Service' agency, which brings him to the attention of women with names like Mrs Bristol. We're talking sexual economies again here, because Gil's sexual prowess is positioned in inverse proportion to his work-related skills. Similarly, as the recession bit harder, sexploitation offered a contrasting utopian boom, a world of plenty.[9] The dominant narrative of the itinerant labourer or salesman can be found in *Secrets of a Door to Door Salesman* (Wolf Rilla, 1973), *Confessions of a Window Cleaner* (Val Guest, 1974), *The Amorous Milkman* (Derren Nesbitt, 1975), *Confessions of a Pop Performer* (Norman Cohen, 1975), *Ups and Downs of a Handyman* (John Sealey, 1975), *Adventures of a Taxi Driver* (Stanley Long, 1976), *Confessions of a Driving Instructor* (Cohen, 1976), *I'm Not Feeling Myself Tonight* (Joe McGrath, 1976), *Secrets of a Superstud* (Martin M. Lewis, 1976), *Adventures of a Private Eye* (Long, 1977), *Confessions from a Holiday Camp* (Cohen, 1977) and *Adventures of a Plumber's Mate* (Long, 1978), while other sex comedies dealt with similar scenarios. *What's Up Nurse* (Derek Ford, 1977), *What's Up Superdoc?* (Ford, 1978) and *Rosie Dixon – Night Nurse* (Justin Cartwright, 1978) return to the *Carry On* films' favourite setting to explore slap-and-tickle amidst the bedpans. The next chapter looks at the most popular incarnation of this cycle, Columbia's *Confessions* films. I shall also look at the genre's final phase, as the sex industries attempted to capitalise on this mainstreaming, particularly in David Sullivan's vehicles for Mary Millington.

7

COMING CLEAN ...

From Robin Askwith to Mary Millington

To the question 'What time is it in pornotopia?' one is tempted to answer, 'It is always bedtime.'

Stephen Marcus (1966: 272)

Cor! Cop a load of that then, eh? What a knocker factory!

Timmy Lea (Robin Askwith), *Confessions of a Window Cleaner*

The *Confessions* films and David Sullivan's vehicles for Mary Millington (*Come Play With Me*, especially) have two things in common – a more or less 'utopian' representation of sex and a commercial success made possible by extensive distribution and the acceptance of sexploitation on the major circuits. But there the similarity ends. The mid-1970s sexcom star is male – Robin Askwith, Barry Evans, Christopher Neil – while the 'pornocrat' narrative of the late 1970s turned to female stars established in top-shelf magazines. The *Confessions* films were backed by Columbia and symbolised industry acceptance of softcore, but the Millington films emerged from the very heart of the sex industries, Sullivan's Roldvale company.

By 1977, the pornocrats were ready for entry into the mainstream – Sullivan's Private Shop empire began matching shops to postal code areas on vast mail order lists the following year. Others were just as ready to stop them – Manchester's chief constable James Anderton was sending the vice squad out on raids from 1977 and the Private Shops regularly attracted protestors of diverse political persuasions. As the Williams Committee revisited pornography and obscenity, this became too discursively combative a time for the sexcom's formula of titillation and light entertainment. Fiona Richmond and Mary Millington are the stars who belong to this moment. Richmond offered an image of emancipated female sexuality tailored to the readership of *Men Only*. Her role as magazine columnist, author of several books, chat show regular and football pin-up contributed to the appearance of autonomous professionalism in concert with her proclamations of pleasure. Millington also gave her name to softcore magazine columns and was 'discovered' by a prominent pornocrat, who promoted her intensively in *Whitehouse*, *Park Lane* and *Playbirds*. But Millington was constructed as the 'real thing' ('Britain's Linda Lovelace') despite her location within the familiar traditions of sex comedy. Her comparative invisibility in her own films and her status as the major casualty of the genre problematise the 'innocence' of the genre and point to some of the shifts taking place.

Confessions of the British

It's now positively orthodox to champion Hammer and *Carry On*, once the sign of a culture-slumming iconoclast; but tell people that you like Robin Askwith and you soon realise you're on to something. The *Confessions* films – there were only four, but their imitators made it seem more – have never quite recovered from the critical disapprobation that met them on their original release. The increasingly exasperated reviews of *The Daily Mail*'s Margaret Hinxman are fairly representative, although few critics projected the same sense that the films had been created for the sole purpose of ruining their day. *Confessions of a Window Cleaner* (Val Guest, 1974) was 'a puerile sex farce' (30 August 1974); ... *Pop Performer* (Norman Cohen, 1975) prompted the judgement that 'If the *Carry On*'s are the equivalent of those harmless smutty seaside postcards, this is the graffiti in the grubby seaside "loo" ' (16 August 1975); ... *Driving Instructor* (Norman Cohen, 1976) was 'cretinously awful, oafishly acted and lumpishly directed' (24 July 1976). But these were minor reservations compared to a memorable outburst by Alexander Stuart:

> They said Rasputin was mad. Maybe he was. They said British cinema was dead. Maybe it is. There's nothing in this sorry tale of the pathetic sexual activities of window-cleaning folk that resembles living matter. *Confessions of a Window Cleaner* might well be retitled *Confessions of the British: What they don't know about Making Films, Making Erotic Images, Making People Laugh and Making Love.* We probably don't clean windows too well either.
>
> (Films and Filming, September 1974: 52)

For a number of film critics, the *Confessions* films were neither one thing nor the other. They were compared unflatteringly with the *Carry Ons*, which could now be patronisingly indulged as harmless, outmoded smut, but even more so with a 'proper' erotic cinema. 'It's a pity that the Mrs Whitehouses are too busy bashing serious permissive films such as *Last Tango in Paris* to bother with this kind of seedy rubbish,' grumbled Margaret Hinxman (Daily Mail, 16 August 1975), sentiments echoed by David Robinson's review of ... *Pop Performer* in which he also reflected contemptuously on 'the sexual infantilism of a sufficient proportion of the public to promise the film the same box-office success as its predecessor' (The Times, 8 August 1975). Images of wayward, disobedient audiences recur in the history of British film criticism, but 'bad Britishness' (sniggering, repressed, infantile) assumed an implicit class identity. Interestingly, *The Morning Star*'s critic Virginia Dignam was one of the few dissenters – she seemed genuinely to like the films, much to the bemusement of Robin Askwith.[1]

Respectability

While critical acclaim was neither forthcoming nor, most likely, expected, the *Confessions* films were, in every other sense, promoted as a respectable part of British

7 Nose pressed against the window of permissiveness: Robin Askwith as Timmy Lea in *Confessions of a Window Cleaner* (1974). (Courtesy of The Kobal Collection.)

cinema. The *Confessions* formula offered overlapping combinations of four ingredients – slapstick (speeded-up sequences, an accident-prone hero), bedroom farce (the alarming regularity with which husbands arrive home early), sitcom (recurring characters, usually the hero's family) and sexploitation (full-frontal female nudity, softcore sex). This is important – the films *appropriated* sexploitation as part of a larger package, rather than offering the genuine article. They filled a very specific and astutely gauged gap in the market as a combination of adult entertainment and good, clean fun. In this respect, their relationship with television was crucial. Like most 'X' films since the 1950s, they foregrounded elements that audiences couldn't yet see on television, but combined them with stars and generic pleasures which had largely been absorbed by television.

The intermediary link here is the sitcom movie. When Nigel Andrews reviewed ... *Window Cleaner* as a 'study piece' in the decline of British comedy, he saw the reliance on television talent as symptomatic of 'feature films that produce the impression of half-hour comedy ideas spun out to a strained and over-anxious ninety minutes' (*Financial Times*, 23 August 1974). The sitcom movies, like stage adaptations, faced the problems of 'opening out' texts designed for a limited range of sets and situations, with the added challenge of combining familiar pleasures with at least the illusion of some degree of product differentiation. Some tried to 'spice up' the formula without losing the family audience made available by the 'A' certificate – *Holiday on the Buses* (1973) throws in the sort of brief nudity that the *Carry Ons* had been getting away with since ... *Camping* in 1969, while *Man About the House*'s (1975) strip poker game has some sexcom potential, but produces nothing more risqué than Robin's declaration that 'I'll raise your skirt with my trousers'. The *Confessions* films, again, did some astute borrowing. When Timmy (Robin Askwith) goes home, he has his very own sitcom family, composed of equal parts *Till Death Us Do Part* and *On the Buses*, two sitcoms with argumentative extended families. Dandy Nicholls, and subsequently Doris Hare, played his mother, Bill Maynard his father and Anthony Booth (initially sold as the series's star) was conniving brother-in-law Sid; only Sheila White, as sister Rosie, didn't have a background in sitcom. The Lea family scenes evoke sitcom's familiarity and repetition – the same sets, the same running gags and conflicts; Sid and 'Dad' at each other's throats, the latter's light-fingered acquisitions from the Lost Property Office he works at (a moose head, a gorilla suit, a Wildlife collecting box he 'found abandoned in the high street'). Other performers from sitcom and variety appeared in sexcoms – John Le Mesurier, Irene Handl, Windsor Davies, the omnipresent Alfie Bass and even Arthur Askey (an important wartime comic star and later television variety performer), appearing to have lost the will to live in *Rosie Dixon – Night Nurse*. But this ensured that the hero had to be generically mobile, capable of functioning in the world of skiving, bigoted fathers and lovable working-class mums as well as of the softcore antics which punctuated the narrative.[2]

The publicity for *Confessions of a Window Cleaner* stressed three pieces of evidence in the case for its 'good taste'. First of all, there was the cast – 'great comedy stars who are known to and loved by audiences everywhere'. Second, while these were scarcely BritLit films, they were adapted from a series of hugely successful paperback novels, 'the publishing phenomenon of the decade'. The *Adventures* films' paperback tie-ins were novelisations, but offered similar advice to exhibitors: 'Local promotions with booksellers result in bigger audiences and provide an ideal opportunity for extra High Street publicity. Make sure you tie-in with Mayflower – it's part of the big Promotion Package.'[3] Most important, however, was the foregrounding of tradition, the sense of lineage within which critics had constructed the *Confessions* films as illegitimate offspring:

> the long tradition in entertainment in this country of good, naughty laughter – from double-entendres in the music-hall (Max Miller is a prime example) to seaside postcards, from West End stage farces (e.g. Robertson Hare) to the 'Carry On' films.

While the films arguably grew out of a convergence of two traditions, admittedly already on speaking terms, this emphasises only the one – the posters make much of the seaside postcard legacy, featuring caricatures of Askwith leering through steamed-up windows or having part of his anatomy painfully mistaken for a gear lever. Sex and nudity were acknowledged simply as a modernising of this tradition. On the one hand, 'the British respond to jokes that make belly-laughs out of sexy situations, always provided the bounds of good taste are recognised', but exhibitors were encouraged to remind local reporters 'how these bounds, themselves, have widened over the years'. This was the image accepted by trade press reviewers, usually more sympathetic to commercial formulas than their newspaper counterparts. Marjorie Bilbow accorded authentic 'roots' to *Confessions of a Pop Performer* – roots which lay in 'the rich earth of English ribaldry where there is plenty of room for growth' (*CinemaTV Today*, 16 August 1975: 13).

Robin Askwith

> Athletic and cheeky-faced, the young actor is so exactly the epitome
> of the author's character that Timothy Lea the writer swears he must
> have been psychic to have created a part so tailor-made for Askwith.
> publicity for *Confessions of a Window Cleaner*

There is an argument to be made for Robin Askwith as the most important performer in mid-1970s British cinema – not such a great claim, perhaps, but worth making anyway.[4] For one thing, he drew together most of what was left of a domestically oriented British cinema – sexploitation (*Cool it Carol!*, *Four Dimensions of Greta*, *Let's Get Laid*), horror (*The Flesh and Blood Show*, *Tower of Evil*, *Horror Hospital*), the Children's Film Foundation (*Scramble*, *Hide and Seek*), sitcom movies (*Bless This House*) and *Carry On Girls*, as well as less predictable work with Pasolini (*Canterbury Tales*, appropriately) and Lindsay Anderson (*If*, *Britannia Hospital*). Here is a CV which offers hints on how Askwith helped the films to 'crossover', to mediate between exploitation and mainstream entertainment.

8 Rolling Stone or 'lecherous goldfish'? Robin Askwith gets the horn in *Confessions of a Pop Performer* (1975). (Courtesy of The Kobal Collection.)

But, as the above quote confirms, Askwith's stardom was inseparable from the role of Timmy Lea, a classic blurring of the line between performer and character. John Ellis makes a distinction between a 'star' and a 'personality', and, while he uses it partly to bolster up the debatable superiority of cinema (with its fascinating stars) over television (reduced to paltry personalities), it also has its uses. The star is 'ordinary and extraordinary, available for desire and unattainable' (1992: 91), which doesn't sound much like our Robin. The 'personality', by implication, is more accessible and knowable – the soap or sitcom star is a case in point, where 'subsidiary forms of circulation' (press, publicity) largely reinforce the impression that what you see is what you get. The Sun adored 'Randy Robin', photographing him with Page 3 girls and breathlessly detailing his real-life 'confessions'. 'Timothy Lea' was both a character and an author, except that the latter was in fact writer Christopher Wood, who later gravitated to Bond movies (someone with that talent for innuendo was destined to meet Roger Moore). But Askwith played Timmy as both character and author in promotional material, referring to 'my books' in trailers or on the ... Pop Performer soundtrack, in between Kipper's glam-punk songs like 'Do the Clapham'. An interview feature in Men Only casts producer Greg Smith as Sid to Askwith's Timmy. The former is portrayed as the astute, money-minded mover-and-shaker who knows how best to deploy his young star's boyish energy – not for nothing does ... Pop Performer's plot pre-empt The Great Rock'n'Roll Swindle. Askwith, meanwhile, is likened to a 'street trader' – 'He's got the buoyancy of somebody who lost his virginity in the communal dressing-room to a stripper between turns, and hasn't looked back since' (Burn 1977: 18–19). As anyone who has seen ... Window Cleaner will know, that's exactly how Timmy attempts to lose his virginity.

In the BBC's 1995 'adaptation' of McGillivray's Doing Rude Things, Askwith claimed that he was not the first choice for the part, and that it had been offered to Dennis Waterman (who is, in fact, closer to the character in the book), Richard O'Sullivan and Richard Beckinsale. Whether this is apocryphal or not, between them they offer different takes on the 1970s Lad – respectively, working-class bit of 'rough', heterosexual fop and sexual beginner, keen but nervous. Beckinsale, in The Lovers, Rising Damp and, to a lesser extent, Porridge, was permissive by inclination but celibate in practice. His ongoing pursuit of 'Percy Filth' in The Lovers (Granada 1970–1) is frustrated by the literally anti-permissive Beryl (Paula Wilcox) – 'N-O spells "No",' she reminds him at least once an episode. Waterman and O'Sullivan had actually done sexploitation films,[5] but, in retrospect, Askwith seemed best placed to draw these different strands of 1970s masculinity together, with a few added extras. If Brian Jones and Sid James were put through the matter transporter from The Fly, Askwith resembles what might emerge at the other end. From a distance, he's fashionably skinny and androgynous, but, up close, his resemblance to a seaside postcard archetype is more apparent – Hinxman likened him to a 'lecherous goldfish'. More than one reviewer saw him as a successor, welcome or otherwise, to Sid James, adding resonance to his performance as Sid's son in the Bless This House film.

Askwith was in many ways a New Lad before his time – an expelled public school boy reconstructed as pseudo-working-class rogue-hero.[6] The Men Only interview emphasises his links with pop and football, two key industries of upward mobility – Askwith played for the Queen's Park Rangers youth team before a leg injury, and managed singer Ronnie Bonds with Greg Smith.[7] While Timmy inherits this cocksure bravado, he's also like Norman Wisdom with testosterone injections. In The Early Bird (Robert Asher, 1965), Wisdom plays a milkman, a 'little man' working for a small dairy threatened by a big one (not unlike the rival driving schools in ... Driv-

ing Instructor). In the *Confessions* films, 'little industry' becomes Sid's dubious scams. They inhabit the fringes of criminality, like a benign version of Charlie Endell and Budgie – Timmy has been to reform school for stealing lead off the church roof in the books. 'You're really not a loser / You just find it hard to win', ... *Window Cleaner's* theme song assures Timmy, asserting his 'little man' status, in an economic or class sense if not a sexual one.

The sexcom hero

> Ever thought about window cleaners? They spend their days looking into hundreds of little boxes, many of which have got people in. All sorts of people!
>
> Timmy, *Confessions of a Window Cleaner*

The fantasy of skilled and semi-skilled labourers encountering endlessly desiring suburban women derives partly from pornography and what Marcus calls the 'sexualisation of all reality' (1966: 244). But the sexcom hero also had a more recent predecessor – the working-class hero of 1950s and 1960s British film, theatre and literature. *Alfie* (Lewis Gilbert, 1966) is especially important, not least for establishing the hero's mode of address: direct-to-camera advice on 'birds', references to some women as 'it', a practice which turns up in *Adventures of a Taxi Driver*. Even more than his Angry Young predecessors, Alfie embodied a new type of male sexuality, a working-class hedonist who approached women as a 'proficient technician' (Walker 1974: 308). Such a masculinity, according to Isobel Quigly, was once 'thought totally un-English, but now being fished out of the proletarian pond where Englishness of the traditional kind never flourished ... he suggests a subterranean national character rising to surprise even the locals' (quoted in Walker, 1974: 306). Alexander Walker wondered what would have happened if *Alfie* had been made in the 1970s 'when Women's Lib was digging its spurs into male flanks' (*ibid.*: 307). But Alfie's 1970s counterparts soften his predatorial approach to pulling, are acted-upon as well as active, and forgo some of his 'proficiency' for callow enthusiasm and a degree of wide-eyed vulnerability. Even more important than *Alfie* is *Here We Go Round the Mulberry Bush* (Clive Donner, 1967) – just how important can be gauged by the way most of its young cast made the transition to sexcoms (Barry Evans, Judy Geeson, Adrienne Posta, Angela Scoular and Sheila White). Barry Evans's Jamie is a sexual innocent in search of rites-of-passage 'experience', a trajectory picked up on by ... *Window Cleaner*. Timmy's origins in the 'proletarian pond' – 63 Scraggs Lane, near Clapham Common – are important for a hero who operates in suburbia without himself being suburban.

A transitional figure can be found in paperback fiction between the late 1960s and early 1970s. Stanley Morgan's Russ Tobin series, beginning with *The Sewing Machine Man* (1969), modifies the working-class hero for door-to-door permissiveness. Tobin has working-class origins in Liverpool, but his upwardly mobile trajectory is indicated by successive titles in the series – *The Courier*, *Tobin on Safari*, *Tobin in Las Vegas*.

His salesman beginnings, though, are important, especially when he re-imagines himself as his own product: 'I was carrying my commodity around with me – sex appeal, and all I had to do now was decide what secondary line to carry – fridges or vacuum cleaners or encyclopedias' (Morgan 1969: 24).

The *Confessions* novels were published between 1971 and 1979 – nineteen 'Timothy Lea' adventures, seven by 'Rosie Dixon' (also Wood) and a separate series by 'Jonathan May' (Laurence James, who also wrote the 'Mick Norman' *Hell's Angel* series for New English Library).[8] ... *Window Cleaner* (1971) clearly had at least one eye on *Alfie*: 'Rule Two: Make them laugh. This is where you can't go wrong. Once you've got a bird laughing – and especially a married one – you can practically hear the bedsprings creaking' (Lea 1971: 66). The book is partly about Timmy's sexual education, both at the hands of his customers and, after his first successful encounter, from that key post-permissive artefact, the sex guide – 'It's very interesting and I'm full of things I didn't know, like birds taking longer to get warmed up than fellows ... I get the message that I'm supposed to stick around a bit longer ...' (*ibid.*: 40). But it is also a very visible response to 'liberated' female sexuality. Timmy encounters a range of women – working-class and 'posh', married and/or bored or lonely, a lesbian couple: in the most anxious episode, not included in the film (although there's a version of it in ... *Taxi Driver*), he nearly ends up in bed with a female impersonator. Two women live outside this flawed utopia. Elizabeth is the nice, virginal girl who makes him think of marriage, but whom Sid gets off with instead. More interesting, and again not in the film, is Sandy, the most overtly feminist presence in the novel. She talks about female orgasms, has lots of lovers (many of them 'spades', as the book so charmingly puts it) and exposes Timmy's hypocrisy for expecting her to be monogamous when he isn't. 'She's so direct, she's like a man,' he muses (*ibid.*: 76), and neither he nor the book knows quite what to do with her.

The first two novels are almost, dare one say it, 'realist' in style, but they broadened into postcard caricature as they went on. The films pushed this further, and Askwith modified Timmy into a more comically stupid character. Even so, he is full of such gems as: 'Birds are funny things, you know. One minute they give you the "No, no, you mustn't" bit, then suddenly it's "Yes, yes, you certainly must, you randy bugger".' Some of this expertise on 'crumpet' is reminiscent of boys' talk in playgrounds (one of the places where *Confessions* books were circulated and consumed). In spite of their 'X' certificates, the films, too, seemed to address an audience prone to the myths that little or no sexual experience helped sustain, a combination of outrageous boasts and palpable terror. Julian Wood (1984) has examined such boys' talk and characterises its attitude to girls as 'a mixture of pursuit, disinterest, patronisation, fear and fixation' (65). One example he gives is a ritualistic 'cataloguing of the female body in alternative terms', a linguistic display he interprets as imparting a 'tenuous sense of control' (*ibid.*: 65). The *Confessions* novels progressively evolved a language so dense in its combination of sexual and rhyming slang that it became positively droog-like in its self-referentiality. Try the following passage from *Confessions of a Private Dick*, for example, for a fairly extensive 'naming of parts':

Nadia Durrant has temporarily stopped remodelling my hampton while she enjoys her burst of conscience but now she starts again and I sink my digits into the inviting cleft between her back bumpers. She opens her legs to make it easier for me and I slide my hand down until it brushes against a few silky lair hairs and makes contact with the lower end of juice junction. The moment I touch her fun box she lets out a long sigh and tightens her grip on my Mad Mick like she is frightened it might make a bolt for it ...

'Kiss me there!' she pants, straining her arms down her body. It is clear that the lady is desirous of a grumble and mumble and, never one to disappoint, I spread apart her luminous bridges [Bridges of Sighs: thighs – Ed.) and prepare to dive.

(Lea 1975: 99-100)

The first third of the film version of Confessions of a Window Cleaner invites comparisons, in particular, with Here We Go Round the Mulberry Bush, a similarity not lost on reviewer Gareth Jones: 'Like Donner's film, Window Cleaner is angled for a teenage market, presenting a gauche and ineffectual young hero whose lack of success is much emphasised, especially with the almost untouchable "girl he loves", and whose eventual successes are elided into farce or fantasy' (Monthly Film Bulletin, September 1974: 196). Each begins with an effervescent title sequence in which its irrepressibly cheerful protagonist cycles through suburbia, marvelling at its seemingly limitless sexual possibilities without quite knowing how to exploit them. ... Window Cleaner ditches the coloured-filter fantasy inserts and replaces Stevie Winwood and Traffic with a title song by what seems to be a Lulu impersonator. 'The whole country is having it off and it's like I'm a leper,' complains Jamie in Mulberry Bush, while Timmy's sex life 'holds about as much sensation as a concrete contraceptive'. Some generic changes have taken place in our hero, however. Jamie is a lower-middle-class suburban grammar-school boy – he lives in Stevenage new town with one of those 1960s R. D. Laing families so popular in 'Swinging' films. Timmy's Scraggs Lane is, as its name suggests, the 'scrag end' of the sort of housing due for demolition in the march to suburbanisation, an appropriate milieu for his On the Buses family. Jamie's near-or-actual conquests are within reach of his own class and age, although he dreams of being seduced by a 'ripe experienced' woman, perhaps during his supermarket delivery job. 'She seems a nice class of person' is his most frequent response to a likely candidate, while a suburban housewife greets him with a stony stare and a telling TRADESMEN ONLY sign. In the final scene, he sets his sights on the 'nice' girl who, like him, is on her way to university.

Timmy's nose is initially pressed literally against the window of permissiveness, like Arthur the plumber in Commuter Husbands, 'looking into hundreds of little boxes', hypnotised by the utopian possibilities of the 'knocker factory'. He has an unhappy first attempt with badly dubbed stripper Lil, an 'initiation' set up by Sid, whose prodigious northern charm evidently serves him well. Timmy succeeds only in penetrating her suspender belt. His real initiation comes courtesy of Mrs Jacqueline Brown

123

(sexcom trouper Sue Longhurst), 'a bit of a nympho' who lives in the promisingly suggestive Lyndhurst Rise. She's an OMO Wife in more ways than one – they have sex in a kitchen engulfed by soap suds and he emerges to the accompaniment of the Hallelujah Chorus ('Well, Jacqui had certainly taught me to come clean'). In between these two episodes, he's seemingly mocked by a billboard milk-promotion which asks 'Are You Getting Enough?' The equation of sex and milk underlines the semi-maternal relationship he enjoys with his 'Nine to Five Widows', an impression that all that foam does little to dispel.

But this maternal power has a potentially threatening underside. The oddest episode in ... *Window Cleaner* concerns Mrs Villiers (Melissa Stribling), whose husband owns some of the biggest blocks of flats serviced by Sid and Timmy. Mrs Villiers, we learn, is 'hygiene-mad' – an inverted Jacqui – and has already ejected Timmy from the house as he learns naked yoga from the Swedish maid. In short, she has 'castrating mother' written all over her. The films and books have a telling phrase for terrifyingly voracious women –'a blind date with a bacon slicer' – and Mrs V threatens to be one of those, too. She lures him into the coal cellar to change a lightbulb, but he falls off the stepladder, removing her skirt in the process and covering it and himself with coal dust. 'You're just a dirty little boy, aren't you,' she sneers icily, and announces her intention to strip him and bath him. This combination of sexual promise fused with the punishment of little boys is too much for Timmy and the film – both turn and run away.

The British experiment

> It's just like riding a bicycle. Once you find you can stay up, there's no problem!
>
> Timmy, *Confessions of a Window Cleaner*

The *Confessions* films have never been repackaged as a 'greatest hits' compilation in the manner of the innumerable compilations called *That's Carry On*. But such a compilation would doubtless give particular prominence to the enduring image of strenuous bouts of sexual activity, often speeded-up, which demolish the immediately surrounding environment. Car wing mirrors revolve like Linda Blair's head in *The Exorcist*, windscreen wipers go into overdrive, bonnets fly off and radiators ejaculate in a kind of mechanical 'money shot'; beds and furniture collapse, kitchens are flooded, clouds of steam pour forth. Sex, in short, is a kind of environmentally unfriendly, rampaging free-for-all. In *The Tall Guy* (Mel Smith, 1989), it doesn't ring quite true when Jeff Goldblum and Emma Thompson perform similarly furniture-threatening intercourse – everyone knows that the middle classes don't shag like that, at least not in British comedy. Such bedroom hooliganism belongs to the realm of what Angela Carter calls 'a sexual folklore of bizarre vitality' (1992: 166). For Carter, this is a nationally specific sexuality – she's talking about the 'bonking' subworld of the British tabloid press. If the middle classes are usually represented through conventions of repression and denial – No Sex, Please, We're Gazing into the Abyss – the 'phallic, aggressive' sexual culture of white, working-class, straight masculinity is the id to the bourgeoisie's superego:

> This orgiastic riotousness is the inversion of the bourgeois culture of repression and is based on the same set of existential premises, on a sense of self with rigidly defined boundaries, on a fear of the expression of emotion as, perhaps, eroding those boundaries.
>
> (ibid.: 167)

Carter is undeniably on to something, although her distinction between the orgiastic and the ecstatic is worryingly close to Roland Barthes's elitist plaisir (implicitly lumpen, 'easy' pleasure) and jouissance (a 'higher' orgasmic pleasure, engendering modernist sensations of ego-dissolution) to reproduce the same elitism. And yet, sexcoms do prescribe sexuality along fairly narrow lines, not only in their homophobic episodes and the lurking fear of the female sexual appetite, but in recoiling from almost anything which departs from a vigorous missionary-positioned workout – little wonder that Askwith's thrusting buttocks became the genre's most enduring image.

In 1972, The Joy of Sex was billed as 'a gourmet guide to lovemaking', a gastronomic analogy anathema to low culture's insistence on stuffing its face with a lot of what it knows and likes, even if the consequences are the sexual equivalent of 'Busman's Stomach' (Timmy examines an article on 'new tools' after one perilously strenuous bout). At least once in each film, he's asked to perform cunnilingus, which is clearly at the more exotic and worrying end of the menu; at best mystifying, at worst a dangerous journey into the unknown ('Talk to her! Talk to her!' implores Miss Prendergast in ... Window Cleaner as Timmy emits suffocating noises). If all that Olympic bounce-and-thrust keeps sexual difference at bay, these scenes bring it right back.

The speeded-up sequences can be seen partly as the legacy of a 1960s popular modernist legacy and the signs of narrative 'disruption' outlined by Robert Murphy – fantasy sequences, slapstick, 'distancing' techniques (which tend not to distance us at all) such as narrators, inter-titles and direct address (1992: 3). Some of these pass into the sexcom, although slapstick, for example, is used for direct comic effect rather than to signal the ironic pop culture literacy of the film-makers. The Sex Thief (Martin Campbell, 1973), a particularly unsavoury sex comedy, is one of the first to include accelerated footage.[9] The hero (David Warbeck) is a gentleman thief with a penchant for rape (which, inevitably, his victims enjoy), which is one of the reasons why its seven-times-in-one-night sequence recalls A Clockwork Orange. Kubrick's film uses a speeded-up sex sequence as one of an array of 'ironic' techniques to establish the impeccable virility and energy of his rebel-rapist hero, as Alex (Malcolm McDowell) has sex with two teenage girls. The Sex Thief, similarly, does not use the device to undercut its hero in the way that the Confessions films do. In another sequence, sex with an initially unwilling victim is intercut with a wrestling match, complete with a disagreeably Eisensteinian use of 'submissions' and 'pin-falls'.

One of Linda Williams's boldest moves in *Hardcore* (1990) is to compare the sex film with the musical, at least in the way it has been conceptualised by Richard Dyer (1981) as a utopian genre. 'To a great extent', she argues, 'the hard-core feature film is a kind of musical, with sexual number taking the place of musical number' (Williams 1990: 124), and pornography or sexploitation celebrates energy, abundance, intensity, transparency and even community (Dyer's utopian categories). Certainly the first two sex scenes in ... *Window Cleaner* conform to Williams's differentiation between 'spontaneous, exciting (good) sex' (Jacqui and the soap suds) and 'unexciting, unspontaneous, phoney or contrived (bad) sex' (Lil the stripper and her voracious suspender strap). We can both gender and historicise this distinction in the sexcom. 'Contrived' sex usually brings with it the pressure to perform, and lurking behind this is the newly politicised female orgasm. In short, the films are much more uncertain when irrepressible male randiness has to negotiate the intricacies of actual female desire.

Nevertheless, the sexcom is utopian in its discovery of numerous opportunities for sexual conquests to compensate for the 'lacks' (exhaustion, scarcity, dreariness, manipulation, fragmentation) associated with work (and, less directly, class) and home. In the opening scene of ... *Pop Performer*, Timmy attempts a rapid escape down his ladder to evade the wrath of a suburban husband. But his ladder is pushed over, depositing him through the window of the house next door and on to the bed Sid is sharing with another housewife. Nothing encapsulates the fantasy of suburban pornotopia more succinctly – keep on going, one infers, and there's a milkman, a salesman or a plumber in every bedroom in the street.

Certainly the sexcom's 'numbers' celebrate energy and spontaneity, in particular (and Timmy is the very model of transparency). But they are also the source of much of the slapstick, which implies a degree of awkwardness – the rise and fall of Askwith's buttocks, as well as the bizarre injuries which seem to befall them (he sits on a hot radiator during one session, and a short-sighted golfer tees-off between them as he makes out in a bunker), the manic gurning and cries of 'Wa-hey!' meant to signify (orgiastic) pleasure. If there is a limit to sexual utopia, it can be located in the body. The body is notoriously treacherous in low comedy – it fails, breaks wind, looks unintentionally ridiculous when it should look its best. Added to this is the threat of punishment from returning husbands and injuries sustained during hasty escapes – in those pre-button-fly days, zipper accidents are especially reliable ('I've been arrested by the fuzz already!' moans Timmy as the police almost catch him on the job in ... *Driving Instructor*). Above all, there's the unstoppable 'escalation' of the female libido. The flip-side of that 'Are You Getting Enough?' poster is a 'Give Generously' tin which catches Timmy's rueful eye – his landlady has just worn him out and her daughter is waiting for him in his room.

If softcore titillation is supposedly about overvaluing the body – beauty, size, performance, energy – low comedy quickly cuts it down to size, sometimes literally: *Adventures of a Private Eye* ia a veritable A to Z of castration gags, ranging from accidents with mouse traps to the electric fan which falls into Jon Pertwee's lap. Richard Dyer sees such a representation of the male body as double-edged. On the one hand, the comic undercutting of masculinity and 'acceptance of male sexual failure' are re-freshing, but, at the same time, not only do they go hand-in-hand with derogatory images of women but 'this itchy, tetchy squeamishness is itself a product of a soci-ety which loathes the human body' (1993: 117). Sex comedy isn't quite so clearcut – its 'body politics' belong to more of a mixed economy, and this is partly to do with their contradictory response to a specific historical moment, a sense of want-ing to embrace a supposedly modern sexual culture while holding on to something which seems to be more permanent. But the Confessions narrative does derive partly from pornography, which already entertains distinct anxieties about the 'perform-ance principle', bringing with it, as it does, what Moye calls 'a pretty gruelling re-gime' (1985: 59). The attendant fears are exacerbated by the discursive visibility of female desire: 'not being able to "get" an erection at the appropriate time, "prema-turely" ejaculating, and the more general sense of having to be ready for sex no matter what the immediate circumstances or feelings' (ibid.: 50). This is the stuff of the sexcom, but also constitutes a highly exploitable 'netherworld of phallic failure' within the sex industries: 'as pornography beats out the tempo of what it takes to be a man so it offers the solace of ointments, pills and plastic equipment to the defeated and the frightened' (ibid.: 63). Sexcoms disavow such alienating solutions and prefer to find solace in utopian energy and spontaneity. But perhaps the penis-with-a-name – Percy, John Thomas, Mad Mick – is the most frequent reminder of phallic desire as 'alien-ated work' (ibid.: 63).

This was, in any case, the end of the line for a certain type of British comedy, the last time it could be enjoyed outside the quotation marks of ironic appropria-tion or the political amnesia of nostalgia. The sexcom flourished for three or four years, but the last phenomenally popular one showed other influences breaking through.

The 'Mousetrap at the Moulin'

If ever there was a missed opportunity for empirical audience research, then Come Play With Me (George Harrison Marks, 1977) was it. In the darkest days of British cinema, when even sex films were no longer a sure bet at the box office, it exerted sufficient pull on the public to run continuously at the Classic Moulin for four years, a feat which, in David McGillivray's words, 'is a source of continued amazement' (1992: 78). The film opened not only during the same week as Fiona Richmond's Hardcore (James Kenelm Clarke, 1977) but at the same cinema. Hardcore is built en-tirely around Richmond, who's rarely off screen – its working title was Frankly, Fiona and it attempts to reproduce the same globetrotting sexploits that ran monthly in her Men Only column and her bestselling book Fiona (1976). Come Play With Me was the first film to be sold on Mary Millington's name, yet she is hardly on screen longer than the bit parts she played in Keep It Up Downstairs and What's Up Superdoc? Come Play With Me occupied an auditorium with a smaller seating capacity than its rival, yet made more than twice as much in its first week. For four weeks, it was in the West End Top Ten, making about £5,000–6,000 a week in a 134-seat auditorium with a

£2 admission price. During its first provincial date, at the Leeds Plaza, it had that cinema's highest take for two years.

The 'Mousetrap at the Moulin' was enough of a phenomenon for The Guardian to send Stanley Reynolds to investigate (9 August 1980). By 1980, clearly no one was surprised by the juxtaposition of 'familiar household faces' (Alfie Bass, Irene Handl, Rita Webb, Ronald Fraser, Cardew Robinson) and 'a Carry On film with tits, mock copulation, and of course that touch of Sappho', and Reynolds was able to locate it as part of an 'authentic' tradition – 'that happy combination of clowns and girls which was mined for so many years just a few yards up the street from the cinema at the old Windmill Theatre'. But despite finding 'the whole thing ... so English in such a homey English way' – Marjorie Bilbow called it 'a goodhearted film, a romp among friends, that the older telly audience can feel safe with' (Screen International, April 1977: 28) – Reynolds did not extend this generosity beyond the film to its audience. 'Very respectable, very ordinary, but very gormless customers' is how he characterised them. He doesn't appear to have spoken to them, to have felt it worth asking what they expected from the film or whether it delivered, whether any of them had seen it more than once. Rather, they were little more than a footnote to the film's low comic heritage, a pseudo-sociological fait accompli. Comedy was the only appropriate companion for sex for these downtrodden punters – an odd inference given the proximity of cinema clubs – whereas 'high drama' would be 'too uncomfortable; perhaps reminding the punters of their own home lives in the suburbs'. Not for these dullards the name-dropping of Chaucer, Shakespeare and Henry Miller.

With its original audience long dispersed – I recently found it on video in Soho, repackaged as 'Swedish erotica', its '18' certificate unexpectedly flanked by two erect penises – Come Play With Me is best approached via the three names which appeared most prominently in its promotion: George Harrison Marks, David Sullivan and Mary Millington. Part of Come Play With Me seeks to move on from the sexcoms and to at least suggest the transition of the Sullivan package on to the screen. But I'm not scoring auteurist points when I suggest that Harrison Marks was making a very different film, one which appears to belong to a time before the Confessions films.

In the first instance, then, Come Play With Me is not only a nostalgic sex film, it's virtually a heritage sex film, a fact which did not go unnoticed in Marjorie Bilbow's characteristically perceptive review:

> I fear that George Harrison Marks must have been asleep like Rip Van Winkle while the sex film scene has rolled away from the nudist camps and strip clubs. In choosing to make a comedy with sex (not to be confused with a sex comedy) he set himself a very difficult task in competition with others who have gone through the trials and errors and learned from them. I love him for sticking his neck out as producer, director, writer and star, but it was a foolhardy venture.
>
> (Screen International, April 1977: 28)

Scott Meek made much the same observation less sympathetically in *Monthly Film Bulletin* – 'third-rate music hall, inferior and outdated pop song, irrelevant comic song and inadequate dance' (May 1977: 95) – describing it as a 'mixture of Ealing comedy and pornography'. There is a sense of *The Ladykillers* engaging in an ill-starred dalliance with *Confessions from a Health Farm*. The film is overplotted to the point of insignificance, but deals with two forgers, Clapworthy (Marks himself, in outrageous wig and teeth) and Kelly (Alfie Bass), masquerading as musicians at the Highland health farm of Lady Bovington (Irene Handl) in order to evade police and villains alike. Soon, Lady Bovington has installed an out-of-work troupe of strippers as nurses and everything is in place. Clapworthy and Kelly are largely kept well away from the sex, as though there's a parallel film they haven't been told about – they never take off vests and long underwear even in the sauna. In a telling scene, they are not invited to the 'swinging' poolside party towards the end of the film. In time-honoured comic tradition, they share a bed, bickering at each other as Clapworthy reads *Whitehouse* and Kelly unleashes a particularly unsalubrious fart. Light entertainment and sexploitation are on strained speaking terms, although the variety duo (they even drive a chugging, vintage car) do get to involve the nurses in the aforementioned 'irrelevant song and inadequate dance', 'It's Great to be Here'.

It's difficult to separate this yearning for variety and burlesque from Marks – there's even a trip to Brighton Pier in one one scene, complete with Rita Webb's fortune teller and a recalcitrant, shitting parrot. It scarcely matters that, his background notwithstanding, comedy was not Marks's strong point. Marks was a pre-permissive figure who never quite made the transition to post-permissiveness – he hadn't made a feature film since 1969's *Nine Ages of Nakedness*, which in any case was like a compilation of glamour films from the early 1960s. In the contemporary porn market, it's significant that it was naughty schoolgirls in 'regulation blue knickers' and stern headmasters oblivious to the banning of corporal punishment who offered a reassuringly familiar world for him.[10] When *Queen of the Blues* (Willy Roe, 1979) summons up burlesque, even down to a bizarre Max Miller impersonation, it's because it minimises the plot in relation to the onstage 'numbers'. *Come Play With Me* invokes music hall within a familiar structure of feeling, as 'a repository of lost values' (Medhurst 1986: 185). The film is like an epitaph for the British sex comedy.

One of David Sullivan's earliest sales techniques was to put 'explicit' front covers on old copies of *Knave*, *Fiesta* and even *Health and Efficiency*. 'All the punters were getting was old stock served up in a new cover,' commented Harrison Marks admiringly (Killick 1994: 13). Is this too cruel an analogy for *Come Play With Me*, even before it found a new life as 'Swedish erotica'? In the 1970s, Sullivan developed two methods of promoting his material. The softcore-packaged-as-hardcore technique later extended to videos in the Private Shops, most notoriously in appropriating the 'color climax' covers from the Danish Rodox company. But Sullivan also extended the boundaries of softcore, in its legal sense. 'Strength sells,' he told a television documentary in 1977, and his magazines departed from the glamour conventions of his top-shelf competitors in two ways – the 'ordinariness' of the models ('they looked as though they could be found in any British town', as Killick puts it, 1994: 23) and the more explicit poses. The crotch now became the centre of the gaze, with labia visible, then parted and later penetrated by a variety of objects (almost anything but a penis, which remained off limits). The class connotations, too, were very different – *Mayfair* and *Penthouse* conjured up a *Jason King* world of high-living men-of-the-world. Sullivan's magazines hinted at the upward mobility of the aspiring pornocrat, but solicited an impatient working-class 'punter' who wanted the goods delivered at an aggressively lower price. The 'Readers' Wives' – Sullivan's invention – grew out of this ethos, and so did Millington, constructed as the suburban wife who was up for anything, sexy but not conventionally glamorous, knowable, accessible – by implication, fuckable (a fantasy developed in her ghost-written travels around Britain).

Come Play With Me and Millington were part of a larger package, and were intended to be consumed alongside the magazines. It isn't just that Sullivan misled people about the sexual content of the film – four inserted scenes for the mythical 'continental' version would 'make Linda Lovelace look like Noddy ... Nothing is simulated' (*Daily Telegraph*, 15 November 1976), a rumour which drew Equity into a fracas as those 'familiar faces' reacted in horror. More importantly, Sullivan could construct a pornographic package which didn't need to be inscribed into the text. This was, according to posters, 'The strongest, funniest sex comedy seen in Britain. Featuring Sex Superstar Mary Millington – the British "Linda Lovelace" – and ten sex-crazed naughty nurses in action!' The poster promoted an 'uncensored and unretouched' photomagazine for £1.25, an intriguing artefact in its own right. For one thing, it builds on these outrageous claims: '*Come Play With Me* features many top TV stars in the most unexpected sequences! But the real action is provided by Mary and twenty or so of the most attractive women in Britain. AND WHEN WE SAY ACTION WE MEAN ACTION!'[11] This was more than a novelisation – it tied the film more closely to the magazines (A *Playbirds* Novel Special) and it packaged the film as hardcore, as the following passage suggests:

> His cock juddered like a plane's joystick and then her hand flashed down to her pussy again. She squeezed it like a damp rag and touched it with her nails. The juice poured out of the clenched skin and laced her thighs. Then Bill started to cream off. Great gouts of semen came spurting from his tortured tool. His gouts almost reached the low ceiling of the stage and one of his spurts hit a lamp that hung over head. When the semen hit the bulb there was a tremendous hiss, rather as though he had poured water on a fire.
>
> (*Playbirds* Magazine 1977: n.p.)

Did anyone actually expect to see this on the screen (there isn't even an equivalent scene)? What seems more important is the tease – as in the myth of the 'continental' version – that such images might be out there somewhere, waiting for an impending censorship breakthrough. The scene embodies the phallic hyperbole of pornography, with its inexhaustible organs and fluids – soon they are in a growing 'pool of spunk' – a world away from the euphemistic abstractions of the *Confessions* novels, but also from a notable scene in the film.

Millington is massaging a muscular patient whose physique is used to convey comic simple-mindedness rather than virility. She straddles him as he lies face down and we get a shot of her which recurs during a similar scene in *The Playbirds* – autoerotically immersed in her own bodily pleasure, rubbing her breasts, the framing separating her from the male partner but offering her directly to the spectator. But the massage concludes with the male receiving an unexpected enema – an unwieldy joke sets up a confusion of colonic irrigation with massage. The punchline could be read as the heterosexual fear of anal eroticism, except that she has earlier inserted a helpful finger to 'relax' him further. Rather, it's the last battle between the grotesque, infantile comic body of the Marks *Come Play With Me* and the promise of pornotopian 'delivery' – later, a strenuous sex scene is staged adjacently to Clapworthy pissing in a sink. While the hardcore inserts are a myth, Sullivan did order additional scenes to be shot and they do have the post-synchronised look that porn inserts often have. An early scene at a burlesque club lingers endlessly over a girl preparing to go on. As she puts on her suspender belt, she starts caressing her body, and the camera looks her up and down. A number of apparently cut-in (or cut-away) scenes have this quality about them – a significant number of performers share scenes without ever being in the same shot. The film literally comes apart at the seams, a 'heritage' sex comedy bent out of shape by scenes celebrating the spoils of the new pornocracy.

Living in a pornocracy

> The pornocrats aren't ashamed to be ostentatious anymore.
>
> *The Playbirds*

If the 'meritocrat' – the 'natural' aristocrat whose success is not beholden to class or background – was a key component in the 1970s mythology, was the pornocrat the 1970s cold-light-of-day equivalent? And if the pornocrat was such a key player and empire builder, does that imply the evolution of a fully fledged pornocracy, a culture organised around the economic logic of pornography? In contrast to the recession, this was the route to economic success for the motivated and the gifted, with the visible rewards of racehorses, wild parties and high living.

The pornocrat controls and selectively distributes sexual capital – thus obscenity laws both help and hinder him – knowledge, 'freedom', sexual technology, the means of stimulation and success. The pornocracy is essentially inhabited by two classes – there are the pornocrats themselves and the swinging elite surrounding them and there are the 'punters' over whom they rule benevolently. The punters can be offered the illusory mobility of a promotion to 'connoisseurs' – the persistent consumers who are ready for a 'stronger' product at a higher price.[12] What looks like a third, intermediary class – the 'playbirds', distinguished by glamour, short-term wealth, fame – actually turns out to constitute part of the sexual capital: aristocratic 'spoils' (the porn star who 'belongs' to a pornocrat).

The pornocracy is, however, precarious, constantly threatened by counter-revolutionaries: feminists, religious groups, a capricious police force taking 'backhanders' and attending parties one minute and acting in the interests of a jealous, repressive rearguard the next. In The Playbirds (Willy Roe, 1978) and Confessions from the David Galaxy Affair (1979), the pornocrat – played, with mandatory medallion in place, by Alan Lake – is arbitrarily and jealously punished for his lifestyle. The later of the two films, in particular, anticipates Sullivan's later imprisonment, and both films display unexpectedly autobiographical details. 'If you make it in any other field, you get the Queen's Award for Industry,' he complained. 'You make it in our industry, they send you to prison' (McGillivray 1992: 78).

The Playbirds, 'A Murder Thriller With Thrilling Bodies', is an extraordinary depiction of the pornocracy from within and of the economic logic of pornography. The fact that it ends with the death of Mary Millington's character gives it an additional chilling resonance. It's a rancid little film, but an extremely interesting one. As a story, it's a virtual remake of quota quickie Cover Girl Killer (Terry Bishop, 1959) in which a pre-Steptoe Harry H. Corbett murders a succession of girls from the covers of a fashion magazine. His glasses are just that little bit too thick, as if to imply that he's spent a lot of time consuming his victims' images before deciding on their punishment. This is an equation that the 1970s pornocrat narrative can warm to. The Playbirds' killer is revealed, in a garbled ending, to be the twin brother of religious zealot Hern (Dudley Sutton). The killer, in short, is morality's evil twin, a demon-worshipping pervert. An earlier suspect is a prominent Tory MP and 'newly elected member of the Decency League', who proclaims on television that 'Pornography is the heroin of the soul', but avidly consumes blue movies which are 'fine for men of the world like ourselves'.

The real interest of the film, however, lies in the mapping of this slasher narrative on to the fictionalisation of the Sullivan empire, with Lake's Harry Dougan, like his real-life counterpart, naming his racehorse after Playbirds magazine, and Millington, on screen a bit more than usual, in a role playing on her good/bad girl image – a policewoman whose undercover activities reveal her also to be a consummate sex performer ('You'd think she'd been born to the life,' comments Gavin Campbell's Inspector Morgan). The thriller plot fizzles out into incoherence, placing greater emphasis on the link between the murders and the production of the magazine – to accompany each murder, there's a prolonged scene of the printing presses rolling on the latest issue: commodification literally equals death.

The opening scenes illustrate the film's logic fairly succinctly. A modelling session cuts to the resulting front cover, as the presses roll and Dougan ponders his empire. The title sequence (discussed in Chapter 2) brings several characters together in the Soho area – Millington's Lucy, Hern with his fire-and-brimstone sandwich board and the model from the opening scene who is murdered just after the final credit. The following 'crime scene' is filled with representations of the murder victim, including her own corpse, numbered in lipstick by the serial killer. The doctor is reading Playbirds as Chief Superintendent Holbourne (Glynn Edwards) arrives. 'Mm, smashing bird,' he remarks appreciatively when someone shows him a photograph of the victim – 'She was pretty,' agrees Lucy/Millington. There is a narrative articulation here of porn's 'spilling over', as solving the crime is constantly paralleled with the consumption of, and later productive participation in, pornography. In the pornification of every aspect of life, bodies alive and dead, photos and pin-ups become interchangeable. Holbourne is shown the *Playbirds* spread – 'This is what she looked like when she was breathing' – and he looks back and forth between the corpse and the centrefold.

The police had, earlier, been publicly and humiliatingly implicated in the spread of Soho 'vice', but that doesn't seem to be the reference point here. Instead, their slide into the logic of the sex industries suggests that it's the only logic that really counts now, the 'spillage' is complete. Although Dougan is finally arrested (off screen) for some undefined offence, and the issue of *Playbirds* featuring Lucy impounded, the rest of the film suggests that the real power lies in those processing plants and the industry they fuel. Holbourne is paralleled with Dougan, albeit as a poor relation, an unsuccessful betting man to the latter's lucrative obsession, and when Morgan evolves the scheme to place Lucy under cover, Holbourne comments, 'If you had your way, we'd be publishing in competition with Dougan.' The preparation is played for laughs – a series of policewomen 'audition' in front of Holbourne and Morgan, and Lucy emerges as the 'natural'. Inevitably, the final section of the film invites comparison with Millington's arrival as top softcore model, culminating in the front cover which spells her demise. After two false leads, the police, like the film, seem to lose interest. Who cares anyway? the film seems to say – nothing can stop those presses rolling, not even the models' deaths, which, we are told, actually help sales. This logic is inadvertently underscored by the final victim being played by the sex industries' most notable casualty, whose death, equally, was easily absorbed, not to say exploited, by the machinery. If rather too much of this relies on gruesome hindsight, it's still a jawdropping moment when the strangling of Lucy is followed immediately by the incongruously cheerful 'Playbirds' theme.

At this point, it's time to turn our attention back to stardom; more specifically, to the British porn star, beginning with Millington's rival Fiona Richmond.

'The frankly sensational adventures of a liberated lady':[13] Fiona Richmond

She does not fuck with *anybody*. They must be special. They must be 'swingers'.
> Angela Carter, on *Inside Linda Lovelace* (1992: 182)

She belongs to a new generation of natural lovers who believe that if you have a beautiful face and a beautiful body you should use them.
> Preface to *Fiona* (Richmond 1976)

Fiona Richmond, a former Playboy Bunny, made her name within the Paul Raymond empire, writing and posing for *Men Only* and appearing in his sexploitation stage farces, although she is probably best remembered for her notorious appearance in the Crystal Palace communal bath. She starred in three films (alongside smaller parts in others), each directed by James Kenelm Clarke – the psychological horror-thriller *Exposé* (1975), the pseudo-autobiographical *Hardcore* (1977) and a wartime sex comedy, *Let's Get Laid* (1977), notable only for Robin Askwith's extraordinary George Formby accent. As the relative fortunes of *Hardcore* and *Come Play With Me* suggest, she was already being eclipsed by Mary Millington in 1977. The peak of her popularity rested on the image perpetuated in her *Men Only* column and her book *Fiona* – a globetrotting swinger who travelled the world 'road-testing men'. If this testing of the equipment, and its owners' deployment of it, constituted a poten-tially threatening scenario for male readers then Fiona assures us interminably that no one worships the Great Cock Almighty quite like she does. Certainly, she en-counters a great many, some extremely distinctive – one is a 'knarled [sic], knotted tree trunk with two well rounded acorns attached to its stumpy stalk' (Richmond 1976: 170). At the end of *Fiona*, she can scarcely contain herself as she reminds us once more: 'Men, I love you and your sublime cocks, and the only way to go is the way I'm going, cocksure and happy!' (1976: 188). Richmond's sexual appetite and expertise operate as a kind of passport, giving her access to the swinging jetset – she's a stewardess in *Fiona* and the first place we see her in *Hardcore* is at an airport. Fiona is an aspirational meritocrat, a vicar's daughter from Norfolk[14] whose libido takes her around the globe and into an economic/sexual elite.

At one point in *Hardcore*, Richmond is described as 'an emancipated female' ush-ering in 'a whole new era of sexual feminism'. It's played half-jokingly, but this claim lurks behind the persona of the 1970s porn star – this is what female liberation is really about, her prodigious sexuality the essence of the post-permissive woman. In her review of *Inside Linda Lovelace*,[15] first published in 1974, Angela Carter ponders the persona of the 'archetypal swinger', for whom sexual freedom is isolated from any other kind of freedom, and moves on from a 'repressive hypothesis' to something like a 'permissive hypothesis':

> the notion of 'permissiveness' can only arise in a society in which authori-tarianism is deeply implicit. Now I am permitted as much libidinal grati-fication as I want. Yippee! But who is it who permits me? Why, the self same institutions that hitherto forbade me! So, I am still in the same boat, though it has been painted a different colour.
>
> (1992: 180)

The question is – and it's a more complicated one with Mary Millington – whom does the porn star speak for, let alone to? Fiona's all-important 'insatiability' is a case in point – when one partner tells her he's going to 'fuck you and fuck you till you beg for mercy', she smiles 'knowingly because I knew that I would last longer than him!' (Richmond 1976: 73). Although Williams (1990) is talking about Ameri-can hardcore, and Marilyn Chambers in particular, she offers two contrasting repre-sentations (or readings) of 'insatiability'. In the first, it disempowers women – like

Hera's anger on learning that men enjoy one-tenth of sexual pleasure to women's 'all ten in full': 'the female loses the game of power if she wins that of pleasure' (ibid.: 153) in an equation where pleasure is simultaneously consolation for lack of power and proof of unsuitability to exercise it. But Williams argues for a second model in which Chambers's cries for 'more, more, more' signify 'the continuous unending pleasures of a utopian world in which the power imbalance between the sexes does not directly enter the represented world of the film' (ibid.: 179). Fiona, like Chambers's Insatiable, 'represents a new view of the active female pursuit of pleasure ... a "paradoxical state of sexual insatiation in the presence of the utmost sexual satisfaction"' (ibid.: 180).

If these floating, ideologically overdetermined fantasies are to be anchored in any way, then audience and context are obviously important. Williams is talking about a moment when hardcore was soliciting a 'couples' audience, so it's not unreasonable to speculate that those films might mean different things to different members of the audience. Fiona Richmond wrote for Men Only – audiences don't get much more clearly circumscribed than that – and the (male) writer of Fiona's preface tells us how she 'has disillusioned me with womanhood' (Richmond 1976: 12). Confronted with the consummate come-and-have-a-go-if-you-think-you're-hard-enough sexuality of Fiona, 'girls should realize that a lot more is expected of them than lying down and opening their legs' (ibid.: 13).

If Richmond speaks of female pleasure for the male pornotopia, that is not the only type of sexual regulation inherent in her persona. Fiona is structured as a sexual travelogue, but she suffers from a xenophobic fear of drinking the water. In Hardcore, she faces the by now obligatory Mary Whitehouse figure in a television interview, but Fiona is as sexually prescriptive, in her way, as Whitehouse, equally convinced of the sanctity of fucking – she even imagines the same kind of allegiances between perverts, paedophiles and queers at the House of Lotus Blossom in Bangkok. In Australia, a female hairdresser moves from shampooing her hair to undressing her and massaging her breasts and pubic hair with a hairdryer and a brush. The book is keen to have it both ways, pruriently playing with the fantasy before vigorously recuperating it – Fiona is soon reminding us, and herself, that 'nothing beats a man's hot, hard penis sticking in the depths of your womb ... I think that although the sensations produced with this girl had been great ... it left me wanting, wanting something only a man can provide. Men, I love you!' (1976: 80). But it's in San Francisco – a Fiona-unfriendly city if ever there was one – that she is least at home. There she witnesses androgynous same-sex couples dancing on a boat, culminating in a lesbian couple performing with a vibrator. Fiona is less than impressed by these 'sad clockwork figures' – 'I couldn't get over the fact that there was no excitement and joy' (ibid.: 123). Once again, the phallus is on hand to redeem the situation, especially when it belongs to the well-endowed Lionel. We learn only gradually that Lionel is black – he's initially described as being 'tall and dark', but soon Fiona is extolling the virtues of his 'bold, black tool', the first part of him, literally, to define him racially. Earlier in the book, black male sexuality is absolutely Other – at the House of Lotus Blossom, a 'gigantic negro' stares at her 'the way a bull looks at a cow' and

reminds her of an ape (ibid.: 88). But racist sexual fantasies have their uses when a
compensatory big dick is required – 'I was a slave girl, giving my powerful black
master the taste of pleasure he had commanded' (ibid.: 124).

Mary Millington was, in many ways, everything Richmond wasn't. For one thing,
she was a much more populist figure. In the first issue of Playbirds, 'she' tells us that
she's not 'another dreary international playgirl, forever having it away with men and
women in an air-conditioned and jet-set style of living' (Millington 1975: 29). Rather,
'I'm never happier than when I am on my home ground of Britain and having fun
and sex sessions with men and women here' – Millington's ghost-written exploits
take her to Leeds, Blackpool, Bradford, Glasgow and Brighton. Twice she emphasises 'men and women'; in contrast to Richmond's homophobia, Millington was
bisexual, a complicated aspect of her stardom, given that it could be (and was)
commodified for heterosexual pornography, but also suggesting that there was more
at stake for Millington's 'liberation' than Richmond's pleasure-seeking. Richmond
always speaks for pleasure, for unmediated hedonism. Millington, on the other hand,
always positioned herself in relation to pornography (which she was still defending
in her suicide note), always acknowledged that she spoke from within an industry.
This problematises her voice, especially given Sullivan's preferred formula of male-
oriented pornography articulated through a female voice, in the nominal female editors
attached to his publications. What are we to make of the major British sex symbol
of the late 1970s?

The Tooting Marilyn

> Mary, if she had nothing else, appeared to enjoy what she was
> doing.
>
> David McGillivray, Sex and Fame – The Mary
> Millington Story (Channel 4, 1996)

To the tabloids, she was the 'queen of porn', in her own words 'a very moral
person' but also 'an exhibitionist', 'the icon of the new sexual liberalism of the
1970s' (Sex and Fame – The Mary Millington Story), 'the only really natural uninhibited
sex symbol that Britain ever produced' (David Sullivan), 'our little bit of Hollywood ... the Tooting Marilyn Monroe' (journalist Colin Wills),[16] 'the British Linda
Lovelace', a 'beautiful puppet' who 'became hooked on glamour, something people who are not sure of themselves often cling to' (Mary Millington's True Blue Confessions). At the end of the 1970s, the considerable success of her four feature vehicles rested on the commercial lure of her name, yet she is extraordinarily absent
from Come Play With Me and Confessions from the David Galaxy Affair, in particular. Comparing the anatomical virtuosity of the German hardcore Miss Bohrloch with her
speaking-clock line delivery in the British films confirms that, even by the standards of the genre, acting was not her forte – indeed, her 'authenticity' rested on a
(sexual) performance which, we were always being told, was not an act but could
be offered directly to us. Agony Aunt Suzie Hayman, in Channel 4's Millington

documentary, describes her as 'a blank sheet upon which men projected their fantasies', but she was also a screen on to which sexual discourses could be projected, discourses which had hardened into unyielding polarities – porn as freedom versus porn as sexual violence, liberation versus exploitation, economic libertarianism versus family values. 'When she died in 1979,' claims McGillivray, 'it's true to say that the era died with her.' A major claim to make, and burden to impose, when no one seems to be able to explain her popularity. Millington has been posthumously constructed as both liberated and doomed, ordinary and poly-morphously insatiable, a male fantasy figure whose persona genuinely belittled male sexuality, a suburban libertine and a child, a girl-next-door and a freak.[17]

Millington's fame has diminished considerably since her death, and her story is worth summarising. She was a veterinary nurse when John Lindsay 'discovered' her, introducing her to glamour photography and subsequently hardcore films for the European market – at various points from here on, she also worked as an expensive prostitute. She worked under a variety of pseudonyms in hardcore. She was born Mary Quilter and buried as Mary Maxted, her married name – she had lived but not slept with husband Bob for a number of years by the time of her death. It was Sullivan who 'recreated' her as Mary Millington, in a pornographic rewrite of the Alfred Hitchcock/Tippi Hedren story. She was named after Roldvale's co-director, Doreen Millington, who had already given her first name to a blow-up doll. The first issue of *Playbirds* calls Mary 'the super sexy younger sister of our editor' (1975: 25). She became Sullivan's most popular model, starring in four films produced by Sullivan and the posthumous 'tribute' *Mary Millington's True Blue Confessions* (Nick Galtress, 1980). She ran two sex shops, which, unlike Sullivan's, openly sold hardcore, including her own. The reasons for her suicide seem legion. She had problems with depression, cocaine and compulsive shoplifting. She was frequently arrested, despite her claims that she was paying the police for protection. The Inland Revenue allegedly hounded and harassed her. In a radio interview, Millington spoke of her dislike of her appear-ance, already modified by plastic surgery. Already alienated from the body which was her one commodity, she was aware that time was diminishing its precarious 'value' on the pornocratic market. In 1979, she wrote four (usually conflated) sui-cide notes – to her husband, to her solicitor, to Sullivan and to Colin Wills of *The Sunday Mirror* – and took a fatal overdose.

Three interlinked constructions of Millington seem to have achieved a particular prominence. First, there's the Monroe comparison – the same initials, an illegiti-mate birth, a fatal overdose, the 'little girl lost' and the manipulative sex bomb, 'naughty one minute and the next a fawn, innocent and wide-eyed' (*Mary Millington's True Blue Confessions*).[18] If John Lindsay's belief, in *True Blue Confessions*, that Millington's sex scenes were the natural successor to Monroe's raised skirt in *The Seven Year Itch* seems particu-larly risible, there are similarities between the way the two stars are taken as 'evi-dence' of a pre-given female sexuality. Second, like Monroe, Millington accommodates a 'decline and fall' narrative in which she is the victim not only of a jealous, repres-sive 'establishment' but of her own beauty and fame. Third, if, as Richard Dyer ar-gues, Monroe was viewed as sexuality itself, or rather 'a vehicle for male sexuality'

(1987: 41), then Millington also became pornography itself, a distillation of its self-justification, its martyrdom and unfulfilled utopian promises.

In his discussion of Monroe's sexuality, Dyer emphasises the coincidence in 1953 of the star's major breakthrough and the first appearance of Playboy, which featured her on the front cover. They are connected by two discourses specific to the 'new' sexuality of the 1950s – a version of Foucault's 'repressive hypothesis' in which sex is subjugated by a hypocritical bourgeoisie and a 'drive reduction model' in which a biologically determined 'natural' sex drive brings health and happiness while 're-pression' brings frustration and psychosis. Monroe was seen as the embodiment of such a 'natural' sexuality – 'Guiltless, natural, not prurient' (Dyer 1987: 31). Millington was even more directly part of a 'glamour package', with an accompanying sexual political agenda, but the porn star's sexuality has to be extraordinary as well as natural – narrator John East describes it as 'magnificent' in True Blue Confessions. A useful, roughly contemporaneous, comparison would be Marilyn Chambers, the former Ivory Soap Queen defiled in Beyond the Green Door, a girl-next-door who proved to be Insatiable. Mark Killick's description of Millington distils the way her 'exhibitionist' persona hangs upon her suburban ordinariness – a reader's-wife-next-door – 'Despite not being conventionally beautiful, the camera liked her and she positively enjoyed showing off her body, as some of her films demonstrate' (1994: 25).

But Mary, like Marilyn, was also 'damaged goods' – True Blue Confessions tells us that she 'loved her mother with an intensity she was never able to equal with any other person, man or woman' and that she never recovered from her death. While Sullivan-related material constructs her unambiguously as porn's martyr – 'the whipping girl of bureaucracy' and victim of a puritanical witch-hunt – she was also 'on a crash course, and there was only one way out'. Mary's phenomenal sexuality, it seems, was also a prison. A scene in True Blue Confessions intercuts a wide-angle orgasmic close-up of Millington from The Playbirds with a camera travelling inexorably up the stair-case of her home to 'discover' a mock-up of her pills and suicide notes. You don't need to be Kuleshov or Eisenstein to figure this one out – Nature has truly woken from its slumbers, exhausted the 'new and wild sensations' available and promptly turned in on itself. There is great emphasis on the 'recesses' of Mary's heart – her love of animals ('love to all animals' concludes one of her suicide notes), her capac-ity for being a 'very moral person' – but she is implicitly doomed by her own de-sires, which have grown too great even for her male 'authors' to contain. Only madness and death can be imagined as the conclusion to such a trajectory.

In Mary Millington's True Blue Confessions, a number of interviewees struggle to encap-sulate her 'talent', visibly give up and fall back on some platitudes about her turning up on time and always being fully prepared. To credit Mary with talent is to attribute to her a 'performance', which, in turn, would short-circuit her authenticity, the fan-tasy that we were getting The Real Thing – 'the message was, "I know what I like and I hope you like it, too".' In this scenario, Millington is the embodiment of pornotopia itself. Three qualities are particularly important: freedom – her life was an 'attack on censorship' according to Alan Lake (Sunday Mirror, 26 August 1979) – modernity and therapy, the benevolent voice of porn. 'If I can help in any way to relieve tension

9 From music hall to pornocracy: Mary Millington in *Come Play With Me* (1977).

in any sexually frustrated men, I'm very pleased to be able to do so,' she said during a radio interview, with reference to her textual manifestations. But even as she cast herself as masturbatory sex aid, her consumers weren't swinging men-of-the-world but 'very lonely men. They've got no chance at all of ever picking up a girl, but they can buy sexy magazines and take them home and masturbate while they look at the pictures, which gives them the relief that I think they need.'

The most frequently cited evidence in the case for Millington's onscreen authenticity, as well as her modernity, was her bisexuality – even *Come Play With Me* includes a (visibly tacked-on) lesbian scene, which, Killick reports straight-faced, has 'added value' for 'so-called "connoisseurs" of porn' because she 'may not have been acting at the time that this lesbian scene was shot' (1994: 26). *True Blue Confessions* encourages a similar reading. The lesbian scene is run after the colonic irrigation scene as evidence that her male partners on screen rarely attracted her – 'She soon became disenchanted with straight sex and lesbian parts like this one satisfied her.' It's easy to read this as a kind of 'coming out' – most observers agree that she preferred women sexually to men – but we aren't invited to see it quite like that. Instead, it's a search for another thrill, and the Sullivan magazines had been selling the fantasy for a while. But the lesbians-for-male-spectators scenario, as in *Monique*, plays with fire and corroborates Millington's 'therapeutic' belittling of the phallic regime.

In her ghost-written trip to Leeds, Mary meets one of her fans, shopkeeper Len, and ostensibly accommodates the fantasy that she is sexually accessible to her fans. But in fact she's more interested in his girlfriend Ena and her thirty-nine-inch bust[19] – 'the moment I set eyes on her I felt the old excitement start through me again. I wanted her, and I think that she knew it as well' (Millington 1975: 30). Fortunately, swinging has made it to Leeds and she has sex with Len in order to get on to the main course with Ena, 'the kind of girl who is closer to lesbianism than she realises'. Slight-shouldered, bandy-legged Len makes it a threesome but 'as so often happens on such occasions we forgot about Len and I'm afraid that we concentrated on each other, excluding him almost completely' (ibid.: 32). Of course, *Playbirds* readers are probably supposed to take more interest in Mary and Ena than Len – punished for being 'rather passive' when his girlfriend is 'evenly balanced on the sexual fence', by implication the same fence that Mary is waiting to be pulled off. But there's a striking consistency about his eventual fate, watching and masturbating as the 'real' action takes place, like those 'lonely' men outside the text. Mary, even in the fantasy, doesn't worship the cock like Fiona – she tolerates it, at best.

Rather than go further back to Marilyn, there's something to be said for coming up to date with another Marilyn-obsessed celebrity. Madonna's stardom has some (invited) similarities to that of the porn star, circulating sexually provocative images and also being the object within those images while having no control over their consumption. 'I'm in charge!' insisted Madonna in 1990 in response to the furore surrounding the 'Justify My Love' video, begging the question: of what? The answer seemed to be the commodification of what were supposed to be her sexual fantasies, a promise taken further in *Sex* (1992). One can play the authenticity game here, contrasting Madonna's modish (and often criticised) appropriation of homoerotic imagery with the way Millington's 'real' bisexuality was exploited for heterosexual pornography. Alternatively, one can adopt a historical superiority and point out that Millington was never 'in charge' of anything, that Madonna has no Sullivan figure to 'create' her, that 'progress' has truly marched on. But what's really at stake is the difference between the slippery, 'postmodern' evasiveness available to Madonna and the cold, hard polarised certainties which characterised the late 1970s. *Mary Millington's True Blue Confessions* correlates Millington's death with the opening of the gay London nightclub Heaven a few months later: 'Mary would have loved the place,' we are told, 'for once she would have been herself.' There's an astonishing 'True Blue Confession' buried here – that there was a far from perfect fit between the (economic) sexual freedom promised by the porn industries and the larger freedoms Millington might have been thinking of. There is, as I have suggested, a confusion of voices about Millington's utterances and values. That she believed in the legalisation of pornography is indisputable – she sold hardcore openly when the more cautious Sullivan wouldn't. Millington's affiliations were visibly with the pornocrats, but we can't assume that she shared all of their interests or even that she was speaking the same language as the one in which her words were often framed.

8

GRIM FLAREY TALES

British horror in the 1970s

> This film is dedicated to those who are disturbed by today's lax moral codes and who eagerly await the return of corporal and capital punishment.
>
> opening title, *House of Whipcord* (1974)

> As for these young people, they come and go like flies these days – dirty ones at that. Their disappearance will hardly be noticed.
>
> Dr Storm, *Horror Hospital* (1973)

The category of the exploitation film is generally taken as comprising a number of generic strands – large evergreen ones like horror, sex and science fiction and more historically or culturally specific ones such as biker movies, blaxploitation, women-in-prison films or kung fu. British exploitation, however, has consisted largely of two, horror and sexploitation – even SF is a pretty sparse output, usually only written about when it crosses over into horror (*Quatermass, Frankenstein*), apparently resisting a satisfactory thematic map of its own.

Linda Wood (1983) estimates that, between 1971 and 1981, horror and sex were the second and third largest categories of British films released, with ninety-one and seventy-nine films respectively – she designates the 'children's film', including the work of the Children's Film Foundation, as the largest output (117 films), while the sex film's nearest rival is the television spin-off with thirty-four films. I cite these figures with some caution, because quantifying generic outputs is a perilous and contentious project. There are problems of definition – is *House of Whipcord* (Pete Walker, 1974) horror, sexploitation or an isolated women-in-prison film? – and of films which cross categories. There is also the question of which categories one employs – Wood excludes comedy, for example, presumably because it pervades most of the others in one form or another. As a rough guide, however, these figures are indicative of some key trends in 1970s British cinema.

If horror was statistically the larger category – it had a longer history and more momentum from the Gothic 'boom' of the 1950s/60s – sex was the dominant one by the end of the decade. By the mid-1970s, the only British horror films making enough money to receive Eady payments (distributed in proportion to relative box-office receipts) had some element of sexploitation built into them – *House of Whipcord, Exposé, Killer's Moon*. It's worth making an admittedly slightly artificial comparison between the fortunes of two films by the same writer, David McGillivray, released in 1976. When Pete Walker's *House of Mortal Sin* opened at the Warner West End, it made £1,483 in its first week; a few weeks later, *I'm Not Feeling Myself Tonight* made £5,004 during its first week at the Classic Moulin.

One might usefully identify three phases in British horror during the 1970s – like Wood, I'm going by year of release rather than production. Up to about 1974–5, there's a sense of continuity from the 1960s – companies such as Hammer, Amicus, Tigon and the UK base of American International were still relatively productive, and these are the films Peter Hutchings focuses on in the last part of *Hammer and Beyond*.

Hutchings suggests that there is a contrast between Hammer's thematic sensitivity to social change – critiques of the family (*Hands of the Ripper*, *Demons of the Mind*), ambivalent responses to female empowerment ('Beautiful temptress ... or Blood-thirsty monster? ... she's the NEW HORROR FROM HAMMER!' declares *The Vampire Lovers*' poster) – and the fact that, unlike their American counterparts, the films were 'usually set in the past, away from everyday reality' (1993: 167). Certainly, their present-day Dracula films, *Dracula A.D. 1972* and *Satanic Rites of Dracula*, seem less comfortable with the perceived social upheavals of the time. *Dracula A.D. 1972* (Alan Gibson, 1972), usually dismissed as beneath discussion, is instructive in this respect. Its endearing attempts at Chelsea hip-talk – 'Dig the music, kids!' is especially cherishable – suggest a belated 'Swinging Sixties' movie. But the counter-culture has already turned ugly in *A.D. 1972*: it's post-Altamont, post-Manson – the police compare Dracula's killings to 'those cult murders' in the States, while the Black Mass summoning the Count culminates in the cry 'I demand an audience with His Satanic Majesty!' as though Jagger and Richards are about to materialise. Dracula, meanwhile, is effectively split in two, between a characteristically austere Christopher Lee and his bohemian helper, Johnny Alucard (Christopher Neame), a name-reversal last used as a disguise for the Count himself in Universal's 1943 *Son of Dracula*. It's a shame the movie doesn't include *Satanic Rites*' one good idea of casting the Count as that quintessential 1970s carnivore, the property developer.

Cushing's Van Helsing, on the other hand, is very much a born-again Selsdon Man, attuned before anyone else to the potential affinities between vampires and 'fringe people'. He both collaborates with the police and provides a metaphysical gloss on the need for law and order, on the need to turn the tide. 'There is evil in the world,' he assures the Police Inspector. 'Of course,' comes the reply, 'Otherwise we wouldn't need a police force, would we?' Van Helsing's granddaughter, Jessica (Stephanie Beacham), a soft hippy at best, belongs to an earlier time – 'I've never dropped acid, I'm not shooting up and I'm not sleeping with anybody yet. The full extent of my wild ways extends to half a pint of lager now and again.' But her friends are an unambiguously 'bad crowd', like the hippies in *Allen's Sorts*, their coffee bar a front for distributing drugs as well as feeding vampires. The Inspector has to crack the youth culture code in order to halt this immoral trajectory, like Detective Inspector Roy Habershon poring over *The Society of the Spectacle* in order to round up the Angry Brigade. He clearly isn't finding it easy to comprehend 'a bunch of kids whose way

143

of life is as foreign to me as …' – Van Helsing completes his sentence for him –'…
as that of a vampire?'

Equally important to this phase is a strain of nostalgic horror. Tyburn's *The Ghoul*
(Freddie Francis, 1975) and *Legend of the Werewolf* (Francis, 1975) constitute a kind of
'heritage' horror, blandly reworking 1960s Hammer narratives as little more than a
longing for simpler generic terrain. More interesting are the vehicles made for Vincent Price, now settled comfortably into permanent self-parody – *The Abominable Dr
Phibes* (Robert Fuest, 1971), *Dr Phibes Rises Again* (Fuest, 1972), *Theatre of Blood* (Douglas
Hickox, 1973) and *Madhouse* (Jim Clark, 1974). In each one, Price 'returns' – from
the dead, from the 'past' – to avenge himself on modernity. The last two films, in
particular, play on Price's potentially anachronistic persona – he's a critically unfashionable, scenery-chewing Shakespearian actor in *Theatre*, an outmoded horror star
attempting a comeback in *Madhouse*. The former is especially magnificent, pitting him
against high culture, embodied both by the petty Critics Circle which denies him a
Best Actor award and by Method acting – a 'twitching mumbling boy' wins the award
instead. There's a kind of violent populism at work here, and not just in the way
Price rewrites Shakespeare by adapting his murders into elaborate serial killings –
Shylock *does* get his pound of flesh this time. Price enlists a grotesque parody of the
critically despised masses, a horde of homeless meths drinkers whom he co-ordi-
nates into a kind of ultra-violent repertory company. More importantly, in terms of
larger generic developments, how can one side with modernity when the 'past' is
embodied in such persuasively flamboyant and wittily elegant form? *Theatre's* flipside
is Pete Walker's *Flesh and Blood Show* (1972), in which another vengeful Shakespearian
actor is on the rampage, this time picking off members of a fringe theatre group,
here equated with sexual modernity – he associates their promiscuity with that of
his unfaithful wife, whose body is hidden in the deserted theatre on the end of a
pier.[1] As in Walker's later, more fully developed films – especially those written by
David McGillivray – an older generation is 'insane and oppressive, cut off from a
world they no longer understand or control' (Chibnall and Hunter 1995: 17). Patrick
Barr is no Vincent Price and, in any case, our sympathies are enlisted very differently by the films; only a scene in which Barr is patronised by the group in a tea
shop opens a space where one might side with the 'old' against the 'modern'.

From 1975 to 1978, two developments can be discerned – the decline or disappearance of Hammer and Amicus, with Tigon continuing as a distributor, and the
sense that horror was either blending with or losing ground to the sex film. There
is a visible shift in the horror films released in 1976 – Hammer's last horror film to
date, *To the Devil a Daughter*, is the odd one out amongst *Symptoms* (aka *Blood Virgin*), *Exposé*,
House of Mortal Sin, *Satan's Slave*, *Schizo* and *Whispers of Fear*. Not only are these films made
by directors with sexploitation backgrounds – Walker, Warren, Kenelm Clarke, Larraz
– but five of them share the same motif of the repressive or claustrophobic country
house, away from the suburban utopia of the flourishing sexcom, but, as Tony Rayns
said of *House of Whipcord*, 'a short train-ride from a naturalistic world of middle-class
adultery, Marks and Spencer's and chintzy restaurants, oozing muzak' (*Monthly Film
Bulletin*, May 1974: 100). The same setting – admittedly partly determined by

10 Selsdon Man(iac) takes centre stage in a Gothic CP movie: Pete Walker's House of Whipcord (1974).

financial considerations and as a way of escaping union restrictions – can be found in *Virgin Witch*, *Horror Hospital*, *Frightmare*, *Prey* and *Terror*.

The years 1979 to 1981 saw the last gasp of British exploitation as a regular theatrical output – David Sullivan's final theatrical feature, *Emmanuelle in Soho* (David Hughes, 1981) was also the last British sex film,[2] and what little British horror there was fell mainly into the category of Hollywood productions such as *Alien*, *Dracula* and *The Shining*.

This thumbnail sketch of the period is worth emphasising, because the two best accounts of British horror start rolling the credits fairly early in the decade. In the case of David Pirie's *Heritage of Horror*, published in 1973, this is to be expected, but Hutchings's final chapter also prioritises films made between 1970 and 1971–1973's *And Now the Screaming Starts* is the last film chronologically to be discussed in any detail. This is not a problem in itself – one has to set textual limits somewhere, and the book is mostly about Hammer – but the 1970s recede from Hutchings's book in a more insistent way. For most of *Hammer and Beyond*, predominantly psychoanalytic or gender-centred readings are mapped scrupulously and convincingly on to a socio-historical background – chapters pointedly specify the periods 1945–55, 1956–64 and 1964–69. But when the final post-1969 chapter is entitled 'Horror and the Family', one is forewarned that otherwise exemplary readings of, say, the Karnstein films or *Hands of the Ripper* are a little more hermetic than the rest of the book.

David Sanjek's 'Twilight of the Monsters: The English Horror Film 1968–1975' (1994) fills two gaps left by Pirie and Hutchings, by including a cultural overview of Britain during the 1970s and by looking at a broader range of films. But Sanjek's approach is limited by a certain prescriptiveness about what British horror should have been doing. 'To remain worthy of attention,' he argues, 'the British horror film would have to embrace the monstrous in audience and viewer alike' (Sanjek 1994: 197), contrasting the 'artificial horror' of the Gothic tradition with the 'real horror' which has been celebrated in the new American horror film, like *Night of the Living Dead* and *The Texas Chainsaw Massacre*. This points to a more specific problem with this prescriptiveness, the setting of agendas drawn from writing about American cinema. In the very first paragraph, he credits *Night of the Living Dead* with 'a radical transformation of the horror genre' (*ibid.*: 195), one which 'helped set in motion the decline of the British horror film and the myth it embodied' (196), namely its Manichean conception of 'good' and 'evil'. This carries some weight when set against the visibly struggling Hammer Gothic, but, given that *Night* has been read most frequently in the light of specifically North American determinants, what sort of tensions might a similarly resonant British horror film explore? Sanjek does identify an 'antiestablishment paranoid' narrative, which is arguably the most visible attempt to create a new 'mythology', albeit one which never quite commanded the same audience support. But Sanjek is overly concerned with credentials and authorship – impressed by Michael Reeves's 'Angry Young Man' image, the fractured narrative of *Scream and Scream Again* (Gordon Hessler, 1969) and the inexplicably overrated *The Wicker Man* (Robin Hardy, 1974), but, like *The Aurum Encyclopedia* (Hardy 1985), reluctant to look beyond the allegedly cynical motivation behind films like Pete Walker's.[3] Walker's films 'substitute shock for substance' and reject 'the opportunity for a systematic discourse upon the abuses of the hegemonic culture ... in order to obliterate another set of undeserving victims' (Sanjek 1994: 204). The films lose out by belonging neither to the Gothic tradition – now 'inoperative' but part of an authentic heritage – or to a cinema which can be interpreted as following the lead of George Romero. This is a little too overdetermined to be entirely helpful.

What I want to do here is exploit the advantage of a narrower focus in order to fill one or two gaps, both by looking outside the Gothic tradition exemplified by Hammer and by tracing some different formations. The 'grim flarey tale', especially prominent in the mid-1970s, has a contemporary setting, it includes or hints at sexploitative elements – thematically, it operates around a similar 'repressive hypothesis' – and it becomes more resonant when considered in the light of the 'crisis', the law-and-order society, the backlash against permissiveness. A film like Killer's Moon (Alan Birkinshaw, 1978) is fairly representative, as a group of schoolgirls are stalked by four escaped psychopaths in the Lake District. The gang includes examples of Whitehouse's bogeymen – a child molester, a homosexual – alongside a more familiar figure in British horror during this period, a religious fanatic. But they are also escapees from a psychiatric experiment, a combination of LSD and dream-therapy allowing them to unleash their violent fantasies in a controlled environment – they still believe that they are dreaming as they rape and murder. These solipsistic psychos are reminiscent of Booker's 1960s dream-generation, resisting the 'explosion into reality', identifiable by an irresponsible disavowal of consequences. But there's also a suggestion that they represent an unleashed permissive unconscious. 'In my dreams, I murder freely – pillage, loot and rape,' says a government minister, outraged by this trendy, do-gooder experiment – 'You do?' replies the psychiatrist, understandably taken aback.

Eaten by Selsdon Man: British horror and the 'crisis'

If 1970s American horror has been conceptualised as operating against the cultural backdrop of Vietnam, Watergate and political protest, some of the most interesting British films can be seen as an ambivalent response to the struggles accompanying the Heath government. While Whitehead (1985) suggests that Heath himself was more moderate than 'Selsdon Man', the punitive, law-and-order-obsessed tyrant recurs in the form of homicidal priests, sadistic prison governors and, above all, the unbalanced judges who appear in both Night After Night After Night and House of Whipcord and are able to re-define the discourses of law and punishment themselves.

Selsdon Man(iac)'s partner-in-crime is the repressive moral reformer – The Sunday Times called the Festival of Light 'the Law and Holy Order March' (Hall et al. 1978: 286). At the time of its release, House of Whipcord was seen by more than one observer as an explicit attack on the Festival; according to Tony Rayns's review, it 'charts the dark side of the Festival of Light with a pop-Freud vengeance' (Monthly Film Bulletin, May 1974: 99). More importantly for a film being sold as a flagellation movie (one character assumes the pseudonym 'Mark E. Dessart'), Stephen Murphy concurred and released it virtually uncut. According to McGillivray, who wrote the film, 'He thought the prison governess, Mrs Wakehurst, was in reality Mary Whitehouse and that her blind, senile husband, Justice Bailey, was anti-porn campaigner Lord Longford. This was news to me' (1991: 131).[4]

Labour's Roy Jenkins had earlier sought both to officialise and to defuse 'permissiveness' by defining it as 'civilisation', 'the achievement of social reform without disruption' (Hall et al. 1978: 250). But such inoculatory pieties got lost in the rigid polarisations that Policing the Crisis attributes to the Heath mythology, in which 'themes of protest, conflict, permissiveness and crime begin to run together into one great, undifferentiated "threat" ' (ibid.: 247). And if the gloves-off assault on this 'threat' is ostensibly in the name of 'decent people', those people begin to look like a rhetorical abstraction. In 'crisis' texts like The Sweeney, Walker's films and Allen's novels, 'decent people' just get in the way, like the couple injured or killed by the body Michael Caine hurls off a tower block in Get Carter, caught in the crossfire between competing carnivores – 'There is precious little left except a vigorous imposition of class interests, a struggle to the death, the turn to repression and control' (ibid.: 262).

In a much-cited essay looking back at the 1951 Festival of Britain, Michael Frayn identified a 'domestic split in the privileged classes' (1963: 320) between what he called the herbivores and the carnivores. The former were characterised as:

> the radical middle-classes – the do-gooders; the readers of the News Chronicle, the Guardian, and the Observer; the signers of petitions; the backbone of the BBC ... who look out from the lush pastures which are their natural station in life with eyes full of sorrow for less fortunate creatures, guiltily conscious of their advantages, though not usually ceasing to eat the grass.
>
> (ibid.: 320)

Meanwhile, their flesh-eating counterparts were:

> the readers of the Daily Express; the Evelyn Waughs; the cast of the Directory of Directors – the members of the upper- and middle-classes who believe that if God had not wished them to prey on all smaller and weaker creatures without scruple he would not have made them as they are.
>
> (ibid.: 320)

Frayn's vegetarian social metaphor has done service at least twice in accounts of popular British cinema. Charles Barr (1977) interprets the Ealing ethos as a predominantly herbivorous one, while Hutchings suggests that the carnivore – 'the authoritative upper- or middle-class male' – is triumphant in Hammer horror. This triumph is primarily over another kind of carnivore – Van Helsing over Dracula, for example – but he correctly points out that the herbivores, 'the decent but fatally narrow-minded and weak inhabitants of the Hammer world are either won over to the side of the no-nonsense authority figure or violently destroyed' (1993: 63).

In the 1970s, the carnivores ('real' and fictional) get hungrier, most literally in *Frightmare* (Pete Walker, 1974) where the Bad Mother is a cannibal – it's a long way from the Festival of Britain to the Festival of Light. The meat-eaters aren't difficult to spot – the New Right, Selsdon Man, the pornocrats who were almost literally swallowing Soho whole. But the 'radical middle classes' of the late 1960s and early 1970s – feminism, gay liberation, the Angry Brigade, student militants – aren't quite so herbivorous. This was a more radical middle-class split, a potential 'revolution led by a key fraction of the dominant class, against the hegemonic culture to which, by any logic, that fraction ought to have made allegiance' (Hall *et al.* 1978: 255). More importantly, the counter-culture consisted largely of 'potential recruits to the *new organic intelligentsia* – those trained to fill intermediary or subaltern positions, but with critical tasks to perform in terms of social reproduction' (ibid.: 254). It was this social power which enabled the radical middle classes to be constructed themselves as carnivores, in the terrifying conspiracies imagined by Mary Whitehouse (who clearly saw her own contingent very much as herbivores-on-the-turn) or the 'real' evil behind pot-smoking dropouts in *Dracula A.D. 1972*.

British horror, however, largely stuck to its herbivores in recruiting its normative heroes and heroines. The villains in these films pick off the last remnants of the 1960s herbivores, domesticated hippies who are easy prey – they all seem like social workers or trendy schoolteachers who insist on being called by their first name. *House of Mortal Sin's* liberal priest, Bernard, is fairly representative – a youth-club priest who smokes, swears, favours words like 'relevant' and longs for the reformation of the Catholic priesthood's vow of celibacy. *Frightmare's* victims answer ads in *Time Out*, while *Horror Hospital's* mad doctor places ads for 'hairy holidays' in what looks like the underground press. The well-meaning or cautiously permissive young things in these films never stand a chance – as the villain in Hammer's *Blood from the Mummy's Tomb* (Seth Holt, 1971) puts it, 'the meek *shan't* inherit the earth – they wouldn't know what to do with it!'

Lewis J. Force's *Night After Night After Night*, made in 1969 and released in 1970, anticipates some of the concerns of the Selsdon Maniac film.' The puritanical Judge Lomax (Jack May) hands out merciless sentences to prostitutes, drug addicts and mentally ill offenders, resisting the consideration of any extenuating circumstances. By night, he dons black leather and what looks suspiciously like a Beatles wig to vicariously explore and exterminate the world of permissive London – he is the slasher killer the police are looking for. His clerk, Carter, inhabits a milder version of the same repressed pathology, his moral rigidity betrayed by porn-addiction and an inability to walk past a strip club without spending the evening:

Carter: 'Permissive Society' they call it, but it's just lack of discipline.
Lomax: That's a very old-fashioned word to use today.
Carter: They must have everything they want. The pill. The National Health. Orange Juice. Contraceptives. Everything for nothing. And when the precautions don't work, the results have to be kept by the tax payer.
Lomax: Quite.
Carter: I blame the women. Walking about the streets half naked. They ask for it.

Lomax is described as a 'modern witchfinder', a nomination which seems to cast him as the descendant of Matthew Hopkins, eponymous villian of *Witchfinder General* (Michael Reeves, 1968), another malignant misogynist who feels compelled to destroy whatever provokes desire in him. Michael Reeves's films, in particular, help to initiate the 'anti-authoritarian' generation-gap strand in British horror, which can be found also in selected against-the-grain Hammer films (*Taste the Blood of Dracula*, *Demons of the Mind*). The elderly couple in *The Sorcerers* (Michael Reeves, 1967) seek to control the film's disaffected, youthful (anti-) hero as a way of vicariously experiencing thrills which would otherwise not be available to them. Reeves's films are angry – as befits the romantic cult surrounding him – but the 1970s version of this scenario is, if anything, resigned, defeated. The endings are increasingly downbeat, suggesting that there is no way out – two of Pete Walker's films end with a door closing ominously, closing off any avenue of literal or ideological escape. *Frightmare* and *Satan's Slave* (Norman J. Warren, 1976) conclude with their respective heroines trapped by their own family, about to be literally or metaphorically consumed. The battle is over and 'youth' has lost.

Made just as the tide was turning, *Night* is equally wary of the still visible counter-culture. The prime suspect for the Soho Ripper is Pete (Donald Sumpter), whose prodigious priapism attracts the loathing of the police and film alike – 'Making birds is like a career with me,' he boasts, 'I bang every bird I meet.' He's designated a rapist, although the sexual encounters we actually see don't support this; his promiscuity and sexual confidence seem to be the real centre of his criminality – 'Must be marvellous being so virile,' sneers Inspector Rowan (Gilbert Wynne) anxiously. Pete is successfully convicted for Lomax's murders and sentenced by him. As the Judge recoils at the memory of Pete's face, the significance of the wig and leather become apparent – Lomax has looked into the face of his own desire, dressed in the clothes of that which he both fears and covets: 'That boy is evil. In his face, I can see the evil and horror of the age. I can smell the evil as though he sweated it. Evil *is*, Carter. Evil *is.*' This allows Pete to be technically 'innocent' while eminently punishable as the real embodiment of that which corrupts the figure of the law – 'Overcome it,' Lomax warns Carter of his pornophilia, 'or it will destroy you', a fate he is destined to live out himself. In the meandering final section, the Judge is clearly meant to be a tragic figure, destroyed by the lure of commercialised sex.

This equation changes and becomes less sympathetic over the next three or four years. As in porn and sexploitation, puritanism is the respectable but transparent mask for the sexually neurotic and perverse, while permissiveness is incontrovertibly 'straight' in every sense of the word. In *House of Mortal Sin*, the psychotic Father Meldrum turns the confessional into a kind of porn booth, from which he demands to know 'everything'. Rayns characterises the villains of *House of Whipcord* thus: 'the prison wardens are a manly, repressed lesbian and a frigid would-be mother; the "arresting officer" is an Oedipal sadist' (*Monthly Film Bulletin*, May 1974: 99). In *Horror Hospital* (Antony Balch, 1973), Dr Storm (Michael Gough) speaks contemptuously of youthful promiscuity and the 'dirty flies' he lures into his web with the promise of 'fun and sun for the under-30s' – the country house is ostensibly that sex comedy standby, the health farm. A kind of demented Pavlovian sexologist, his lobotomising experiments in 'controlling human desire' are ultimately motivated by the bending of youth's collective libido to 'whatever my will desires' – his projected final victim is played, with iconic appropriateness, by Robin Askwith.[6]

It would be hard to find a more prescient film from the first half of the 1970s than House of Whipcord – it stands in bracing contrast to such lumbering allegories as A Clockwork Orange or O Lucky Man.[7] A private, secret prison, run by a retired judge (Patrick Barr), blind and senile, and a disgraced prison warden (Barbara Markham) is designed expressly for the punishment of permissiveness:

> We are constituted here by private charter ... to pass what we regard as proper sentence on depraved females of every category with whom the effete and misguided courts of Great Britain today have been too lenient ... We do not countenance here reformers, prison welfare visitors or chaplains. We do not provide comfortable rooms with chintz curtains, televisions [pronounces it 'tell-ee-visions' as though incomprehensibly exotic]. This, young woman, is a real prison.

The prison is organised around a hierarchy of punishments, which also structure the narrative – solitary confinement for a first offence; for the second, what the audience has ostensibly paid to see – a whipping administered by sadistic lesbian warden, Walker (Sheila Keith); finally, hanging. When the film's apparent heroine, Ann-Marie (Penny Irving), endures the first two, we might assume, not unreasonably, that she is guaranteed to escape or be rescued before capital punishment – not in this film, however, and not in this bleak strain of British horror.

The references to the Festival of Light seem so blatant that it's surprising that they were unintentional, but indicative of the time, perhaps, that these themes could seemingly emerge from exploitation's unconscious; Justice Bailey passes sentence in front of a 'WORLD FOR CHRIST' banner. But hindsight has given the film an additional resonance, and I want to offer another reading. The prison is the Heath government – is this the sort of thing the Selsdon Park think tank might have fantasised about? Justice Bailey is Ted Heath, the hardliner in decline, about to be displaced by a tougher, explicitly female (but not 'feminine') regime. Just as Whitehead characterised Heath as a little softer than some of his cabinet, Bailey holds on to a belief in the potential reformation of deviants, whereas Mrs Wakehurst – Margaret Wakehurst – believes in the obliteration of the middle-class right's Others. 'I find it very difficult to tell the King from the Queen – they both feel the same,' Bailey rambles as he plays chess, 'I expect that one is taller than the other.' Margaret is tough enough to finish the job he can no longer handle, the shape of things to come; she even has a son called Mark, with whom she enjoys a semi-incestuous relationship, fondling him while Ann-Marie is whipped. As the police – Wilson's precarious second term? – arrive to round up whoever's still alive, the tone is hardly reassuring, only able to replace 'hard' law with a more moderate one. In any case, the shadow of Thatcher seems to be distributed across two characters because of the casting as Walker of Sheila Keith, who, unlike Wakehurst, survives at the end of the film. Keith's astonishing performances for Walker – she made five films with him – are uncannily Thatcher-like, with a steely, demented glint in her eye and a voice which hardens and rises when one least expects it. She dominates Frightmare as the devouring wicked stepmother, Dorothy – Thatcher's initial popular incarnation as the Milk Snatcher was, of course, full of connotations of the monstrous mother (see Hunt 1996).

Hutchings (1993) places particular emphasis on 'terrible mother' and 'terrible father' films, with, for example, Countess Dracula as an example of the former and Hands of the Ripper of the latter. Booker, too, interestingly, has much to say about mothers and fathers in relation to 1970s British politics. Permissiveness is the result of too much mother – 'narcissism, self-love, weakness, irrationality' (1980: 139) – with the politics of the radical left characterised as 'the attitude of children who cannot grow up, who expect society to protect and shelter them indefinitely, while at the same time shrilly rebelling against anyone or anything which can be represented as the brutal tyranny of "Father" ' (ibid.: 137). 'All men want to kill their mothers,' suggests one of the escaped psychopaths in Killer's Moon – 'So they say,' replies his friend, 'I think what I wanted was worse.' There's a sense with Booker of the welfare state being the worst mother of all, spawning a generation of petulant, spoilt children who would have come of age in the late 1960s or early 1970s – Hutchings has explored 'monstrous' echoes of the welfare state in earlier British horror films. However, when Booker pathologises Thatcher, he does so in terms of her investing too much in father, an authoritarianism reeking of uncertainty and instability. If Thatcher was understood as both milk-snatching mother and father-in-drag, it might explain why bad mothers and bad fathers seem to act as fronts for one another in mid-1970s horror.

In House of Mortal Sin, Father Meldrum's (Anthony Sharp) homicidal deployment of incense burners, rosary beads and (poisoned) communion wafers is attributed to the repressiveness of his now silent, bed-ridden mother, who thwarted an earlier romance with housekeeper Miss Brabazon (Sheila Keith) by forcing him into the priesthood – 'Mother said "No". Mother knew best.' But just as we have to take Norman Bates's word for mother's evil nature, Meldrum seems well-practised in transferring guilt away from himself. His mother lives in a state of perpetual punishment at the vengeful hands of Miss Brabazon, but Meldrum outlives them both. Mrs Meldrum is despatched after she tries to alert outsiders to her son's murders, killings motivated by and devoted to the extermination of desire. Father Meldrum reneges on a suicide pact with Miss Brabazon and shifts all the blame for the murders on to her – she's an accomplice at best. In the final scene, we see him setting off to murder heroine Jenny (Susan Penhaligon).

Repressive power is a little more protean in Mortal Sin, the most extraordinary of the Walker–McGillivray films. The usual representatives of a jealous, frustrated 'older generation' carry out the crimes – the one attack which diverges from Catholic paraphernalia turns fashionable accoutrements (a coffee percolator and stereo headphones) against the victim. But Meldrum's irresistible power operates via the ability to define boundaries and thresholds, especially through omnipresent surveillance – he tapes his parishioners' confessions in order to control and discipline them. This allies him more overtly with the institution itself – although Bailey and Wakehurst were named, parodically, after punitive institutions (Old Bailey, Wakehurst Prison) – as opposed to pure generic psychological determinism. While the Catholic Church is the iconographic focus, Meldrum is able to command the support of other kinds of institutionalised power. He openly kills one of Jenny's friends during a hospital visit, but is still able to convince the resident psychiatrist that Jenny has a paranoid persecution complex.

Meldrum's soft-permissive counterpart is the trendy priest Father Bernard Cutler (Norman Eshley), whose views on celibacy are partly motivated by a budding romance with Jenny's sister Vanessa (Stephanie Beacham) – they've got as far as kissing before she's throttled with a rosary. But the institution determines Bernard's allegiances and proclivities as firmly as they do Meldrum's – his decision to leave the priesthood is closed off by the murder of Vanessa. A breathtakingly gruesome irony pervades the final scene in which Meldrum explains to Bernard that 'If she was all you wanted, there is no longer any reason for you to leave the church', and helps him destroy his letter of resignation. This time, the herbivore is fully implicated, and Bernard is paralleled with Meldrum throughout the film. During an early stalking scene, Meldrum's presence is signalled by an iridescent crucifix in a darkened room – as Jenny runs downstairs, she is met by a similar glowing cross (it actually seems to be the same zoom shot), namely Bernard's. Her visit to the church for an informal chat with Bernard about her wayward boyfriend leads inadvertently to her 'confessing' to Meldrum about pre-marital sex and an abortion. Similarly, the invitation to Bernard to live temporarily with the sisters mirrors Jenny accidentally leaving her keys with Meldrum.

Bernard, in other words, plays a key intermediary role in the institution's invasion of the private home – the middle-class liberal is co-opted in the name of repression; those middle-class liberals who aren't co-opted are destroyed, an even more brutal and cynical equation than the one Hutchings notes in classic Hammer. *Mortal Sin* was poorly distributed – perhaps because it's rather slow and talky for an exploitation thriller – but it isn't difficult to speculate on why, *Whipcord* apart, Pete Walker's horror films didn't make much money, despite McGillivray likening his sensibilities to those of a used car salesman (McGillivray 1991: 129). Walker's earlier sex films (*School for Sex, Cool it Carol!, Four Dimensions of Greta*) did much better than these bleak, dispirited but fascinating films. But if this is starting to sound like a 'progressive' body of films, some notes of caution need to be sounded. Chibnall and Hunter describe these films as 'cogent critiques of the Establishment and the outdated values of the older generation ... outrageous assaults on the church, the legal system and cosy images of old people' (1995: 4). Certainly the films invite such a response, and it would be foolish to chide them for not being more politically sophisticated in their representation of 'the establishment' than one has any right to expect of commercial thrillers. In any case, *Mortal Sin* does nod in the direction of a comparatively more complex depiction of repressive power. But these films' affiliations with sexploitation are significant in terms of what they say and how. If, at one level, this grubby alliance is what teases out their thematic interest, it also explains why the model of 'repression' is usually reminiscent of Al Goldstein's comments in *Naughty!* about 'people whose hard-ons are memories from thirty years ago ... Catholics and homosexuals who don't want to admit what they are ... frightened, impotent people'.

This ageist and/or homophobic conception of the opponents of (commercial) permissiveness is most evident in *House of Whipcord* as Sheila Keith's Walker takes a particular interest in Ann-Marie's punishment – 'I'm going to make you ashamed of your body ... I'm going to see to that *personally*' – and she does, indeed, wield the whip. Ann-Marie's 'crime', too, is significant – posing naked for a public photo session (*The Sun* seem to imagine critics of Page 3 similarly). She is stripped on her arrival: it is apparent that 'sexual liberation' is here largely cosmetic as Walker makes an inventory of her clothes, culminating with some attention-getting yellow platform shoes – 'One trouser suit, suede, with cap and belt to match. One pair of panties, black, one blouse, black, and one pair of [exasperated pause] *shoes*'. In *Frightmare*, the 'anti-establishment' theme disappears revealingly – institutions are too 'soft' in this film, releasing mentally ill murderers – to lay bare a conception of the old as ugly, pathetic and predatory.

Even so, these antiquated carnivores have a power and authority attributed to them that is somehow inevitable. My Heath–Thatcher reading of *Whipcord* owes more than a little to Charles Barr's 'admittedly fanciful' reading of Ealing's *The Ladykillers*, where he likens Alec Guinness's motley gang of crooks to the postwar Labour government briefly taking over 'the House' which belongs 'naturally' to old Mrs Wilberforce (1977: 171). They lose both because of their own irreconcilable, implicitly class, conflicts and the 'startling, paralysing charisma of the "natural" governing class' (ibid.: 171). Walker and McGillivray's carnivores, too, are 'natural' leaders – Mrs Wilberforce with power drills and sexual hang-ups – only temporarily 'rounded-up' in *Whipcord* as though worse was to come. It was.

The country house has another use in 1970s British horror; rather than a site of repression, it is, if anything, closer to *The Rocky Horror Show*'s 'hunting lodge for rich weirdos'[8] in its magnification of sexual perversity. These films suggest that Swinging Suburbia's monstrous Other wasn't just imagined as the pathologically censorious, but others disenfranchised by or posing a sexual-political 'threat' to the (heterosexual) 'revolution'. It is to that body of sex-horror films that I now want to turn my attention.

A house in the country: gender carnivores

Just as the pornocracy had two sets of opponents – moral fundamentalists and feminists – so too does the sex-horror film locate female power in the same locale as the malevolent, envious 'older generation'. While there is a danger of overdetermining these films on the basis of their setting, it is striking that in *Virgin Witch* (Ray Austin, 1971), *Symptoms* aka *Blood Virgin* (José Larraz, 1976), *Exposé* (James Kenelm Clarke, 1976), *Vampyres* (José Larraz, 1976) and *Prey* (Norman J. Warren, 1978), the country house is the site of dangerous female sexuality, bisexual or lesbian, unstable or jealous, murderous and castrating. The house in *Virgin Witch*, Witchworld, consistently disempowers men, and the real struggle is between competing high priestesses of a swinging coven. Sybil (Patricia Haynes) is a svelte lesbian fashion photographer for *Nova*. Christine (Ann Michelle), the 'bad' half of twin sisters, is a provincial girl in London for the first time – her necromantic power, undefeated at the film's climax, grows out of her insatiable desire for permissive experience. Men tend not to emerge very sympathetically either – control freaks (*Exposé*), rapacious carnivores (*Prey*) or middle-aged travelling salesmen undone by excursions into the permissive zone (*Vampyres*) – but the misogyny tends to be a bit more consistent and unified. The latter four films deal with a small group of characters – usually a triangle – whose sexual tensions are exacerbated by their isolation from city or suburb. Self-consciously slow-moving, this is a noticeably 'artier' group of films – *Prey*'s bizarre grafting of a flesh-eating alien on to what seems to be D. H. Lawrence's *The Fox* is not untypical in its mixed menu of conceit and titillation.

Exposé announces its sexploitation credentials most overtly in its release title and promotional material, which emphasised the role played by Fiona Richmond: 'Britain's No. 1 Sex Symbol. Miss Fiona Richmond in her first Screen Role! Nothing, but nothing, is left to the imagination.' But the film's original title, *House on Straw Hill*, invites associations with *Straw Dogs*, as does its rape scene, rural violence and bookish hero on the defensive. Paul (Udo Kier) is a writer with one successful, if stolen, novel behind him; the country house here also suggests the *nouveau riche* lifestyle which might have been associated particularly with the 1970s AristRockracy. Paul shuts himself away with girlfriend Suzanne (Richmond), and they engage in rough sex while he wears surgical gloves. As he works on that difficult second novel – especially difficult given that he has to write it himself this time – he employs Linda as a secretary, not recognising her as the vengeful wife of the real author of his bestseller, now dead. She's played by Linda Hayden, a minor but interesting figure in British exploitation. As a teenager, Hayden incarnated a precocious jailbait sexuality, most notably in *Baby Love* (Alistair Reid, 1969), *Blood on Satan's Claw* (Piers Haggard, 1971) and *Something to Hide* (Alistair Reid, 1973). 'Linda Hayden pouts evilly even while remaining innocently wide-eyed,' claimed Scott Meek (*Monthly Film Bulletin*, April 1976: 80), perhaps with her earlier roles in mind, although the impression is reinforced by her owning knickers with the days of the week on them. Linda seems to incarnate a number of anxieties. She acts for the dead husband, masturbating over a photo of him, but seemingly possessed and phallicised by him like the metaphysically transsexual 'monster' in Hammer's *Frankenstein Created Woman*, a resurrected woman with a 'male soul' (Hutchings 1993: 110). The vibrator Paul finds amongst her luggage seems to epitomise her ambiguous sexual identity – a totem representing the dead male she 'serves' or a 'hidden' penis? His discovery is intercut with her masturbating, watched by two local youths who accosted her in an earlier scene. They rape her at gunpoint, while she fondles the end of the shotgun. She manages to get it away from them, killing one and maiming the other – rather unconvincingly, he returns to kill her during the final confrontation with Paul, as though only a 'dead' man can put her out of action.

The sense of a female automaton acting for a vengeful male partly spills over into Linda's seduction of Suzanne, framed as an appropriation of Paul's property – 'You're here for me,' he reminds Suzanne after catching them caressing each other in the kitchen, 'for my pleasure, at my expense, to do what I want.' Paul's need for control – 'the tranquillity derived from order ... carefully planned, well organised, well executed, no snags, nothing unexpected to put you off' – has been established earlier in the film, and Linda's consummation of the seduction is intercut with his losing control of his brake-tampered car. But the 'authorship' of Linda's actions is complicated by a dictation scene, where she starts to write the book for Paul and, by implication, for her husband, before revealing her identity and homicidal intentions. If Paul's precarious insertion into the 'champagne set' recalls the newfound economic and cultural capital of the (male) rock celebrity – his book even contains a ludicrous sexual-musical image of someone 'playing on Anna like a virtuoso on a Stradivarius' in a 'great crescendo of lust' – Linda could be seen as a pathologised version of the manipulative rock wife, transgressing the space of male creativity and threatening its power base.

Prey goes even further in opposing a psychotic woman with a now literally monstrous male character, but again seems to ally itself with what it knows, even if, in generic terms, the implications are apocalyptic. Jo (Sally Faulkner) has already killed one man who threatened to come between her and Jessica (Glory Annen), and there are hints that she's spent time in an institution. 'Anders Anderson' (Barry Stokes) is the name assumed by a carnivorous alien in search of meat for an impending alien invasion, but it's specifically female rather than generally human flesh which seems to provide the most satisfactory 'nutrition'. Appropriately, he assumes the body of a man who isn't getting on (or, rather, off) with his girlfriend in a car on a lonely road.[9] Carnivorous masculinity, by implication, grows out of the 'natural' sexual play between hunter and prey – Anderson starts eating Jessica at the climax of a bout of violent sex.

A similar equation is made in the film's unofficial and rather unexpected high cultural source, D. H. Lawrence's story The Fox (1923). Jo and Jessica's predecessors are March and Banford, who live in (more latently) homoerotic seclusion on virtually the same chicken farm. Banford, 'a small, thin, delicate thing' (Lawrence 1923/ 1994: 7) is physically closer to Jessica and, like her, has obtained the farm via her father's wealth; March is 'more robust' – 'She would be the man about the place' (ibid.: 7) – suggesting the tougher, flick-knife-wielding Jo. But, structurally, their roles are reversed – Banford, like Jo, is the more possessive and has to fight to hold on to March, who succumbs to heterosexual temptation. This enclosed world is threatened by two predators – the eponymous fox who eats their chickens and Henry, the unpersuasively magnetic young soldier who 'preys' sexually on March and manages to kill Banford as part of a staged 'accident' while chopping down a tree. Lest we miss the heavyhanded metaphor, Lawrence spells it out for us:

> to March he was the fox. Whether it was the thrusting forward of the head, or the glisten of fine, whitish hairs on the ruddy cheek-bones, or the

bright, keen eyes, that can never be said: but the boy was to her the fox, and she could not see him otherwise.

(ibid.: 14)

Not too surprisingly, this translates into a distinctive understanding of gender:

He was a huntsman in spirit, not a farmer, and not a soldier stuck in a regiment. And it was as a young hunter, that he wanted to bring down March as his quarry, to make her his wife ... March was suspicious as a hare. So he remained in appearance just the nice, odd stranger-youth staying for a fortnight on the place.

(ibid.: 24)

Masculinity is nasty and brutish in Lawrence, but also the 'natural' way of things, the winning team to invest in. Prey's generic determinants make it a little more ambiguous. Anderson, too, poses as the 'odd stranger-youth' as he assimilates human – 'feminine' – culture. His 'natural' carnivorousness nearly gives him away – in contrast to the women's vegetarianism, muesli literally makes him vomit. He's like a parody of straight masculinity, childlike voyeur and rapacious consumer in one body.

But this is also an invasion-of-Earth film, which, as is often the case with the admittedly small number of British 'invasion' movies, is staged through its impact on a small, usually volatile social group. In the final scene, having killed Jessica and Jo, Anderson reports to his planet – 'Have now established humans high in protein and easy prey' – and there's a final shot of children playing to add a suitably chilling note.

But there's another trajectory in the film, another battle taking place. Anderson is dangerous – the literal threat to civilisation-as-we-know-it – but the film has also cast him as the 'innocent' at large in the world of the feminine, a world over which he triumphs. If Anderson – and, concomitantly, masculinity – exhibit too much Nature, then Jessica and, in particular, Jo are supposedly alienated from it, their back-to-the-land lifestyle notwithstanding. Jo's vegetarianism is equated with her separatism: 'Ours is a pure love,' she tells Anderson of her relationship with Jessica, 'without the foul animal function of breeding.' Eating meat is condemned because 'if we are to appreciate the real inner beauty of life, we cannot allow ourselves to behave like animals'. If Lawrence's chicken farm has become a kind of rad-fem commune, then brutal masculinity has to become doubly so to compensate.

Prey, in other words, is another competing carnivore movie, and it's here that it really counts that Jo is not the 'small, thin, delicate' Banford, but a man-hating, castrating psychotic who, by the end of the film, is prepared to kill Jessica rather than let her leave with Anderson – when she falls into the grave she has dug for her former lover, there is a macabre sense of poetic justice. After Anderson kills the fox, there is a celebratory party, during which Jo dresses him in drag – he cradles Jessica's toy rabbit, the sign of the sexual herbivore. A subsequent scene underlines the sense of a threatening immersion in the feminine as Anderson nearly drowns in a murky

157

lake and has to be rescued, a scene prolonged into a seeming eternity by its slow-motion photography. If Anderson is to be either predator or victim – and Jessica's fate suggests that unaffiliated herbivores are even more vulnerable than usual – *Prey* has no qualms about the preferable outcome, even if Planet Earth has to be sacrificed in the name of gender restoration.

Vampyres, made in 1974 but not released until 1976, reintroduces the lesbian or bisexual vampire, the female monster most closely associated with the 1970s (Zimmerman 1981), here breaking free of Hammer's Gothic trappings and taking up residence in a house which is equal parts uncanny place and swingers' pad. Fran (Marianne Morris) and Miriam (Anulka) share this house to which, in the guise of hitch-hikers, they lure mostly male, middle-aged travellers, usually exsanguinating them in a single night. The exception is Ted (Murray Brown), whose consumption is prolonged both by Fran, in spite of Miriam's advice – 'You're playing a dangerous game – kill him before it's too late!' – and Ted himself, who wilfully forgoes several opportunities to escape. This characteristic triangle, however, also draws in two outside observers, a caravanning couple Harriet (Sally Faulkner) and John (Brian Deacon), who seem to stand in for the honeymooners of earlier vampire films.

According to Tanya Krzywinska, 'the queer female vampire presents us with a du-plicitous message – she is both the production of patriarchal and heterosexist fear and, at the same time as she foregrounds the fears and terrors of the dominant ideology, she is also a popular articulation which breaks the silence about same sex desire' (1995: 100). *Vampyres* captures this ambivalence in the question mark it places over whose fantasy has summoned up the twin succubi and, by extension, what kind of fantasy it is offer-ing to the audience. In an early scene, we are presented with a point-of-view shot of Fran and Miriam by the roadside from John and Harriet's car. The 'view' initially ap-pears to belong to John – it's preceded by a shot of him looking and he comments on Fran's appearance. But the gaze is re-allocated to Harriet – the point-of-view shot ends with a view over John's shoulder and there's a cut to Harriet, looking. Furthermore, only she – corroborated by the image – has seen both women; John sees only Fran. 'Perhaps you're seeing things,' he suggests, and Harriet is cast in the role of 'sensitive' woman, perceptive to the uncanny. She dreams of Fran and Miriam, almost wills them into being, paints the house in which 'no normal person would live'. 'I always knew we'd find each other,' Fran tells Harriet, appearing seemingly from nowhere and making an invisible mark on her forehead – 'By this sign I'll recognise you.' But the film never follows up this apparent erotic promise – Harriet is butchered ignominiously, not granted the languorous draining that Ted undergoes.

The male heterosexual narrative of *Vampyres* (the one which would sell the film) is an explicitly masochistic one, as evinced both by Ted's complicity and by the film's overall investment in exciting, dangerous pick-ups. The story is given at least a to-ken 'frame' as Ted's fantasy/daydream in the final scene as he wakes unharmed in the grounds of the mansion. Krzywinska argues that:

> the sex scenes between the two women are shown with no 'model' male voyeur present. This differs from most 'heterosexual' hard-core pornogra-

phy, in which a man will generally watch, then intervene, participate and conclude, through his orgasm, the 'action'.

(1995: 108)

What's equally striking, however, is how knowing *Vampyres*, like Monique, seems to be about this pornographic convention, not least in representing the male as unable to see it through.[10] Undressing for another bout of sex, Ted collapses instead on the bed – detumescence is spreading to his whole body. Fran kisses and licks his prone body, draws more blood from an earlier wound, shares it with Miriam as she joins in – if anything, it's Miriam who 'intervenes, participates and concludes'. Gradually, Ted's body becomes little more than a prop for Fran and Miriam's sex, until they finally ignore him altogether.

Away from the period setting of Hammer's Karnstein films, and also without those films' 'authority' figures, like the band of patriarchs who behead Ingrid Pitt's Carmilla, the two women in *Vampyres* suggest a collision of the timeless and the timely. Fran is on the one hand outside time – clocks and watches stop as her victims expire, and Ted tells her, 'You remind me very much of someone I knew a long time ago.' A psychoanalytic reading might make much of the intimations of the pre-oedipal, with the house's inter-uterine tunnels and womb-like centre. But the centre of the uncanny house is also, pointedly, a swingers' pad, the purple wallpaper, zebra-skin rugs and modish antiques a striking contrast to the surrounding dilapidated Gothic trappings. The vampires speak the language of the permissive as well as the uncanny – 'Nothing's too good to be true – the only trouble is life's too short' – somewhere between fashionable Chelsea girls, with their flowing dresses and maxi coats, and the softcore pin-up (which is where the two actresses were 'discovered'). Ted is our old friend Terylene Man, testing out this new sexual licence, this promise of no questions and no ties – 'You're not easy to understand,' he tells Fran, again conflating the supernatural and sexual-political. But if the lesbian vampire film toys with the overthrow of heterosexual masculinity, *Vampyres* suggests that this might be what men want, at least for a while, at least until he wakes up, safely 'outside' the fantasy.

The Selsdon Maniac and sex-horror films perhaps most of all signal the split in 'permissiveness': on the one hand, object of a rearguard attack, on the other hand complicated by more specific agendas than heterosexual hedonism. If the second group suggests a more conservative development within the genre, then it should be emphasised that the first group of films still have some purchase on the rightward swing of the 1970s. In any case, *Vampyres* is a complex mix of sexual fantasies and sexual anxieties, placing it in closer proximity to the perverse sex-horror films being made in Europe at the same time. And even *Prey* combines its misogyny with a fascinating representation of threatened masculinity turning ugly – if Jo incarnates the stereotypical castrating lesbian, can Anderson be seen as the carnivorous pornocrat, finally persuaded to bare his teeth?

POSTSCRIPT

Academics behaving badly?

This isn't really the kind of book to lend itself to a neat 'Conclusion' (which is why I've opted for a more modish 'Postscript'). I had considered the option of surveying the remaining 'traces' of this 'low heritage'. Certainly, one could point to the success of David Sullivan's *Daily Sport* and *Sunday Sport* as an enduring 'pornification' of everyday life as tabloid readers are recast as 'punters' to be sold telephone sex lines, softcore videos and the magazines Sullivan claims he no longer owns. Equally, one might cite an isolated example of low comic cinema like Roy 'Chubby' Brown's *U.F.O. The Movie* (Tony Dow, 1993) – with its tale of the sexist comedian kidnapped by feminist aliens, it was as though *Zeta One* had exerted a cinematic influence in a parallel universe. But it's easier to be confident about demarcations of the 'low' at a historical distance. At the time of writing, everyone from *Smash Hits* to *The Guardian* seems agreed on the trash-pop magnificence of The Spice Girls – I love them, too, admittedly, but this looks alarmingly like a critical consensus (or an uncritical one). To disagree runs the risk of seeming grey, dull and humourless. Meanwhile, it's the 'middlebrow' – arguably always the real set of 'easy' pleasures, in Bourdieu's terms – which has been recast as the low, the indefensible: 'Blander than popular culture and even less hip than high art, the middlebrow is favoured by all of those people who find Céline and Cilla too fast for their blood' (Charlotte Raven, 'The Soft Centre', *The Observer: Life*, 21 January 1996: 12). If you really wanted to find the populist cutting edge now, you might try writing about *Heartbeat*, Andrew Lloyd Webber or Wet Wet Wet. Perhaps John Carey might give it a go in his next book; perhaps *The Daily Mail* already has done.

Instead, I want to return briefly to questions of nostalgia and popularity, given that one of the contexts for this book is contemporary mass media's deployment of what *Time Out* called 'the flares principle' – the belief that 'however unfashionable and horrendous something is, given enough time, it will be looked back on with kitsch affection' (no. 1360, 1996: 87). These thoughts have been prompted largely by Simon Frith and Jon Savage's bracing 'Pearls and Swine: Intellectuals and the Mass Media' (1997), which appeared just as I was completing this book. Here, indeed, is an essay designed to pull you up short if you've just written a book in which the words 'popular' and 'populism' figure prominently. Frith and Savage's essay, in turn, was prompted by three texts – McGuigan's *Cultural Populism*, Carey's *The Intellectuals and the Masses* (a kind of hymn to middlebrow populism) and the now-defunct magazine the *Modern Review*, which offered 'low culture for highbrows' via 'a knowing middlebrow consumer guide' (Frith and Savage 1997: 7).

Cultural populism, for Frith and Savage, is the triumph of journalistic over academic discourses, of the masses as the mythically 'normal' pitted against difference, of 'experience' over critical analysis: 'The defence of the masses against the intellectual depends ... on a particular kind of nostalgia. The commonplace acts as a bulwark against all sorts of social change, against a permanent fear of unrest at the margins' (ibid.: 9). The true legacy of populism, they imply, is to be found in the *Modern Review*, in the features pages of the 'quality' press (which have 'bought in' pop-culture 'experts') and programmes like *The Late Show*:

> For all the populist tone of, say, the *Guardian*'s art pages, popular culture is actually treated with a distinct lack of seriousness – at least on its own terms. It becomes, rather, a source of populist credibility ('I loved *Batman*'), of self-serving nostalgia (most obvious in television's treatment of its own history), and of intellectual idleness (to treat pop culture *theoretically* is, it seems, to deprive it of its 'fun').
>
> (ibid.: 14)

Frith and Savage's essay belongs to a larger critical agenda which seeks to serve time on cultural populism. Yet while there is much to agree with, I'm not sure that populism itself, for all its limitations, is the real enemy here. The *Modern Review*, as they suggest, was far from populist except in its cynical anti-intellectualism – rather, it shifted cultural capital from the object to the consumer-critic, an interesting hijacking of academic populism's 'audience empowerment'. Has the academic story of popular culture achieved closure, then? I don't think so, any more than that critical theory and cultural history cannot be on speaking terms with memory, pleasure and 'experience' – Savage's own exemplary *England's Dreaming* benefits greatly from a dialogue between 'having been there and bought that' and a more distanced critical-historical perspective.

An earlier response to McGuigan's book concluded that 'now that teaching popular culture has itself become an orthodoxy, it is perhaps time to give it a rest' (Donald 1992: 36). I find two things especially resistible here, leaving aside the breathtaking audacity in sweeping aside a huge and diverse cultural output which has already only been studied cautiously and highly selectively. First, there's the sense of having successfully colonised uncivilised territory and then moving on. Second, popular culture becomes a short-term intellectual fad – an exotic bit of rough – an impression common to the *Modern Review* and academics itching to get back to more 'serious' matters.

The 'lower' end of the popular is still considered too banal to be more than a past-its-sell-by-date trend for many in the academy – their intellectual patronage won't be missed. And it's too important to leave to the *Modern Review* or critical slummers in the 'quality' press. This material still has much to tell us, and we haven't finished talking about it just yet.

NOTES

1 'THE DECADE THAT TASTE FORGOT'?

1 I'm being a little disingenuous here. Allen and Altman constitute a kind of high-popular cinema. Fellini achieved considerable popular success in Italy, where the cultural field operates slightly differently, but in Anglo-American film culture he belongs unambiguously to art cinema.

2 It 'insists on being enjoyed' (Bourdieu 1979/1984: 489), again suggesting an unseemly and unwelcome control over the body.

3 Frith and Horne (1987) provide a useful account of the British pop–art-school interface.

4 Prolific pop biographer George Tremlett wrote in 1975, 'In a few years' time we may all be saying that Slade are the most important rock group to have emerged since The Beatles' (Tremlett 1975: 7). It didn't quite turn out that way, because Slade were a specifically British success story and never really broke America.

5 Simon Frith has a nice phrase for the way 'time-bound' pop music works – as 'news and nostalgia' (Frith and Gillett 1996: 7) – which is, I think, applicable to a broader range of 'disposable' texts; television, in particular, but also some especially 'dated' films.

2 PERMISSIVE POPULISM

1 Fantasy, escapism and infantilism are, for Booker, very 1960s sensibilities – he's no great fan of either decade.

2 These measures allowed for imprisonment without trial, for example. More damningly, there were allegations of torture, and the British government was criticised by the European Court of Human Rights and Amnesty International.

3 The Act introduced the notion of 'patriality', which limited the right of abode in Britain to those with a parent or grandparent in Britain, effectively prioritising white 'patrials'. 'Non-patrials' had to wait for work permits. Whitehead (1985) notes that Labour never really reversed the racist subtext of the Act, simply removing the retrospective power to deport long-term 'illegal' immigrants and allowing in husbands and families of women residents.

4 The 'sus' law was suggested by a provision in the 1824 Vagrancy Act – loitering with suspicious intent. In the more volatile 1970s, it served predominantly racist practices. The ethnicity of those considered 'suspicious' was remarkably consistent – see Hall *et al.* (1978) and Whitehead (1985) for more detailed accounts. The Special Patrol Group had been in existence since 1965, but the confrontations of the 1970s made them more visible – they were inconclusively implicated in the death of Blair Peach during the 1979 Southall counter-demo against the National Front.

5 'The Politics of a Sad Little Island' is one of Booker's chapter headings.

6 Booker sees *Upstairs Downstairs* as a 'day-dream vision of a world in which the two realms, upper and lower, could still coexist in happy, interdependent harmony – such a striking contrast to the bleak, envious, divided, class-racked society of today' (1980: 164).

7 George Harrison Marks talking to Jonathan Green (1993: 165).

8 A more detailed account of Lindsay's trials can be pieced together from McGillivray (1992), Ferris (1993) and Thompson (1994). Lindsay appears as a kind of permissive spokesman in *Naughty!* (Stanley Long, 1971) and *Mary Millington's True Blue Confessions* aka *The Naked Truth* (Nick Galtress, 1980).

9 Medhurst (1992) and Healy (1995) offer interesting readings of the ostensibly 'negative' stereotypes performed by Inman, Charles Hawtrey and Kenneth Williams.

10 Producer Peter Rogers had been warned that they would no longer receive 'A' certificates if the age gap continued to widen between the male *Carry On* stars and the objects of their lecherous gazes. *Carry On England* was the first to receive a 'AA' certificate, although an 'A' certificate version was also distributed – neither did very well.

11 'Murphy Must Go' was *CinemaTV Today*'s headline on 11 March 1972, with Kenneth Rive, president of the Cinematograph Exhibitors Association leading the call for his resignation.

12 Alexander Walker and John Walker (both 1985) both look at the 1970s and 1980s together and are fairly keen to skip over the mid-1970s; the latter at least acknowledges the 'low' cycles. There are no film books purely about the 1970s (excluding catalogues like Wood 1983), despite its larger output. It's simply the 'wrong' output.

13 One should also note, as Higson does, a fragmented body of British pop movies, which can be subdivided into art films with rock star leads (Mick Jagger in *Performance*, David Bowie in *The Man Who Fell to Earth*, Roger Daltrey in *Lisztomania*, which appears to be Ken Russell's sex comedy); attempts at something like a glam *Hard Day's Night* (Slade's excellent *Flame*, *Never Too Young to Rock*, which features Mud – also in *Side By Side* – The Rubettes and The Glitter Band); and films which drew on pop's cultishness such as *Jubilee* and *Quadrophenia*, anticipating 1990s hits like *Trainspotting*. The most notable box office successes were Ken Russell's barnstorming *Tommy* and the two David Essex films, *That'll Be the Day* and *Stardust*.

14 The 1927 Cinematograph Films Act established the quota system, ensuring that the distribution and exhibition of British films did not drop below a given (varying) percentage. The Eady levy, statutory from 1957, was a tax on each cinema admission which was fed back into production – the more successful the film, the greater the production company's entitlement to Eady funds. By the late 1970s, British-based Hollywood productions like *Superman* and *Alien* were taking the lion's share.

15 Sarah Street (1997) acknowledges the success of some of these films, but points to the relative fortunes of sequels as evidence of 'how far audience expectations were not met' (98) by the originals. This 'audience', which slips from the textual to the social, is based on box-office figures from twenty years ago, and, in any case, the success of *Mutiny on the Buses* rather complicates the argument. The sitcom movies were hardly unique as comedies derived from non-cinematic sources which offered pleasures not necessarily sustained (or sustainable) for feature duration – the vehicles for music hall performers and stand-ups (and most of the *Carry Ons*) share this overstretched quality, but we cannot assume that audiences felt let down by the lack of a 'proper' narrative curve.

16 EMI's *Keep It Up Downstairs* was written by *Crossroads*' Hazel Adair – 'It's a sad fact that if you are going to make films cheaply those kinds of films are the only sort which are likely to make money' (*Screen International*, 11 October 1975: 1). The *Crossroads* hard sell clearly hadn't deserted her.

3 FROM CARNIVAL TO CRUMPET

1 *Convenience* progresses to sex education films, which were a bit more contemporary. The fictitious *Sweet Glory of Love* is framed by an increasingly dishevelled 'well known and

practising doctor' introducing (offscreen) sexual positions. Significantly, it has been passed only by the local council.

2 Presumably a reference to *Oh! Calcutta!*

3 *Zeta One* also satirises feminism, with its space-age separatists, the Angvians (Angry Ones?), but they, too, emerge triumphant, not least over a parodied James Bond figure.

4 Female conductors.

5 Theories of the abject are most closely associated with Julia Kristeva, but some of the most useful ideas are presented more clearly by Mary Douglas: 'all margins are dangerous. If they are pulled this way or that, the shape of fundamental experience is altered. Any structure of ideas is vulnerable at its margins. We should expect the orifices of the body to symbolise its especially vulnerable points' (1966/1991: 121).

6 Dennis Kirkland (with Hilary Bonner 1992) goes further – according to one of his chapter headings, Hill was 'Born for TV'.

7 *The Sun* (11 September 1972) reported that a taxi driver told Nina Baden-Semper that she was his 'favourite dolly bird' – 'He was white, too,' emphasised the actress.

8 There's an interesting scene in the *Man About the House* film. George comes across Smethurst and Walker, in cameo roles as themselves, in the Thames studio bar. He recognises them, and starts referring to Walker as 'sambo the nignog, straight from the jungle'. It's Smethurst who intervenes on behalf of the ostensibly 'enlightened' discourse, and a chastened George leaves. But the scene doesn't end there. Smethurst asks Walker what he wants to drink – 'I think I fancy a White Lady,' comes the reply, and Smethurst chokes on his drink. Even this 'inoculatory' scene can't close off that particular set of anxieties.

4 LADS AND LOUNGERS

1 The BBC's history of British advertising, *Washes Whiter*, deserves some credit here. Although I haven't quoted from it directly, I'm indebted to its juxtaposition of ads for suggesting some of these 'types'.

2 In the original outline for the series, Dennis Waterman's Detective Sergeant George Carter was described as: 'A working-class lad on the make. Were it not for the fact that a concerned school teacher had instilled in him notions of public service, he might have ended up on the other side. Several of his friends have' (Alvarado and Stewart 1985: 63).

3 Slade, too, capitalised on a soccer-populist image. Nick Kent cited their 'empathy with football' as part of a 'strong working-class consciousness' (Tremlett 1975: 78) and, manager Chas Chandler claimed, 'For a period, there were no groups around that knew the same wage-packet type of background as the football fans ... Now it is back to the people' (Taylor and Wall 1976: 110).

4 In one episode, we learn that his full name is Robin Oswald Tripp, and Chrissie immediately notices an acronym in the making. It's difficult to resist invoking here *North by Northwest*, where Cary Grant's Roger Thornhill shares the same initials (except that his 'O' stands for 'absolutely nothing'). This style-over-content masculinity, signified as an absence, seems tied to his status as an advertising executive, and Robin, too, is almost a (new) demographic consumer-type – laddishly heterosexual, but suitably responsive to aftershaves and 'unisex' fashions.

5 Prior to playing Jason King, Peter Wyngarde's career included some intriguing cameos. In *The Avengers'* 'A Touch of Brimstone', he revives the Hellfire Club, a key signifier of aristocratic excess. In an episode of *The Saint*, 'The Man Who Liked Lions', he worships Roman masculinity for its 'strength' and 'discipline' and can't wait to get Roger Moore into a toga for some gladiatorial wrestling.

6 *The Persuaders'* dynamic is essentially right-wing – Judge Fulton has his flip-side in 'Bad Judge' movies like *House of Whipcord*. 'The Time and the Place', however, does deal with a far-right group of disaffected aristocrats planning a coup. Prepared to counter 'anarchy,

strikes, demonstrations, civil disorder' with martial law, they plan to assassinate the Heath-like prime minister during a television debate on his Law and Order Bill. The plot is foiled, but has the effect of making 'Heath' seem reassuringly moderate in comparison with the fascist Lord Croxley (Ian Hendry) and the rowdy bearded lefties in the audience.

7 One can only speculate as to what the programme would have been like if Danny had been played by Rock Hudson, as originally planned.

5 'KNUCKLE CRAZY'

1 'He must have been a thug himself,' speculates one of *Bookmark*'s interviewees, before adding an intriguing qualifier: 'even if he wasn't, he *thought* like one in his head, so he was a secret thug.' Frank, a fourteen-year-old Skin when interviewed, offers a more negotiated sense of the 'authentic' appeal of *Skinhead* – 'it was really good, but it was a load of bollocks as well, if you know what I mean' (Robins and Cohen 1982: 485).

2 *Dragon Skins*, as its title suggests, taps into the kung fu fever of the mid-1970s with a tale of martial-arts-trained soccer hooligans – Robins and Cohen (1982) provide an interesting account of Bruce Lee's impact on skinhead 'crews'.

3 The 'classic realist text', its 'hierarchy of discourses' and its 'metalalanguage', is explained in more detail in Colin MacCabe's 'Realism and the Cinema: Notes on some Brechtian Theses' (1981). 'A classic realist text may be defined as one in which there is a hierarchy amongst the discourses which compose the text and this hierarchy is defined in terms of an empirical notion of truth' (217). Most of these discourses are partial, open to interpretation – the ones which appear in inverted commas in a novel or newspaper ('accessed voices'), the dialogue in a Hollywood film. But the 'metalanguage' – the narration outside speech marks in either the novel or newspaper, the *image* in film, which is usually taken as more 'reliable' than dialogue – presents itself as 'unwritten prose', as a transparent window on to the 'truth', 'dematerialised to achieve perfect representation' (ibid.: 218). This involves not appearing to 'speak' at all, which is clearly not the case either with Allen or the 'third voice' in the press, the editorial.

4 'Mick Norman' was, in fact, NEL editor Laurence James, who later wrote a *Confessions* series for Sphere as 'Jonathan May'.

5 Headline from *The Daily Mirror*, 4 June 1973.

6 Jon Savage (1988a and 1990) provides a more detailed account of the impact of male homosexuality on British youth subcultures.

7 In *Hell's Angels*, Hunter S. Thompson describes the invariable 'defiling of the initiate's new uniform' amongst the original (American) Angels: 'A bucket of dung and urine will be collected during the meeting, then poured over the newcomer's head in solemn baptismal ... These are his "originals", to be worn every day until they rot ... It takes a year or two before they get ripe enough to make a man feel he has really made the grade' (1967: 54–5).

8 There's a palpable longing for America in the Angel books, 'a hog with a full tank and a coupla thousand miles of nothing but highway ahead of you ... Christ! It makes you realise what a pissy little island we live on' (*Mama* (Cave 1972/1995): 80.) British 'Angels' are usually seen as a pale imitation of their American counterparts, at best Rockers with pretensions – the back cover of the Penguin edition of Thompson's *Hell's Angels* holds up the American Angels as 'a phenomenon which relegates our Rockers to the nursery'. Part of Mick Norman's fantasy scenario is the conceit that The Last Gang in Town is British.

9 Amongst Theweleit's fascists, homosexual activity (usually, but not always, rape) was permissible as domination or as transgression – proof of being 'above' society's 'norms' – but it had to be purged of all traces of desire: *desiring* homosexuals were fit only for the camps.

10 Thompson (1967) is less than happy about gay appropriations of Angel imagery, not least in Kenneth Anger's *Scorpio Rising* – 'one of the keenest talents in the homosexual repertoire', he snaps, 'is the ability to recognize homosexuality in others, very nearly without exception' (95). But while the 'secret-queer factor' is dismissed as bitchy innuendo, it also further empowers the Angels' transgressive image – 'More than ever before, they were wreathed in an aura of violent and erotic mystery ... brawling satyrs, ready to attempt congress with any living thing, and in any orifice' (ibid.: 95).

6 CAN YOU KEEP IT UP FOR A DECADE?

1 This description also suggests an aesthetic precursor to the 'reader's wife'.
2 Sexploitation, significantly, had a star system before pornography did, from Betty Page and Pamela Green to 'Page 3' stars like Samantha Fox. Mary Millington arguably belonged to both fields, constructed as an accessible personality and an anonymous, insatiable body.
3 While these films are thought of as being quintessentially (and unflatteringly) British in style and attitude, the suburban films seem to have absorbed and adapted generic influences from Europe. I have called them the 'report' films because of certain similarities to the German *Schulmädchen* (schoolgirl) and *Hausfrauen* (housewife report) films which did play in Britain in dubbed, retitled versions. *Hausfrauen Report 4.Teil*, for example, played as *Housewives on the Job* on a double bill with the British *I'm Not Feeling Myself Tonight* (Joseph McGrath, 1976). These films, too, appear to have developed from pseudo-documentary to exposé to comedy. There is often, in British sexploitation, a sense of sex arriving from a geographical 'elsewhere', brought over by uninhibited au pair girls or embedded in *La Ronde* narratives imported from Euro-softcore. It was comedy, that most culturally specific mode of expression, which brought sex 'home'.
4 For the left, this posed a dilemma – they should, in principle, have been in favour of the cheaper housing made available by the newer suburbs and necessitated by slum clearance, but found their aesthetic sensibilities assaulted none the less. Later, there is a more romantic tradition where suburban relocation is part of an erosion of 'authentic' working-class communities. There are traces of this in *Whatever Happened to the Likely Lads?* but the programme doesn't buy into it uncritically.
5 Similar sentiments can be found in Hanif Kureishi's *The Buddha of Suburbia* (1990), which covers the same period.
6 The coexistence of conformist and idiosyncratic character traits often seems to be represented as a quintessentially British quality.
7 *Suburban Wives* contains more of a 'hunter' figure in a story about a photographer who preys on housewives, charming and then sexually blackmailing them. The young photographer played by Dennis Waterman in *A Promise of Bed* is closer to the sexcom hero.
8 *Escort Girls* (actually a misnomer because three of them are male) invests in a different kind of non-suburban masculinity. Vicky (Veronica Doran) is a wealthy but unglamorous heiress who runs a Mayfair pet shop. She employs Lester (Ken Gajadhar) to accompany her to a school reunion with his snobbish, bigoted 'friends'. Unusually for the genre, Lester is black – sexploitation treads a careful path around race except for some ill-advised jokes in one or two of the comedies. Vicky knows exactly the effect Lester will have at the party, and in an unexpected fantasy sequence he 'performs' each of their constructions of black masculinity – Lester as tennis player (following a comment about sporting prowess), Lester as a boxer (the 'black is beautiful' fantasies of Vicky's girlfriends), Lester in Zulu war dress, Lester as a 'soulful' singer. But Vicky's fantasies are equally overdetermined and she has the financial power to pursue them. She insists that he 'rape' her – 'don't you know how, *black boy?*' she taunts as he hesitates. Finally, we see them lying in bed together as she lowers her hand pointedly beneath the sheets – 'you're mine, remember? You're mine.'

9 Interestingly, sexcom's key phase coincides with Harold Wilson's second term of office, as though there was a brief, precarious optimism in the air; certainly, the genre's decline parallels Callaghan's downfall, and this bleak period seems to be reflected more appropriately in the hard-nosed David Sullivan films.

7 COMING CLEAN ...

1 'Look, I've got a punter's taste. The only notoriety I'm going to get is to be slagged. Like Stan Bowles. I mean I'm just slagged by everybody. Except the Morning Star who think I'm the epitome of the working lad, which is very strange as I'm a true-blue Conservative' (Burn 1977: 20).

2 According to executive producer Michael Klinger, mid-way between Compton-Cameo and international productions like Gold and Shout at the Devil, 'because the main character, Timmy Lea, comes from a recognisable family background and is surrounded by good stock comedy figures, the situations provoke universal laughter and you could take your maiden aunt to see them' (Film Review, July 1976: 6). Askwith's one sitcom vehicle, ITV's The Bottle Boys (1983, 1985) was an ill-advised attempt to graft aspects of the sexcom world (he played a milkman) back on to prime-time sitcom, but the time was all wrong, as indeed was everything else about it.

3 Mayflower was a subsidiary of Granada, who also owned a chain of cinemas.

4 In 1975, he was voted Best Newcomer in the Evening News film awards, a populist trophy determined by public voting.

5 Waterman plays a virtual sexcom hero in A Promise of Bed; O'Sullivan lusts after Gabrielle Drake in Au Pair Girls and camps it up in Can You Keep It Up for a Week?

6 The public-school background and small role in If ... invite comparison with Malcolm McDowell, the last young star of 'high' British cinema. Askwith is like McDowell's 'low' counterpart, the rampaging sexual 'outlaw' of Clockwork Orange re-written as the sexcom hero, the opaque salesman-at-large picaresque narrative of O Lucky Man transformed into the Confessions milieu.

7 Askwith plays a footballer in The Four Dimensions of Greta and a musician of sorts in Horror Hospital and Confessions of a Pop Performer.

8 The 'Timothy Lea' novels are Confessions of a Window Cleaner (1971), ... Driving Instructor (1972), ... from a Holiday Camp (1972), ... from a Hotel (1973), ... Travelling Salesman (1973), ... Film Extra (1973), ... from the Clink (1973), ... Private Soldier (1973) – all published by Sphere. Futura subsequently published Confessions from the Pop Scene (alternative title ... Pop Performer) (1974), ... from a Health Farm (1974), ... from the Shop Floor (1974), ... Long Distance Lorry Driver (1975), ... Plumber's Mate (1975), ... Private Dick (1975), ... from a Luxury Liner (1976), ... from a Nudist Colony (1976), ... Milkman (1976) and ... Ice Cream Man (1977). Confessions from a Haunted House (1979) was a bizarre attempt to revive the series, evidently without much success. Confessions of a Night Nurse (Futura, 1974) was the basis for Rosie Dixon – Night Nurse, and Rosie also served as/with a Gym Mistress (1974), Escort Agency (1975), Lady Courier (1975), Package Tour (1975), Physical WRAC (1976) and Baby Sitter (1976). Her co-star Penny Sutton spun off into an air hostess series, beginning with I'm Penny, Fly Me (Futura, 1975).

9 It's also the one British film I know of – David Sullivan's publicity claims notwithstanding – to be released abroad with hardcore inserts, under the jaw-droppingly Freudian title Her Family Jewels.

10 The 'CP' genre is the only category of porn marketed abroad for its Britishness – they don't call it le vice anglais for nothing. Marks was already making spanking loops – often shown in Soho's 'Spankarama' – by the late 1970s. This isn't the theoretically fashionable 'sadomasochism' – no one could call it transgressive – but Ramsey Campbell (1996) has bravely (or recklessly) opened up the genre to analysis. It remains to be seen whether anyone takes up the invitation.

11 There are also some priceless 'reviews' cited – most of them, funnily enough, attributed to magazines like *Park Lane* and *Playbirds*: 'first British porno film', 'The strongest film ever' and the unintentionally apt 'I'm amazed this sort of thing is allowed!' Given the Trades Description Act, so am I.

12 Killick (1994: 44–6) provides a useful account of the Private Shops' practice of 'marking up' – extracting as much money as possible from customers by offering additional items at 'discount' prices; it was not uncommon to take them from £10 up to £100. Refunds were out of the question – disappointing goods were dismissed as 'punters' merchandise, while material for 'connoisseurs' replaced them at a higher price.

13 *Hardcore*'s subtitle.

14 I have no idea whether she actually was a vicar's daughter, but it was part of her image – the unpromising beginnings from which the 'sensual woman' blossoms.

15 *Fiona* was clearly meant to be a British *Inside Linda Lovelace* – Millington also 'wrote' a book, which I have not been able to find, *The Amazing Mary Millington* – and Lovelace was obviously an important reference point in defining a British porn star.

16 Sullivan and Wills, interviewed on *Sex and Fame – The Mary Millington Story*.

17 Surprisingly, given her historical moment, there is no feminist anti-porn writing about Millington that I know of; surprising, also, because the 'British Linda Lovelace' tag lends itself to other readings, given Lovelace/Marchiano's later allegations about the violently coercive nature of her career. Millington, however, was a recalcitrant 'sex worker' who never recanted.

18 She even gets credited with a Monroe joke – asked what she had on while posing for the infamous 'Golden Dreams' calendar, Marilyn is supposed to have replied, 'I had the radio on'. In the Millington version, the radio became a record player.

19 I say 'girlfriend', but she turns rather abruptly into a wife halfway through the story, as though the 'swinging couple' fantasy starts writing itself in its sleep.

8 GRIM FLAREY TALES

1 Both films share another figure – the dutiful daughter who collaborates, ambiguously, in the killings: Diana Rigg in *Theatre of Blood*, Jenny Hanley in *Flesh and Blood*.

2 Two final theatrical shorts – The Hellcat Mud Wrestlers (1982) and The Female Foxy Boxers (1983) – seem to point the way to video porn/sexploitation packages, not least in their specialisation.

3 According to *Aurum*, *House of Whipcord*, *Frightmare* and *House of Mortal Sin* 'adopt a brutally cynical approach loosely related to sixties, anti-authoritarian ideologies and ruthlessly exploit the theme for all the gore and sex [they] can possibly yield within a commercially saleable format' (Hardy 1985: 302). One could easily describe *Night of the Living Dead*, apart from the sex, in the same way.

4 McGillivray claims that Walker added the pre-credits 'dedication' after his meeting with Murphy (1991: 131).

5 'Lewis J. Force' was actually a pseudonym for the prolific Lindsay Shonteff.

6 One of *Horror Hospital*'s final images is of Askwith emerging from behind Gough/Dr Storm's House-of-Wax-like mask – there's an irresistible sense of British exploitation shedding its skin, with Gough an icon of downmarket horror and Askwith symbolic of the generic shift about to happen.

7 Even the murky day-for-night photography works for the film, creating the sense of a permanent power-cut, a perfect mid-1970s 'look'.

8 *Vampyres* literally inhabits the same house as *Rocky Horror* – Oakley Court, in Bray, which also opened its doors to some of Hammer's horrors.

9 Equally appropriately, Barry Stokes also played the hero in *Ups and Downs of a Handyman*.

10 Given that the vampire attacks are more often slashing, tearing (fangless) ones than seductions, it isn't even as though the hypothetical male viewer would be able to imagine 'taking over'.

SELECT FILMOGRAPHY

List of abbreviations

d.	Director
dist.	Distributor
l.p.	Leading players
p.	Producer
p.c.	Production company
rel.	Year of release
sc.	Script

Carry on at Your Convenience rel. 1971
p.c. A Peter Rogers Production; dist. Rank; p. Peter Rogers; d. Gerald Thomas; sc. Talbot Rothwell; l.p. Sidney James (Sid Plummer), Kenneth Williams (W. C. Boggs), Charles Hawtrey (Charles Coote), Hattie Jacques (Beattie Plummer), Joan Sims (Chloe Moore), Bernard Bresslaw (Bernie Hulke), Kenneth Cope (Vic Spanner), Jacki Piper (Myrtle Plummer), Richard O'Callaghan (Lewis Boggs), Patsy Rowlands (Hortense Withering).

Carry on Camping rel. 1969
p.c. A Peter Rogers Production; dist. Rank; p. Peter Rogers; d. Gerald Thomas; sc. Talbot Rothwell; l.p. Sidney James (Sid Boggle), Kenneth Williams (Dr Kenneth Soper), Joan Sims (Joan Fussey), Charles Hawtrey (Charlie Muggins), Terry Scott (Peter Potter), Barbara Windsor (Babs), Bernard Bresslaw (Bernie Lugg), Hattie Jacques (Matron/Miss Haggerd), Peter Butterworth (Josh Fiddler).

Carry on Girls rel. 1973
p.c. A Peter Rogers Production; dist. Rank; p. Peter Rogers; d. Gerald Thomas; sc. Talbot Rothwell; l.p. Sidney James (Sidney Fiddler), Barbara Windsor (Hope Springs), Joan Sims (Connie Philpotts), Kenneth Connor (Mayor Frederick Bumble), Bernard Bresslaw (Peter Potter), Peter Butterworth (Admiral), June Whitfield (Augusta Prodworthy), Jack Douglas (William), Patsy Rowlands (Mildred Bumble), Valerie Leon (Paula Perkins), Margaret Nolan (Dawn Breaks), Robin Askwith (Larry Prodworthy).

Carry on Loving rel. 1970
p.c. A Peter Rogers Production; dist. Rank; p. Peter Rogers; d. Gerald Thomas; sc. Talbot Rothwell; l.p. Sidney James (Sidney Bliss), Kenneth Williams (Percival Snooper), Charles

Hawtrey (James Bedsop), Hattie Jacques (Sophie Bliss), Joan Sims (Esme Crowfoot), Bernard Bresslaw (Gripper Burke), Terry Scott (Terence Philpot), Jacki Piper (Sally Martin), Richard O'Callaghan (Bertie Muffet), Imogen Hassall (Jenny Grubb).

Carry on Matron   rel. 1972
p.c. A Peter Rogers Production; dist. Rank; p. Peter Rogers; d. Gerald Thomas; sc. Talbot Rothwell; l.p. Sidney James (Sid Carter), Kenneth Williams (Sir Bernard Cutting), Charles Hawtrey (Dr Francis A. Goode), Hattie Jacques (Matron), Joan Sims (Mrs Tidey), Bernard Bresslaw (Ernie Bragg), Barbara Windsor (Nurse Susan Ball), Kenneth Connor (Mr Tidey), Terry Scott (Dr Prodd), Kenneth Cope (Cyril Carter).

Come Play With Me   rel. 1977
p.c. Roldvale; dist. Tigon; p./d./sc. George Harrison Marks; l.p. Irene Handl (Lady Bovington), Alfie Bass (Kelly), George Harrison Marks (Clapworthy), Ronald Fraser (Slasher), Ken Parry (Podsnap), Tommy Godfrey (Blitt), Bob Todd (Vicar), Rita Webb (Madame Rita), Cardew Robinson (McIvor), Sue Longhurst (Christina), Mary Millington (Sue), Suzy Mandell (Rena).

Commuter Husbands   rel. 1973
p.c. Blackwater; dist. Chilton; p. Morton Lewis; d./sc. Derek Ford; l.p. Gabrielle Drake (Carol Appleby), Robin Bailey (Dennis), Jane Cardew (Dennis's Secretary), Heather Chasen (Dennis's Wife), Dick Hayden (Arthur Benbow), Claire Gordon (Carla Berlin).

Confessions from a Holiday Camp   rel. 1977
p.c. Swiftdown, for Columbia; dist. Columbia-Warner; p. Greg Smith; d. Norman Cohen; sc. Christopher Wood, from the Timothy Lea novel; l.p. Robin Askwith (Timothy Lea), Anthony Booth (Sidney Noggett), Doris Hare (Mum), Bill Maynard (Dad), Sheila White (Rosie), Colin Crompton (Roughage), Liz Fraser (Mrs Whitemonk), Linda Hayden (Brigitte), John Junkin (Mr Whitemonk), Lance Percival (Lionel).

Confessions of a Driving Instructor   rel. 1976
p.c. Swiftdown, for Columbia; dist. Columbia-Warner; p. Greg Smith; d. Norman Cohen; sc. Christopher Wood, from the Timothy Lea novel; l.p. Robin Askwith (Timothy Lea), Anthony Booth (Sidney Noggett), Sheila White (Rosie), Doris Hare (Mum), Bill Maynard (Dad), Windsor Davies (Mr Truscott), Liz Fraser (Mrs Chalmers), Irene Handl (Miss Slenderparts), George Layton (Tony Bender), Lynda Bellingham (Mary Truscott), Suzy Mandel (Mrs Hargreaves).

Confessions of a Pop Performer   rel. 1975
p.c. Swiftdown, for Columbia; dist. Columbia-Warner; p. Greg Smith; d. Norman Cohen; sc. Christopher Wood, from *Confessions from the Pop Scene* by Timothy Lea; l.p. Robin Askwith (Timothy Lea), Anthony Booth (Sidney Noggett), Bill Maynard (Mr Lea), Doris Hare (Mrs Lea), Sheila White (Rosie), Bob Todd (Mr Barnwell), Jill Gascoigne (Mrs Barnwell), Peter Cleall (Nutter Normington), Carol Hawkins (Jill Brown).

Confessions of a Window Cleaner   rel. 1974
p.c. Swiftdown, for Columbia; dist. Columbia-Warner; p. Greg Smith; d. Val Guest; sc. Christoher Wood and Val Guest, from the Timothy Lea novel; l.p. Robin Askwith (Timothy Lea), Anthony Booth (Sidney Noggett), Linda Hayden (Elizabeth Radlett), Bill Maynard (Mr Lea), Dandy Nicholls (Mrs Lea), Sheila White (Rosie), John Le Mesurier (Inspector Radlett), Melissa Stribling (Mrs Villiers), Sue Longhurst (Jacqui), Katya Wyeth (Carole).

171

Cool it Carol!   rel. 1970
p.c. Pete Walker Film Productions; dist. Miracle; p./d. Pete Walker; sc. Murray Smith; l.p. Janet Lyn (Carol Thatcher), Robin Askwith (Joe Sickles), Jess Conrad (Jonathan), Stubby Kaye (Rod Strangeways).

Dracula A.D. 1972   rel. 1972
p.c. Hammer; dist. Columbia–Warner; p. Josephine Douglas; d. Alan Gibson; sc. Don Houghton; l.p. Christopher Lee (Count Dracula), Peter Cushing (Prof. Van Helsing), Stephanie Beacham (Jessica Van Helsing), Michael Coles (Inspector), Christopher Neame (Johnny Alucard).

Escort Girls   rel. 1974
p.c. Donwin Productions; dist. Variety; p./d./sc. Donovan Winter; l.p. David Dixon (Hugh), Maria O'Brien (Susan), Marika Mann (Emma Gouldman), Gil Barber (Wayne), Veronica Doran (Vicky), Ken Gajadhar (Lester).

Exposé   rel. 1976
p.c. Norfolk International Pictures; dist. Target; p. Brian Smedley-Aston; d./sc. James Kenelm Clarke; l.p. Udo Kier (Paul Martin), Linda Hayden (Linda Hindstatt), Fiona Richmond (Suzanne).

Frightmare   rel. 1974
p.c. Peter Walker (Heritage) Ltd; dist. Miracle; p./d. Pete Walker; sc. David McGillivray; l.p. Rupert Davies (Edmund Yates), Sheila Keith (Dorothy Yates), Paul Greenwood (Graham), Deborah Fairfax (Jackie), Kim Butcher (Debbie).

Groupie Girl   rel. 1970
p.c. Salon Productions; dist. Eagle; p. Stanley Long; d. Derek Ford; sc. Derek Ford, Suzanne Mercer; l.p. Esme Johns (Sally), Billy Boyle (Wes), Richard Shaw (Morrie), Neil Hallett (Detective Sergeant), Donald Sumpter (Steve).

House of Mortal Sin aka The Confessional   rel. 1976
p.c. Pete Walker (Heritage) Ltd; dist. Columbia–Warner; p./d. Pete Walker; sc. David McGillivray, from a story by Pete Walker; l.p. Anthony Sharp (Father Xavier Meldrum), Susan Penhaligon (Jenny Welch), Stephanie Beacham (Vanessa Welch), Norman Eshley (Father Bernard Cutler), Sheila Keith (Miss Brabazon).

House of Whipcord   rel. 1974
p.c. Peter Walker (Heritage) Ltd; dist. Miracle; p./d. Pete Walker; sc. David McGillivray, from a story by Pete Walker; l.p. Barbara Markham (Mrs Wakehurst), Patrick Barr (Justice Bailey), Ray Brooks (Tony), Ann Michelle (Julia), Penny Irving (Ann-Marie de Vernay), Sheila Keith (Walker), Dorothy Gordon (Bates), Robert Tayman (Mark E. Dessart).

Horror Hospital   rel. 1973
p.c. Noteworthy Films; dist. Antony Balch; p. Richard Gordon; d. Antony Balch; sc. Antony Balch, Alan Watson; l.p. Michael Gough (Dr Storm), Robin Askwith (Jason Jones), Vanessa Shaw (Judy Peters), Ellen Pollock (Aunt Harris), Skip Martin (Frederick), Dennis Price (Pollock).

Killer's Moon   rel. 1978
p.c. Rothernorth Productions; dist. Rothernorth; p. Alan Birkinshaw, Gordon Keymer; d./sc. Alan Birkinshaw; l.p. Anthony Forrest (Pete), Tom Marshall (Mike), Georgina Keen (Agatha), Alison Elliot (Sandy).

Love Thy Neighbour rel. 1973
p.c. Hammer/EMI; dist. MGM–EMI; p. Roy Skeggs; d. John Robins; sc. Vince Powell and Harry Driver; l.p. Jack Smethurst (Eddie Booth), Rudolph Walker (Bill Reynolds), Nina Baden-Semper (Barbie Reynolds), Kate Williams (Joan Booth), Keith Marsh (Jacko), Tommy Godfrey (Arthur).

Man About the House rel. 1974
p.c. Hammer/EMI; dist. EMI; p. Roy Skeggs; d. John Robins; sc. John Mortimer and Brian Cooke; l.p. Richard O'Sullivan (Robin Tripp), Paula Wilcox (Chrissie), Sally Thomsett (Jo), Yootha Joyce (Mildred Roper), Brian Murphy (George Roper), Jack Smethurst, Rudolph Walker (Themselves), Arthur Lowe (Spiros), Bill Maynard (Chef), Spike Milligan (Himself), Doug Fisher (Larry).

Mary Millington's True Blue Confessions aka The Naked Truth rel. 1980
p.c. Roldvale; dist. Jay Jay; p. David C. Kenton; d. Nick Galtress; sc. John M. East; narrated by John M. East, featuring John Lindsay, John M. East, David Sullivan, Tom Hayes, Cathie Green.

Monique rel. 1970
p.c. Tigon British; dist. Tigon; p. Michael Style; d./sc. John Bown; l.p. Sibylla Kay (Monique), Joan Alcorn (Jean), David Sumner (Bill).

Naughty! rel. 1971
p.c. Salon; dist. Eagle; p./d. Stanley Long; sc. Stanley Long, Suzanne Mercer; l.p. C. Lethbridge-Baker (Horace), Lee Donald (Papa), Brenda Peters (Mama), Nina Francis (Daughter), Shane Raggett (Son), Jim O'Connor (Henry Ashbee), David Gray (Henry Hayler), John Lindsay (Himself).

Night After Night After Night rel. 1970
p.c. Dudley Birch Films; dist. Butcher's; p. James Mellor; d. Lewis B. Force (Lindsay Shonteff); sc. Dail Ambler; l.p. Jack May (Judge Charles Lomax), Justine Lord (Helena Lomax), Gilbert Wynne (Det. Inspector Bill Rowan), Linda Marlowe (Jenny Rowan), Terry Scully (Carter), Donald Sumpter (Pete Laver).

On the Buses rel. 1971
p.c. Hammer/EMI; dist. MGM–EMI; p. Ronald Wolfe, Ronald Chesney; d. Harry Booth; sc. Ronald Wolfe, Ronald Chesney; l.p. Reg Varney (Stan Butler), Doris Hare (Mrs Butler), Michael Robbins (Arthur), Anna Karen (Olive), Stephen Lewis (Blakey), Bob Grant (Jack).

Permissive rel. 1970
p.c. Shonteff Films; dist. Tigon; p. Jack Shulton; d. Lindsay Shonteff; sc. Jeremy Craig Dryden; l.p. Maggie Stride (Suzy), Gay Singleton (Fiona), Gilbert Wynne (Jimmy), Alan Gorrie (Lee), Robert Daubigny (Hippie), Forever More (Group).

The Playbirds rel. 1978
p.c. Roldvale; dist. Tigon; p./d. Willy Roe; sc. Bud Tobin, Robin O'Connor; l.p. Mary Millington (Lucy Sheridan), Glynn Edwards (Chief Superintendent Jack Holbourne), Gavin Campbell (Inspector Morgan), Alan Lake (Harry Dougan), Windsor Davies (Assistant Police Commissioner), Derren Nesbitt (Jeremy), Kenny Lynch (Police Doctor), Suzy Mandel (Lena Cunningham), Dudley Sutton (Hern).

Prey rel. 1978
p.c. Tymar Film Productions; dist. Supreme; p. Terence Marcel, David Wimburg; d. Norman J. Warren; sc. Max Cuff, story by Quinn Donoghue from an idea by David Wimburg, Terence Marcel; l.p. Glory Annen (Jessica), Sally Faulkner (Jo), Barry Stokes (Anderson).

Suburban Wives rel. 1972

p.c. Blackwater; dist. Butcher's; p. Morton Lewis; d./sc. Derek Ford; l.p. Eva Whishaw (Sarah), Maggie Wright (Irene), Heather Chasen (Kathy), Gabrielle Drake (Secretary), Robin Culver (Photographer).

Vampyres rel. 1976

p.c. Essay Films; dist. Fox–Rank; p. Brian Smedley-Aston; d. Joseph (José) Larraz; sc. D. Daubenay (José Larraz); l.p. Marianne Morris (Fran), Anulka (Miriam), Murray Brown (Ted), Brian Deacon (John), Sally Faulkner (Harriet), Karl Lanchbury (Rupert), Michael Byrne (Playboy).

The Wife Swappers rel. 1970

p.c. Salon Productions; dist. Eagle; p. Stanley Long; d. Derek Ford; sc. Derek Ford, Stanley Long; l.p. James Donnelly (Paul), Larry Taylor (Leonard), Valerie St John (Ellen), Denys Hawthorne (Cliff), Bunty Garland (Sheila).

Selected television programmes

Department 'S' ATV/ITC 1969–70 (28 episodes)

p. Monty Berman; sc. various (story consultant: Dennis Spooner); l.p. Peter Wyngarde (Jason King), Joel Fabiani (Stewart Sullivan), Rosemary Nicols (Annabelle Hurst), Dennis Alaba Peters (Curtis Seretse).

Jason King ATV/ITC/Scoton 1971–2 (26 episodes)

p. Monty Berman; sc. various (story consultant: Dennis Spooner); l.p. Peter Wyngarde (Jason King), Anne Sharp (Nicola Harvester).

Love Thy Neighbour Thames 1972–6

p. Stuart Allen, Ronnie Baxter, Anthony Parker; sc. Vince Powell and Harry Driver; l.p. Jack Smethurst (Eddie Booth), Kate Williams (Joan Booth), Rudolph Walker (Bill Reynolds), Nina Baden-Semper (Barbie Reynolds).

Man About the House Thames 1973–6

p. Peter Frazer-Jones; sc. Johnnie Mortimer and Brian Cooke; l.p. Richard O'Sullivan (Robin Tripp), Paula Wilcox (Chrissie), Sally Thomsett (Jo), Yootha Joyce (Mildred Roper), Brian Murphy (George Roper), Doug Fisher (Larry).

On the Buses LWT 1969–73

p. Stuart Allen (first four series), Derrick Goodwin, Bryan Izzard; sc. Ronald Wolfe and Ronald Chesney; l.p. Reg Varney (Stan Butler), Cicely Courtneidge (Mrs Butler – first series), Doris Hare (Mrs Butler – remaining episodes), Stephen Lewis (Inspector Blake), Michael Robbins (Arthur), Anna Karen (Olive), Bob Grant (Jack).

The Persuaders! ATV/Tribune/ITC 1971–2 (24 episodes)

p. Robert S. Baker; sc. various; l.p. Roger Moore (Lord Brett Sinclair), Tony Curtis (Danny Wilde), Laurence Naismith (Judge Fulton).

Rising Damp Yorkshire 1974–8

p. Ronnie Baxter; sc. Eric Chappell; l.p. Leonard Rossiter (Rigsby), Richard Beckinsale (Alan), Don Warrington (Philip), Frances De La Tour (Ruth Jones).

Whatever Happened to the Likely Lads?   BBC1 1973—4
p. James Gilbert and Bernard Thompson; sc. Dick Clement and Ian La Frenais; l.p. James Bolam
(Terry Collier), Rodney Bewes (Bob Ferris), Brigit Forsyth (Thelma).

BIBLIOGRAPHY

Selected fiction

Allen, Richard (1970, 1971, 1972/1992) *The Complete Richard Allen Volume One: Skinhead/Suedehead/Skinhead Escapes*, Dunoon: STP.

—— (1972, 1973, 1977/1993) *The Complete Richard Allen Volume Two: Skinhead Girls/Sorts/Knuckle Girls*, Dunoon: STP.

—— (1973, 1974/1994) *The Complete Richard Allen Volume Three: Trouble For Skinhead/Skinhead Farewell/Top-Gear Skin*, Dunoon: STP.

—— (1972, 1973, 1975/1994) *The Complete Richard Allen Volume Four: Boot Boys/Smoothies/Terrace Terrors*, Dunoon: STP.

—— (1980, 1977, 1975/1996) *The Complete Richard Allen Volume Five: Mod Rule/Punk Rock/Dragon Skins*, Dunoon: STP.

Barlas, Chris, Cooke, Brian and Mortimer, Johnnie (1977) *Man About the House*, London: Sphere.

Cave, Peter (1971/1995) *Chopper*, London: Redemption.

—— (1972/1995) *Mama*, London: Redemption.

Dixon, Rosie (Christopher Wood) (1974) *Confessions of a Night Nurse*, London: Futura.

Home, Stewart (1989) *Pure Mania*, Edinburgh: Polygon.

Kureishi, Hanif (1990) *The Buddha of Suburbia*, London: Faber.

Lawrence, D. H. (1923/1994) *The Fox/The Captain's Doll/The Ladybird*, London: Penguin.

Lea, Timothy (Christopher Wood) (1971) *Confessions of a Window Cleaner*, London: Sphere.

—— (1972) *Confessions of a Driving Instructor*, London: Sphere.

—— (1972) *Confessions from a Holiday Camp*, London: Sphere.

—— (1974) *Confessions from the Pop Scene* (reprinted in 1975 as *Confessions of a Pop Performer*), London: Futura.

—— (1975) *Confessions of a Private Dick*, London: Futura.

Miall, Robert (1972) *Jason King*, London: Pan.

—— (1972) *Kill Jason King!*, London: Pan.

Morgan, Stanley (1969) *The Sewing Machine Man*, Frogmore: Mayflower.

Norman, Mick (1973, 1974/1994) *Angels from Hell: The Angel Chronicles* (*Angels from Hell, Angel Challenge, Guardian Angels, Angels on My Mind*), London: Creation Books

Playbirds Magazine (author unknown) (1977) *Come Play With Me: Playbirds Novel Special*, London: Kelerfern.

Richmond, Fiona (1976) *Fiona*, London: Star.

Weldon, David (1978) *The Playbirds*, London: Playbirds Magazine.

Secondary sources

Abraham, Ian (1996) 'Oh ... Miss Jones!' A Rising Damp Magazine.

Aldgate, Anthony (1995) Censorship and the Permissive Society: British Cinema and Theatre 1955–1965, Oxford: Oxford University Press.

Alvarado, Manuel and Stewart, John (1985) Made for Television: Euston Films Limited, London: BFI.

Bakhtin, Mikhail (1984) Rabelais and His World, Bloomington, IN: Indiana University Press.

Barker, Martin and Beezer, Anne (eds) (1992) Reading Into Cultural Studies, London and New York: Routledge.

Barr, Charles (1977) Ealing Studios, London: Cameron and Tayleur.

—— (ed.) (1986) All Our Yesterdays: 90 Years of British Cinema, London: BFI.

Bennett, Tony and Woollacott, Janet (1987) Bond and Beyond: The Political Career of a Popular Hero, Basingstoke and London: Macmillan.

Booker, Christopher (1980) The Seventies: Portrait of a Decade, London: Allen Lane

Boot, Andy (1996) Fragments of Fear: An Illustrated History of British Horror Films, London: Creation Books.

Bourdieu, Pierre (1979/1984) Distinction: A Social Critique of the Judgement of Taste, Cambridge, MA: Harvard University Press.

Braham, Peter (1982) 'How the Media Report Race' in Gurevitch, Michael, Bennett, Tony, Curran, James and Woollacott, Janet (eds) (1982) Culture, Society and the Media, London and New York: Methuen.

Briggs, Asa (1995) The History of Broadcasting in the United Kingdom Volume V: Competition 1955–1974, Oxford: Oxford University Press

Brown, Paul J. (1995) All You Need is Blood: The Films of Norman J. Warren, London: Midnight Media.

Bryson, Bill (1995) Notes from a Small Island, London: Black Swan.

Burn, Gordon (1977) 'The Men Only Interview: Robin Askwith', Men Only 42, 1: 18–20.

Buxton, David (1990) From The Avengers to Miami Vice: Form and Ideology in Television Series, Manchester: Manchester University Press.

Campbell, Ramsey (1996) 'Pulsating Posteriors and Masochistic Misses' in Jaworzyn, Stefan (ed.) Shock, London: Titan.

Carey, John (1992) The Intellectuals and the Masses: Pride and Prejudice Among the Literary Intelligentsia 1880–1939, London: Faber.

Carter, Angela (1982/1992) Nothing Sacred: Selected Writings, London: Virago

Centre for Contemporary Cultural Studies (1982) Making Histories: Studies in History-Writing and Politics, London: Hutchinson.

Chambers, Iain (1985) Urban Rhythms: Pop Music and Popular Culture, Basingstoke and London: Macmillan.

—— (1986) Popular Culture: The Metropolitan Experience, London and New York: Routledge.

Chartham, Robert (1970) Sex Manners for the Young Generation, London: New English Library.

Chernin, Rowan (1996) "Arroooollldd!!! Video Marathon: Sitcom Films', Loaded 27: 192–3.

Chibnall, Steve and Hunter, I. Q. (1995) A Naughty Business: The British Cinema of Exploitation, Leicester: Phoenix Arts.

Chippindale, Peter and Horrie, Chris (1990) Stick It Up Your Punter! The Rise and Fall of The Sun, London: Mandarin.

Clark, Katrina and Holquist, Michael (1984) Mikhail Bakhtin, Cambridge, MA and London: Harvard University Press.

Clarke, Alan (1992) '"You're nicked!" Television Police Series and the Fictional Representations of Law and Order' in Strinati, Dominic and Wagg, Steve (eds) Come on Down? Popular Media Culture in Post-War Britain, London and New York: Routledge.

Clarke, John (1976) 'The Skinheads and the Magical Recovery of Community' in Hall and Jefferson (eds) (1976).

Clarke, Sue (1976) 'My Crazy Life as Timmy Lea: Robin Askwith', Photoplay (July): 52–3, 59.

Cohen, Phil (1972) 'Subcultural Conflict and Working Class Community', reprinted in Gelder and Thornton (eds) (1997).

Cohen, Stanley (1972/1980) Folk Devils and Moral Panics: The Creation of the Mods and Rockers, Oxford: Martin Robertson.

Cohen, Stanley and Taylor, Laurie (1992) Escape Attempts: The Theory and Practice of Resistance to Everyday Life, 2nd ed., London and New York: Routledge.

Comfort, Alex (1972) The Joy of Sex, London: Quartet.

Coniam, Matthew (1996) 'The Great British Sitcom Movie', Comedy Review 3: 40–2.

Cook, Jim (ed.) (1982) Television Situation Comedy, BFI Dossier no. 17, London: BFI.

Cook, Jim and North, Nicky (eds) (1985) Teaching TV Sitcom, London: BFI.

Cook, Pam (1996) Fashioning the Nation: Costume and Identity in British Cinema, London: BFI.

Crowther, Bruce and Pinfold, Mike (1987) Bring Me Laughter: Four Decades of TV Comedy, London: Columbus.

Curran, James and Porter, Vincent (eds) (1983) British Film History, London: Weidenfeld and Nicolson.

Daniels, Thérèse and Gerson, Jane (eds) (1989) The Colour Black: Black Images in British Television, London: BFI.

Davis, Anthony (1989) TV Laughtermakers, London: Boxtree.

Dawson, Graham (1994) Soldier Heroes: British Adventure, Empire and the Imagining of Masculinities, London and New York: Routledge.

Dewe Mathews, Tom (1994) Censored: The Story of Film Censorship in Britain, London: Chatto and Windus.

Doherty, Thomas (1988) Teenagers and Teenpics: The Juvenilisation of American Movies in the 1950s, Boston: Unwin Hyman.

Donald, James (1985) 'Anxious Moments: The Sweeney in 1975' in Alvarado and Stewart (eds) (1985).

—— (1992) 'Culture Vultures', Sight and Sound 2, 7: 35–6.

Douglas, Mary (1966/1991) Purity and Danger: An Analysis of the Concepts of Pollution and Taboo, London and New York: Routledge.

Drummond, Philip (1976) 'Structural and Narrative Constraints in The Sweeney', Screen Education 20.

Dyer, Richard (1981) 'Entertainment and Utopia' in Altman, Rick (ed.) Genre: The Musical, London: Routledge.

—— (1987) Heavenly Bodies: Film Stars and Society, London and Basingstoke: BFI/Macmillan.

—— (1993) The Matter of Images: Essays on Representation, London: Routledge.

Easthope, Antony (1994) 'The Impact of Radical Theory on Britain in the 1970s' in Moore-Gilbert (ed.) (1994a).

Ellis, John (1992) Visible Fictions, London: Routledge.

Featherstone, Mike (1982) 'The Body in Consumer Culture', Theory, Culture & Society 1, 2: 18–33.

Ferris, Paul (1993) Sex and the British: A Twentieth-Century History, London: Mandarin.

Foucault, Michel (1976/1981) The History of Sexuality vol. 1, London: Penguin.

Fowler, Pete (1972/1996) 'Skins Rule' in Frith and Gillett (eds) (1996).

Fox, Arthur (1962) Striptease With the Lid Off, Manchester: Empso Ltd.

Frayn, Michael (1963) 'Festival' in Sissons, Michael and French, Philip (eds) (1963) Age of Austerity 1945–1951, London: Hodder and Stoughton.

Frith, Simon (1983/1989) 'Only Dancing: David Bowie Flirts With the Issues' in McRobbie (ed.) (1989).

—— (1997) 'The Suburban Sensibility in British Rock and Pop' in Silverstone (ed.) (1997).

Frith, Simon and Gillett, Charlie (eds) (1996) *The Beat Goes On: The Rock File Reader*, London: Pluto.

Frith, Simon and Goodwin, Andrew (eds) (1990) *On Record: Rock, Pop and the Written Word*, London: Routledge.

Frith, Simon and Horne, Howard (1987) *Art Into Pop*, London: Methuen.

Frith, Simon and Savage, Jon (1997) 'Pearls and Swine: Intellectuals and the Mass Media' in Redhead, Steve (ed.) (1997) *The Clubcultures Reader*, Oxford: Blackwell.

Frow, John (1995) *Cultural Studies and Cultural Value*, Oxford: Oxford University Press.

Gabor, Mark (1972/1996) *The Pin-Up: A Modest History*, Cologne: Evergreen.

Garfield, Simon (1996) *The Wrestling*, London: Faber.

Garratt, Sheryl (1984/1990) 'Teenage Dreams' in Frith and Goodwin (eds) (1990).

Gaudreault, André (1990) 'Showing and Telling: Image and Word in Early Cinema' in Elsaesser, Thomas (ed.) *Early Cinema: Space Frame Narrative*, London: BFI.

Gelder, Ken and Thornton, Sarah (eds) (1997) *The Subcultures Reader*, London and New York: Routledge.

Gibbs, David (ed.) (1993) *Nova 1965–1975*, London: Pavilion.

Gray, Frances (1994a) 'A Body, a Bosom and a Joke? The Actress and the Carry Ons', unpublished paper, Leicester Film and Television Summer School.

—— (1994b) *Women and Laughter*, London: Macmillan.

Green, Jonathan (1993) *It: Sex Since the Sixties*, London: Secker and Warburg.

Green, Pamela (1996) 'Peeping Tom', *Femme Fatales* 5, 1: 8–10, 15–21, 60.

Greer, Germaine (1970) *The Female Eunuch*, London: Paladin.

Gripsrud, Jostein (1989) '"High Culture" Revisited', *Cultural Studies* 3, 2: 194–207.

Guirdham, Quentin and Allen, Robert (1971) 'How to Pull Birds in London', *Penthouse* 6, 2: 18–20, 64.

Gunning, Tom (1990) 'The Cinema of Attractions: Early Film, its Spectator and the Avant-Garde' in Elsaesser, Thomas (ed.) *Early Cinema: Space Frame Narrative*, London: BFI.

Hall, Stuart (1981/1990) 'The Whites of Their Eyes: Racist Ideologies and the Media' in Alvarado, Manuel and Thompson, John O. (eds) (1990) *The Media Reader*, London: BFI.

Hall, Stuart, Critcher, Chas, Jefferson, Tony, Clarke, John and Roberts, Brian (1978) *Policing the Crisis: Mugging, the State and Law and Order*, London: Macmillan.

Hall, Stuart and Jefferson, Tony (eds) (1976) *Resistance Through Rituals: Youth Subcultures in Post-War Britain*, London: Hutchinson.

Harbord, Jane and Wright, Jeff (1995) *40 Years of British Television*, rev. ed., London: Boxtree.

Hardy, Phil (ed.) (1985) *The Aurum Film Encyclopedia: Horror*, London: Aurum Press.

Harker, Dave (1994) 'Blood on the Tracks: Popular Music in the 1970s' in Moore-Gilbert (ed.) (1994a).

Harris, David (1992) *From Class Struggle to the Politics of Pleasure: The Effects of Gramscianism on Cultural Studies*, London and New York: Routledge.

Haskell, Molly (1974) *From Reverence to Rape: The Treatment of Women in the Movies*, New York: Penguin.

Haufen, Graf (1994) 'Sexy Schoolgirls: The Sequel', *Highball* 2, 1: 14–19.

Healy, Murray (1995) 'Were We Being Served? Homosexual Representation in Popular British Comedy', *Screen* 36, 3: 243–56.

—— (1996) *Gay Skins: Class, Masculinity and Queer Appropriation*, London and New York: Cassell.

Heath, Ashley (1993) 'That Tank Top Feeling', *The Face* 53: 48–53.

Hebdige, Dick (1979) *Subculture: The Meaning of Style*, London and New York: Routledge.

—— (1982) 'This is England! And They Don't Live Here' in Knight (ed.) (1982).

—— (1988) *Hiding in the Light*, London: Routledge.

Hewison, Robert (1986) *Too Much: Art and Society in the Sixties 1960–1975*, London: Methuen

Higson, Andrew (1994) 'A Diversity of Film Practices: Renewing British Cinema in the 1970s' in Moore-Gilbert (ed.) (1994a).

Hill, John (1985) 'The British "Social Problem" Film – *Violent Playground and Sapphire*', *Screen* 26, 1: 34–48.

—— (1986) *Sex, Class and Realism: British Cinema 1956–1963*, London: BFI.

Hoch, Paul (1979) *White Hero Black Beast: Racism, Sexism and the Mask of Masculinity*, London: Pluto.

Holland, Patricia (1983) 'The Page Three Girl Speaks to Women, Too: A Sun-Sational Survey', *Screen* 24, 3: 84–102.

Holland, Steve (1995) 'Jim Moffatt', *Paperbacks, Pulps and Comics* 3: 51–7.

Home, Stewart (1995) *Neoism, Plagiarism and Praxis*, Edinburgh and San Francisco: AK Press.

Hornby, Nick (1992) *Fever Pitch*, London: Indigo.

—— (1994) 'Sparing the Rod' in Roberts, Chris (ed.) *Idle Worship*, London: Harper Collins.

Humm, Maggie (ed.) *Feminisms: A Reader*, Hemel Hemstead: Harvester Wheatsheaf.

Hunt, Leon (1994) 'Coming Clean About the '70s: Robin Askwith and the British Sex Comedy', unpublished paper, Leicester Film and Television Summer School.

—— (1996) 'Frightmare' in Black, Andy (ed.) *Necronomicon Book One*, London: Creation Books.

Hurd, Geoffrey (1981) 'The Television Presentation of the Police' in Bennett, Tony, Boyd-Bowman, Susan, Mercer, Colin and Woollacott, Janet (eds) *Popular Television and Film*, London: Open University/BFI.

Hutchings, Peter (1986) 'Frenzy: A Return to Britain' in Barr (ed.) (1986).

—— (1993) *Hammer and Beyond: The British Horror Film*, Manchester and New York: Manchester University Press.

Jones, Dylan (1997) *Easy! The Lexicon of Lounge*, London: Pavilion.

Jordan, Marion (1983) 'Carry On ... Follow That Stereotype' in Curran and Porter (eds) (1983).

Killick, Mark (1994) *The Sultan of Sleaze: The Story of David Sullivan's Sex and Media Empire*, London: Penguin.

Kingsley, Hilary and Tibballs, Geoff (1989) *Box of Delights: The Golden Age of Television*, London: Macmillan.

Kirkland, Dennis (with Bonner, Hilary) (1992) *Benny: The True Story*, Sevenoaks: Coronet.

Knight, Nick (ed.) (1982) *Skinhead*, London, New York and Sydney: Omnibus Press.

Kohn, Marek (1981/1989) 'The Best Uniforms' in McRobbie (ed.) (1989).

Krzywinska, Tanya (1995) 'La Belle Dame Sans Merci?' in Burston, Colin and Richardson, Colin (eds) *A Queer Romance: Lesbians, Gay Men and Popular Culture*, London and New York: Routledge.

Laing, Stuart (1994) 'The Politics of Change: Institutional Change in the 1970s' in Moore-Gilbert (ed.) (1994a)

Lappin, Tom (1993) 'TV Bygones: *Man About the House*', *The Modern Review* 1, 11: 11.

—— (1994) 'TV Bygones: *On the Buses*', *The Modern Review* 1, 14: 18.

Lebeau, Vicky (1997) 'The Worst of All Possible Worlds?' in Silverstone (ed.) (1997).

'The Loafer' (1995) 'Confessions of a Marathon Man (The Works of Robin Askwith)', *Loaded* 11: 102–3.

Longford Committee Investigating Pornography (1972) *Pornography: The Longford Report*, London: Coronet.

MacCabe, Colin (1981) 'Realism and the Cinema: Notes on some Brechtian Theses', reprinted in Bennett, Tony, Boyd-Bowman, Susan, Mercer, Colin and Woollacott, Janet (eds) *Popular Television and Film*, London: BFI/Open University.

—— (ed.) (1986) *High Theory/Low Culture: Analysing Popular Television and Film*, Manchester: Manchester University Press.

McArthur, Colin (1982) *Dialectic: Left Film Criticism from Tribune*, London: Key Texts.

McClellan, Jim (1995) 'Are You Being Served?', *The Face* 86: 79–81.

McGillivray, David (1974) 'Horrible Things', *Films and Filming* 21, 3: 44–8.

—— (1982) 'History of British Sex Movies Part 1', *Cinema* 1: 50–3.

—— (1982) 'History of British Sex Movies Part 2', *Cinema* 3: 38–42.

—— (1982) 'History of British Sex Movies Part 3', *Cinema* 4: 38–43.

—— (1991) 'Spawn of Tarantula!' in Jaworzyn, Stefan (ed.) *Shock Xpress*, London: Titan.

—— (1992) *Doing Rude Things: The History of the British Sex Film 1957–1981*, London: Sun Tavern Fields.

—— (1994) 'Carry On: Sexual Perversity in Great Britain', *Highball* 2, 1: 11–13.

—— (1994) 'Spawn of Tarantula! Part 2' in Jaworzyn, Stefan (ed.) *Shock Xpress 2*, London: Titan.

—— (1996) 'Spawn of Tarantula! Part 3' in Jaworzyn, Stefan (ed.) *Shock*, London: Titan.

McGuigan, Jim (1992) *Cultural Populism*, London: Routledge.

McRobbie, Angela (ed.) (1989) *Zoot Suits and Second-Hand Dresses: An Anthology of Fashion and Music*, Basingstoke and London: Macmillan.

Marcus, Steven (1966) *The Other Victorians: A Study of Sexuality and Pornography in Mid-Nineteenth Century England*, London: Corgi.

Marwick, Arthur (1982) *British Society Since 1945*, Harmondsworth: Penguin.

Medhurst, Andy (1986) 'Music Hall and British Cinema' in Barr (ed.) (1986).

—— (1989a) 'Introduction to Situation Comedy' in Daniels and Gerson (eds) (1989).

—— (1989b) 'Sunsational', *Marxism Today* (November): 40–1.

—— (1992) 'Carry On Camp', *Sight and Sound* 2, 4: 16–19.

—— (1994) 'Home Amusement', *Are We Having Fun Yet? The Sight and Sound Comedy Supplement* (March): 3.

—— (1995) 'Inside the British Wardrobe', *Sight and Sound* 5, 3: 16–17.

—— (1997) 'Negotiating the Gnome Zone: Versions of Suburbia in British Popular Culture' in Silverstone (ed.) (1997).

Medhurst, Andy and Tuck, Lucy (1982) 'The Gender Game' in Cook (ed.) (1982).

Millington, Mary (1975) 'Modelling Mary Millington Goes UK – Leeds', *Playbirds* 1: 29–32.

Modleski, Tania (1988) *The Women Who Knew Too Much: Hitchcock and Feminist Theory*, New York and London: Methuen.

Moore, Roger (1973) *Roger Moore as James Bond 007*, London: Pan.

Moore-Gilbert, Bart (ed.) (1994a) *The Arts in the 1970s: Cultural Closure?*, London: Routledge.

—— (1994b) 'Apocalypse Now?: The Novel in the 1970s' in Moore-Gilbert (ed.) (1994a).

Moore-Gilbert, Bart and Seed, John (eds) (1992) *Cultural Revolution? The Challenge of the Arts in the 1960s*, London: Routledge.

Moye, Andy (1985) 'Pornography' in Metcalf, Andy and Humphries, Martin (eds) *The Sexuality of Men*, London: Pluto.

Muller, Eddie and Faris, Daniel (1996) *Grindhouse: The Forbidden World of 'Adults Only' Cinema*, New York: St Martin's/Griffin.

Mungham, Geoff and Pearson, Geoff (eds) (1976) *Working Class Youth Culture*, London: Routledge.

Murphy, Robert (1992) *Sixties British Cinema*, London: BFI.

Murray, Charles Shaar (1991) *Shots from the Hip*, London: Penguin.

Neale, Steve and Krutnik, Frank (1990) *Popular Film and Television Comedy*, London: Routledge.

Newman, Bill (ed.) (1993) *The Art of Page 3*, London: Michael O'Mara.

Nuttall, Jeff and Carmichael, Rodick (1977) *Common Factors/Vulgar Factions*, London, Henley and Boston: Routledge and Kegan Paul.

Oldfield, Paul (1985) 'Glitter', *Monitor* 4.

Orwell, George (1941/1965) 'The Art of Donald McGill', reprinted in *Decline of the English Murder and Other Essays*, Harmondsworth: Penguin.

Parkinson, Michael (1975) *Best: An Intimate Biography*, London: Arrow.

Pearson, Geoff (1976) '"Paki-Bashing" in a North East Lancashire Cotton Town: A Case Study and its History' in Mungham and Pearson (eds) (1976).

Penman, Ian (1988) 'All Content and No Style: Being There', *The Face* 94: 61–3.

—— (1989) 'The Shattered Glass: Notes on Brian Ferry' in McRobbie (ed.) (1989).

Perry, George (1985) *The Great British Picture Show*, London: Pavilion.

Petley, Julian (1986) 'The Lost Continent' in Barr (ed.) (1986).

Pfeil, Fred (1995) *White Guys: Studies in Postmodern Domination and Difference*, New York: Verso.

Phelps, Guy (1975) *Film Censorship*, London: Victor Gollancz.

Pines, Jim (ed.) (1992) *Black and White in Colour: Black People in British Television Since 1936*, London: BFI.

Pirie, David (1973) *A Heritage of Horror: The English Gothic Cinema 1946–1972*, London: Gordon Fraser.

Polhemus, Ted (1994) *Street Style*, London: Thames and Hudson.

Popular Memory Group (1982) 'Popular Memory: Theory, Politics, Method' in Centre for Contemporary Cultural Studies (1982).

Potter, Jeremy (1990) *Independent Television in Britain Volume 4: Companies and Programmes 1968–1980*, London: Macmillan

Pulver, Andrew (1996) 'Men Behaving Sadly', *The Face* 94: 165.

Rabinow, Paul (ed.) (1984) *The Foucault Reader*, London: Penguin.

Redhead, Steve (1990) *The End of the Century Party: Youth and Pop Towards 2000*, Manchester: Manchester University Press.

Reynolds, Simon and Press, Joy (1995) *The Sex Revolts: Gender, Rebellion and Rock'n'Roll*, London: Serpent's Tail.

Ridgman, Jeremy (1992) 'Inside the Liberal Heartland: Television and the Popular Imagination in the 1960s' in Moore-Gilbert and Seed (eds) (1992).

Rigelsford, Adrian (1996) *Carry On Laughing: A Celebration*, London: Virgin.

Robins, David and Cohen, Philip (1982) 'Enter the Dragon' in Cohen, Stanley and Young, Jock (eds) *The Manufacture of News: Deviance, Social Problems and the Mass Media*, rev. ed., London: Constable.

Roddick, Nick (1982/3) 'Soho: Two Weeks in Another Town', *Sight and Sound* 52, 1: 18–22.

Root, Jane (1984) *Pictures of Women: Sexuality*, London, Boston, Melbourne and Henley: Pandora Press.

Ross, Robert (1996) *The Carry On Companion*, London: Batsford.

Russo, Mary (1994) *Female Grotesques: Risk, Excess and Modernity*, London and New York: Routledge.

Sanjek, David (1994) 'Twilight of the Monsters: The English Horror Film 1968–1975' in Dixon, Wheeler Winston (ed.) (1994) *Re-Viewing British Cinema 1900–1992*, Albany, NY: State University of New York Press.

Savage, Jon (1988a) 'The Enemy Within: Sex, Rock and Identity' in Frith, Simon (ed.) *Facing the Music: Essays on Pop, Rock and Culture*, London: Mandarin.

—— (1988b) 'The Way We Wore: Fashion', *The Face* 94: 66–7.

—— (1990) 'Tainted Love: The Influence of Male Homosexuality and Sexual Divergence on Pop Music and Culture since the War' in Tomlinson, Alan (ed.) *Consumption, Identity and Style*, London and New York: Routledge.

—— (1991) *England's Dreaming: Sex Pistols and Punk Rock*, London: Faber.

Schaefer, Eric (1997) 'The Obscene Seen: Spectacle and Transgression in Postwar Burlesque Films', *Cinema Journal* 36, 2: 41–66.

Sconce, Jeffrey (1995) '"Trashing" the Academy: Taste, Excess, and an Emerging Politics of Cinematic Style', *Screen* 36, 4: 371–93.

Segal, Lynne (1990) *Slow Motion: Changing Masculinities*, London: Virago.

Sgammato, Joseph (1973) 'The Discreet Qualms of the Bourgeoisie', *Sight and Sound* (summer): 134–7.

Silverstone, Roger (ed.) (1997) *Visions of Suburbia*, London and New York: Routledge.

Simpson, Mark (1994) *Male Impersonators*, London: Cassell.

Smith, Anthony (ed.) (1974) *British Broadcasting*, London: David and Charles.

Spigel, Lynn (1995) 'From the Dark Ages to the Golden Age: Women's Memories and Television Reruns', *Screen* 36, 1: 16–33.

Street, Harry (1982) *Freedom, The Individual and The Law*, London: Penguin.

Street, Sarah (1997) *British National Cinema*, London and New York: Routledge.

Tannock, Stuart (1995) 'Nostalgia Critique', *Cultural Studies* 9, 3: 453–64.

Taylor, Ian and Wall, David (1976) 'Beyond the Skinheads: Comments on the Emergence and Significance of the Glamrock Cult' in Mungham and Pearson (eds) (1976).

Theweleit, Klaus (1987) *Male Fantasies Volume 1: Women Floods Bodies History*, Minneapolis: University of Minnesota Press.

—— (1989) *Male Fantasies Volume 2: Male Bodies – Psychoanalyzing the White Terror*, Oxford: Polity Press.

Thompson, Ben (1993) 'Crumpet and Flares', *Sight and Sound* 3, 9: 59.

Thompson, Bill (1994) *Softcore*, London: Cassell.

Thompson, Hunter S. (1967) *Hell's Angels*, Harmondsworth: Penguin.

Thornton, Sarah (1995) *Club Cultures: Music, Media and Subcultural Capital*, Cambridge: Polity Press.

Tibballs, Geoff (1994) *Randall and Hopkirk (Deceased)*, London: Boxtree/ITC.

Tolson, Andrew (1977) *The Limits of Masculinity*, London: Tavistock.

Took, Barry (1992) *Star Turns: The Life and Times of Benny Hill and Frankie Howerd*, London: Weidenfeld and Nicolson.

Toop, David (1988) 'Too Much of Everything: Music', *The Face* 94: 64–5.

Tremlett, George (1974) *The David Bowie Story*, London: Futura.

—— (1974) *The Gary Glitter Story*, London: Futura.

—— (1975) *The Slade Story*, London: Futura.

—— (1976) *The Rod Stewart Story*, London: Futura.

TV Times (1971) *On the Buses Souvenir Extra*.

Vahimagi, Tise (1994) *British Television: An Illustrated Guide*, Oxford: BFI/Oxford University Press.

Walker, Alexander (1974) *Hollywood England: The British Film Industry in the Sixties*, London: Harrap.

—— (1985) *National Heroes: British Cinema in the Seventies and Eighties*, London: Harrap.

Walker, John (1985) *The Once and Future Film: British Cinema in the Seventies and Eighties*, London: Methuen.

Ward, Micky (1975) 'Confessions of Robin Askwith', Film Review 25, 10: 14–15.

Weeks, Jeffrey (1977) Coming Out: Homosexual Politics in Britain from the Nineteenth Century to the Present Day, London: Quartet.

—— (1985) Sexuality and its Discontents, London: Routledge.

—— (1989) Sex, Politics and Society: The Regulation of Sexuality Since 1800, 2nd ed., London: Longman.

Whannel, Garry (1994) 'Boxed In: Television in the 1970s' in Moore-Gilbert (ed.) (1994a).

Wheelock, Alan S. (1976) 'Good Night, Nurse', Film Heritage 11, 3: 23–6.

Whitehead, Phillip (1985) The Writing on the Wall: Britain in the Seventies, London: Michael Joseph/ Channel Four.

Whitehead, Tony (1994) 'Among Certain Classes: Class and the Carry On Films', unpublished paper, Leicester Film and Television Summer School.

Whitehouse, Mary (1977) Whatever Happened to Sex? London: Hodder and Stoughton.

Williams, Linda (1990) Hardcore, London: Pandora.

Willis, Paul (1977) Learning to Labour, Aldershot: Gower.

—— (1978) Profane Culture, London: Routledge and Kegan Paul.

Wood, Julian (1984) 'Groping Towards Sexism: Boys' Sex Talk' in McRobbie, Angela and Nava, Mica (eds) (1984) Gender and Generation, Basingstoke and London: Macmillan.

Wood, Linda (ed.) (1983) British Films 1971–1981, London: BFI.

Woodhead, Colin (ed.) (1996) Dressed to Kill: James Bond the Suited Hero, Paris and New York: Flammarion.

Woollacott, Janet (1983) 'The James Bond Films: Conditions of Production' in Curran and Porter (eds) (1983).

Young, Lola (1996) Fear of the Dark: 'Race', Gender and Sexuality in the Cinema, London and New York: Routledge.

Zimmerman, Bonnie (1981) 'Daughters of Darkness: The Lesbian Vampire on Film', reprinted in Grant, Barry Keith (ed.) (1984) Planks of Reason: Essays on the Horror Film, Metuchen and London: Scarecrow Press.

INDEX

Entries in **bold type** indicate illustrations.

Printed in the United Kingdom
by Lightning Source UK Ltd.
109174UKS00002B/26